Judith J. Thompson

Tennessee Williams' Plays: Memory, Myth, and Symbol

PETER LANG
New York · Bern · Frankfurt am Main · Paris

Library of Congress Cataloging-in-Publication Data

Thompson, Judith
  Tennessee Williams' plays.

  (University of Kansas humanistic studies; vol. 54)
  Bibliography: p.
  1. Williams, Tennessee, 1911- —Criticism and
interpretation.   2. Williams, Tennessee, 1911-
—Technique. 3. Myth in literature.   4. Archetype
(Psychology) in literature.   I. Title.   II. Series:
University of Kansas publications. Humanistic
studies ; 54.
PS3545.I5365Z849   1987   812'.54   87-3745

  ISBN 0-8204-0476-4
  ISSN 0085-2473

CIP-Kurztitelaufnahme der Deutschen Bibliothek

Thompson, Judith J.:
Tennessee Williams' plays : Memory, myth, and
symbol / Judith J. Thompson. – New York;
Bern; Frankfurt am Main; Paris: Lang, 1987.
  (University of Kansas Humanistic Studies;
  Vol. 54)
  ISBN 0-8204-0476-4

NE: University of Kansas [Lawrence, Kan.] :
University of Kansas . . .

Cover design by Beth Reussner

© Peter Lang Publishing, Inc., New York 1987

Printed by Weihert-Druck GmbH, Darmstadt, West Germany

University of Kansas Humanistic Studies

David M. Bergeron
General Editor

Vol. 54

PETER LANG
New York · Bern · Frankfurt am Main · Paris

Tennessee Williams' Plays:
Memory, Myth, and Symbol

To Peter, Sarah, and Rachel

ACKNOWLEDGMENTS

I am indebted to the Hall Center for the Humanities at the University of Kansas for generously providing resources and facilities during the preparation of this book; and to Prof. David Bergeron, especially, for his editorial advice and his patient overseeing of this project. I thank also David Fidler and Stephen Miller for their computer expertise and cooperation in preparing and printing the text.

I wish to express my gratitude to several members of the University of Kansas Department of English for their contributions to this study at earlier stages in its development. I am deeply grateful to Prof. Charles G. Masinton, who guided my doctoral dissertation on Williams, and whose continuous support of my study and generous efforts on my behalf are in no small part responsible for this book. I am indebted to Prof. Elizabeth Schultz and Prof. Gerhard Zuther for their astute criticism of my study and their heartening encouragement. I thank also Prof. James Carothers and Prof. Ronald Willis, Director of the University Theatre, for their thoughtful comments on and enthusiastic response to my study. Not least, I am grateful to Prof. John Bush Jones, formerly of the University of Kansas, for his encouraging evaluation of my earliest expression of this study as presented in a paper for his 1973 seminar on Williams, thereby setting in motion a course of events of which this book represents the culmination.

Certain parts of this book were previously published in somewhat altered form as the essay "Symbol, Myth, and Ritual in *The Glass Menagerie*, *The Rose Tattoo*, and *Orpheus Descending*," in *Tennessee Williams: A Tribute*, ed. Jac Tharpe (Jackson: Univ. Press of Mississippi, 1977); rpt. in *Tennessee Williams: 13 Essays* (1980).

Although I assume full responsibility for the ideas expressed in this study, as well as for all idiosyncrasies, errors, and omissions, I must acknowledge my debt to the many scholars whose previous studies of Williams' use of myth and symbol lent support, inspiration, or illumination to my own analyses. Among those of value were works by Esther Jackson, Benjamin Nelson, Richard Vowles, Henry Popkin, John J. Fritscher, Leonard Quirino, Gilbert Debusscher, Peter L. Hays, Thomas P. Adler, and Glenn Embrey; the specific contributions to my study by these and other Williams scholars are documented in the Notes to the text. Several of these previous studies interpret discrete aspects of Williams' use of memory, myth, and symbol in ways which approach my own; however, no work that I know of has noted or explored the recurrent structural pattern I have discerned in Williams' plays and set forth in this book.

A special tribute is due the members of my family without whose abiding confidence and generous assistance I could not have undertaken this project: to my husband, Peter, for unselfishly encouraging my preoccupation with this work and for providing valuable criticisms of my study; and to our daughters, Sarah and Rachel, for their patience, good humor, and loving support.

CONTENTS

NOTE ON THE TEXT

Except as otherwise noted, the source of the Williams plays cited
is *The Theatre of Tennessee Williams*, 7 vols. (New York: New
Directions, 1971-81); parenthetical documentation appears in the
text. Within a chapter or section devoted to the analysis of a
single play, first reference to the play includes both volume and
page number in *Theatre*; subsequent references to the same play cite
page number only. In chapters or sections discussing more than one
play, references to each play include both its volume and page
number in *Theatre*.

Essays by Williams which appear as Forewords, Afterwords, or Notes
to his plays in *Theatre* are documented similarly to the plays.

INTRODUCTION

This book examines a recurrent structural pattern in Tennessee Williams' plays that gives organic integrity to the discrete elements of memory, myth, and symbol evoked in his dramatic works. While the book explores seventeen full-length Williams plays informed by the pattern (or variations of it) and traces its evolution through his works of the '60s and '70s, the analysis focuses on eight plays from Williams' most successful period of 1945-1961 in which the pattern is most fully realized: *The Glass Menagerie* (1944-45), *A Streetcar Named Desire* (1947), *The Rose Tattoo* (1950-51), *Cat on a Hot Tin Roof* (1955), *Orpheus Descending* (1957), *Suddenly Last Summer* (1958), *Sweet Bird of Youth* (1959), and *The Night of the Iguana* (1961). Although the specific manifestations of the recurrent structural elements are richly varied and evolve organically within each play, all eight of these plays conform in their essential organization to a single structural pattern: a pattern based on the narration of a past event in the memory of a play's protagonist that invests both tale and teller with mythic significance, followed by the memory's dramatization, or reenactment, in a demythicized and consequently ironic version. The nature and content of the mythicized memory-story determines the play's symbolic characterization, mythical allusions, and archetypal images, whereas the memory's demythicized reenactment decides the play's outcome, theme, and mode. This pattern of recollection and reenactment is fundamental to the dual vision of Williams' drama: its evocation of past and present, romanticism and realism, the mythic and the mundane.

I. The Structural Pattern

In its paradigmatic form, the structural pattern that recurs in these eight plays adheres to the following sequence. An "idyllic," " demonic,"[1] or otherwise mythicized memory of a past event in the life of the protagonist is recounted in the course of each play, usually delivered in monologue by the protagonist himself or herself as part of the exposition at the play's beginning. The *idyllic* memory reflects the protagonist's psychological quest to recapture a romanticized past. Accordingly, the content of this memory-story recalls archetypal myths of primordial wholeness, evoking nostalgia for a once-perfect human condition and a unified cosmos free of antinomies between heaven and earth, spirit and flesh, the sacred and the profane. The *demonic* memory recalls a corrupt past which the guilt-haunted protagonist seeks to escape or transcend. The content of this memory-story thus evokes archetypal myths of a deep and irrevocable division between body and soul, mortals and their gods, suffered by the inhabitants of a fallen or fragmented world.

The mythicized memory, idyllic or demonic, creates an "arrest of time"[2] in the development of the play's characters and action. Because of the traumatic nature of the memory, Williams' protagonists appear transfixed or frozen in the act of looking backward in ecstasy or fear, their emotional growth arrested, and their psychological state thus rendered abnormal, neurotic, or otherwise disturbed.[3] Each is marked by a single obsession: to recapture or escape from the one significant experience in his or her past.

At the same time, the archetypal nature of the memory serves to inflate the characters' human dimensions to mythic or godlike proportions. This enlargement is effected primarily through allusive imagery--drawn from religious, mythological, historical, and literary sources--which endows a character with the attributes of multiple mythical prototypes. In Williams' own words, "All my *great* characters are larger than life, not realistic."[4] In those plays structured by an *idyllic* memory, the protagonists are elevated to the mythic stature of Greek gods or goddesses of beauty, fertility, and rebirth; of Biblical saints and saviors; and of heroic figures in fairytale, folktale, and popular culture. In plays structured by a *demonic* memory, the protagonists assume the archetypal roles of guilt-haunted wanderers and underworld gods, or represent debased versions of Christian saints and martyrs.

The memory-story recollected in the first half of each play is reenacted in its second half, its reenactment forming the major dramatic action of the play. For example, Amanda's mythicized memory of seventeen gentlemen callers is reenacted by Laura and Jim in *The Glass Menagerie*; Serafina's idealized account of her transcendent relationship with her husband Rosario is reenacted by Serafina and Alvaro in *The Rose Tattoo*; and in *A Streetcar Named Desire*, Blanche DuBois's demonic memory of her cruel exposure of Allan Grey is reenacted twice in retributive versions, with Blanche as the victim of humiliations similar to Allan's. The structural pattern of a story told, then "performed" or reenacted in a dramatized version may itself be considered an analogue of myth and ritual: through an infusion of allusive imagery, the protagonist's

2

personal story assumes the dimensions of myth, its reenactment a ritual which parallels the events of the myth.[5] Furthermore, the story itself acts as a prophecy, its reenactment thus made to seem inevitable. According to Northrop Frye, "the device of making a whole story the fulfilment of a prophecy given at the beginning . . . suggests, in its existential projection, a conception of ineluctable fate or hidden omnipotent will."[6] Unlike the ancient prophecies, myths, or rituals of initiation, fertility, sacrificial atonement, and rebirth which these stories suggest, however, the reenactment in these plays rarely culminates in fulfilled or successfully realized aspirations. Instead, the elevated memory-story told at the play's beginning is reenacted in a realistic, naturalistic, existential, or otherwise diminished version of its mythicized original.

The diminished myth or flawed ritual that is reenacted renders ironic the relationship of mythic symbolism to character, action, and theme in these plays. In short, Williams' characters are invested with mythic stature only to be divested of it in the course of the play. In their movement from inflation to debasement, from illusion to reality, the protagonists of these plays recapitulate the archetypal pattern of a fall, emerging finally as representatives of modern anti-heroic humanity. In "Foreword" to *Camino Real*, Williams describes that play in terms which are applicable to all his plays and their characters; all are dramatizations of

> nothing more nor less than my conception of the time and world that I live in, and its people are mostly archetypes of certain basic attitudes and qualities with those mutations that would occur if they had continued along the road to this hypothetical terminal point in it (II, 419).

Like the faded Camille and aging Casanova of *Camino Real*, the protagonists of these plays are ultimately revealed to be debased versions or "shadow-images" of mythical, legendary, and archetypal figures who once provided exempla of humankind's potential for courage, honor, gentility, and love, but who have since been diminished and demythicized by time, history, and circumstance.[7]

The ironic or illusory nature of the protagonists' mythic dimensions is anticipated at the play's beginning by a method of composite characterization;[8] for, even as Williams symbolizes the illusions, delusions, and romantic aspirations of his protagonists

3

Introduction

to transcend their human limitations, he continually invokes their psychological abnormalities, their inherently animal or instinctual natures, and the flesh-and-blood needs that keep them earthbound. Their characterization partakes, then, of both idealized and ironic elements, as they are simultaneously elevated and debased. Thus, Rosario in *The Rose Tattoo* is a composite of the Dionysian god, the popular film star Valentino, and the lecherous goat. Maggie in *Cat on a Hot Tin Roof* is simultaneously elevated to a modern version of the Roman goddess Diana and reduced to a "cat in heat." The diverse images surrounding Chance Wayne in *Sweet Bird of Youth* include those of the Greek god Adonis, the fairy-tale hero of "Jack and the Beanstalk," and an aging romance knight become beach-boy, lothario, and stud.

Concrete symbols provide a further method of revealing the illusory nature of the characters' inflated self-images and the futility of their attempts to transcend the constraints of existential reality. Unlike the allusive imagery which renders the characters' subjective worlds metaphorically expansive and mythically transcendent, concrete symbols anchor their psychic realities to substantial sensory forms which by their very nature are subject to time, accident, and inevitable dissolution. The characters' subjective worlds are thus physically embodied by the very constructs or props of the stage set, by the costumes and other accoutrements of the actors, and by the sensory effects of light, color, and music. They constitute what T. S. Eliot has defined as the "objective correlatives" of states of mind or feeling: that "set of objects, a situation, a chain of events which shall be the formula of that *particular* emotion; such that when the external facts . . . are given, the emotion is immediately evoked."[9] Thus, Laura Wingfield's otherworldliness and arrested development are symbolically encased in an "old-fashioned whatnot" (I, 144) displaying fragile glass animals which, like her own psychic state, are frozen in time; Serafina delle Rose's dreams of transcendent love are literally enshrined in an urn filled with her late husband's ashes; the Reverend T. Lawrence Shannon's attempt to regress to infantile innocence is objectified by a womb-like canvas hammock; and Blanche DuBois's romantic illusions are reflected in the soft glow from a rose-colored Chinese paper lantern.

The characters' subjective worlds, idyllic or demonic, are also evoked by music and other expressionistic auditory effects: the urgent bleating of the unleashed goat in *The Rose Tattoo* signals the necessity of Serafina's fulfilling the animal instincts she vainly tries to repress or sublimate; the "Lament" (IV, 9) which informs *Sweet Bird of Youth* anticipates the inevitability of Chance Wayne's loss of youth, beauty, and sexuality; and the haunting strains of the Varsouviana polka in *A Streetcar Named Desire* serve as an aural symbol of Blanche DuBois's guilt-ridden memories of the past, even as she attempts to escape them by singing "Make-Believe" (I, 360). The futility of a character's attempt to recapture the past or transcend the present may be revealed by details of costume: Amanda Wingfield's yellowed dress and bouquet of jonquils; Serafina's outgrown girdle; Brick Pollitt's bathrobe and crutch; Val Xavier's inescapable snakeskin jacket; or the defrocked Shannon's clerical collar that will not stay fastened. By their combined appeal to the senses--visual and aural--concrete symbols elicit an intensely emotional response to the illusory, ironic, and often pathetic attempts of the characters to transcend phenomenal reality and their own inherently flawed natures.

The climax of each play, then, resides in an *anagnorisis* or recognition scene: that moment when the protagonist is divested of mythic or godlike dimensions, stripped of illusions and delusions, and forced to acknowledge his or her inherently anti-heroic nature. This symbolic moment of demythicization, or rite of divestiture, is generally dramatized by a gesture of breaking, rending, or otherwise shattering the concrete symbol which has been identified as the objective correlative of the protagonist's psychic reality, his means of entry to the subjective world of idyllic memory or of escape from the nightmares of a demonic one.[10] Thus, Jim's breaking of Laura's unicorn in *The Glass Menagerie*, Mitch's tearing of Blanche's paper lantern from the naked light bulb in *A Streetcar Named Desire*, Maggie's disposal of Brick's crutch and liquor bottles in *Cat on a Hot Tin Roof*, Shannon's breaking free from his roped-in situation in the canvas hammock as well as his cutting loose the similarly tied-up iguana in *The Night of the Iguana*, and the literal dismemberment of Chance Wayne in *Sweet Bird of Youth* and of Sebastian Venable in *Suddenly Last Summer* are all symbolic acts which divest the characters of their inflated dimensions, liberate them from their deluded hopes and dreams, and force them to confront an existential reality devoid of transcendent redemption.

Paradoxically, it is this moment of truth which generally affords the protagonist an opportunity to assume a new, more fully human, stature in the expression of love, sympathy, or compassion for another. But for those who cannot or will not accept their personal limitations or the compromise of their mythicized worlds, their lost Edens, the result is physical destruction or psychological withdrawal. Ultimately, the particular way the protagonists of these plays respond to their confrontation with a demythicized reality determines the dramatic outcome of each play, its emotional ambience, and its dominant mode: comic, tragic, or tragicomic.

Central to all these plays, then, is the "descent theme" of romance,[11] which presents as inexorable and inevitable the defeat of the romantic imagination in a modern world inimical to transcendent ideals and aspirations. Accordingly, most of these plays are predominately tragic in mode, evoking pity for the loss of mythic illusions and terror at the primeval savagery and violence underlying the world's civilized veneer. None of these plays presents an exclusively tragic view, however, and not all of them end with their protagonists' destruction. Both *The Rose Tattoo* and *The Night of the Iguana* conclude with an essentially comic vision which offers a viable alternative to existential *angst* and tragic despair: a vision based on the attitudes of acceptance, accommodation, and endurance. In Serafina's embrace of the all-too-human Alvaro, in Shannon's acceptance of being "stuck here" (IV, 354) with the down-to-earth Maxine, and in Hannah's stoical decision to "go on" (IV, 358) resides a comic affirmation of life's inherent value and a strategy for survival. And, in *Cat on a Hot Tin Roof*, the determined efforts of Maggie--the life-force personified-- restore to a semblance of health and wholeness the divided self of Brick Pollitt.

This tragicomic vision is never wholly absent even from Williams' darkest plays, whose protagonists are destroyed by their own warring instincts and the world's inherent corruption. Set against the shattered psyche of Blanche DuBois, the crucifixion of Val Xavier, or the cannibalism of Sebastian Venable are images of rebirth, regeneration, or rescue (though often ironic) or gestures of human kindness (though briefly sustained). The comic alternative to romantic tragedy is embodied by Stanley Kowalski's irrepressible sexuality in *Streetcar*, as well as by Stella's pragmatic realization that "Life has got to go on. No matter what happens, you've got to keep on going" (I, 406), a stoical attitude echoed in *Sweet Bird* by Alexandra del Lago's unillusioned decision to continue her "comeback" by "going . . . on" (IV, 121), though bereft of youth and beauty. A vestige of the comic miracle of rebirth attends even the survival of Val Xavier's snakeskin jacket and its inheritance by Carol Cutrere in *Orpheus Descending* and informs as well Catharine Holly's rescue from the world's cannibalism in *Suddenly Last Summer*. The amelioration of romantic disillusionment and tragic despair is accomplished through the expression of mutual compassion by the members of the Wingfield family at the conclusion of *The Glass Menagerie*. Although the emphasis in these eight plays, then, is on the romantic tragedies of their protagonists, all contain elements of comic consolation. The alternative to tragic despair resides in an existential comedy of survival, however, rather than in a divine comedy of salvation, in resignation rather than redemption, and in endurance rather than transcendence. Through this dual vision, Williams simultaneously evokes a painful sense of mythic loss and offers a measure of human solace.

The structural pattern of Williams' plays--based on a remembered event and its subsequent reenactment--is as old as myth itself and its reenactment in ritual. Its literary antecedents include the analogical interpretations of Old Testament events as prefigurations of the New; and it reaches back in classical literature at least as far as *The Odyssey*, in which mortals reenact (and sometimes transcend) the amoral antics of the Homeric gods. Williams' plays do not simply recall old myths and rituals, however; they transform them in their reenactment. Many of these plays are based on myths of dying gods; but unlike the original myths, they culminate most often in neither rebirth nor resurrection. Similarly, these plays are structured as ritual; but theirs is a ritual of divestment, the divestment of old myths and old gods. Their archetypal pattern is an ironic version of the romance quest, whose destination in an age of disbelief is what Northrop Frye calls the "demonic epiphany" of the *tour abolie*, "the goal of the quest that isn't there."[12] The genre of these plays, then, may be defined as that of ironic myth, described by Frye as "a parody of romance: the application of romantic mythical forms to a more realistic content which fits them in unexpected ways."[13] At the same time, Williams' plays attempt to invest new, human, and sometimes shocking meaning into those *rites de passage* which have become conventional and lost their mythic resonance: the rites of initiation, marriage, and sacrificial atonement.

Thus, Williams constructs from the old myths and rituals new meanings relevant to an age and culture bereft of a commonly shared *mythos*. Seeking to restore symbolic meaning to the modern existential condition, Williams offers a dramatic experience in these plays that encourages our granting religious significance and value to merely human relationships, however limited and compensatory they may seem. Williams' drama offers no solution for metaphysical loneliness other than the rare and transient embrace with one's fellow "isolato," but in this embrace resides a redemptive humanism: a belief in the inherent potential of human communion, to achieve not epiphany but empathy through mutual compassion and understanding. In its sympathetic portrayal of his characters' romantic yearnings for transcendence, its ritualistic depiction of their inevitable confrontation with existential limitations, and its endowing with religious value transient acts of human kindness, Williams' drama imparts a mythic significance to modern secular experience.[14]

II. The Psychological Significance of the Pattern: Jungian Archetypes

In "Foreword" to *Camino Real*, Williams attests to the symbolic nature of his theater, asserting that "symbols are nothing but the natural speech of drama" (II, 421). According to Williams, "We all have in our conscious and unconscious minds a great vocabulary of images, and I think all human communication is based on these images as are our dreams" (II, 421). In a 1967 interview, he added, "I think I write mainly from my unconscious mind."[15] Thus, although Williams places the origin of creative motivation in "the particular and sometimes peculiar concerns of the artist himself" (III, 3) and readily confirms the autobiographical sources of his plays, he attempts to rise "above the singular to the plural concern, from personal to general import" (III, 4) through the use of universally evocative symbols and images.

Williams' belief in a "great vocabulary of images" that derive from the unconscious closely resembles the fundamental assumption of Jungian psychology of a "collective unconscious":[16] that psychic system beyond the personal unconscious of a "collective, universal, and impersonal nature which is identical in all individuals," and which serves as the repository of universal symbols or "archetypes" --those "mental forms . . . which seem to be aboriginal, innate, and inherited shapes of the human mind."[17] Based on archetypal religious, mythical, and literary images, Williams' symbols tap what Jung called a "wider 'unconscious' aspect that is never precisely defined or fully explained,"[18] which serves to universalize their meaning: elevating his characters' personal plights to mythic significance, the structure of his plays to ritual.

8

Moreover, as Williams' protagonists move from illusion to reality, from mythic elevation to existential limitations, they may be said to undergo the successive stages of inflation and alienation encountered in the Jungian psychological process of "individuation": that process of psychic development "arising out of the conflict between the two fundamental psychic facts"--the conscious and the unconscious--whose reconciliation leads to the realization of the personality as "a separate, indivisible unity or 'whole.'"[19] The *idyllic* myth which inflates the memories and self-images of Williams' protagonists in these plays is, according to Jungian psychology, one that is fundamental to the human psyche. According to Jungian scholar Edward Edinger, we emerge from the womb with just such an inflated sense of totality or at-one-ness with the universe: "This is the original state of unconscious wholeness and perfection which is responsible for the nostalgia we all have toward our origins, both personal and historical."[20] Such an "oceanic sense" is experienced by the infantile or immature ego before its necessary realization of itself as an individual entity, differentiated alike from any other human consciousness and the world at large.

Images which indicate a yearning for such primordial wholeness appear in Amanda's memory of "Blue Mountain" and of paradisiacal fields of flowers; in Serafina's *rosa mystica*; in Brick's Platonic idealization of Skipper; in Val Xavier's transcendent bird of Paradise; and in multiple projections of a play's character as an archetypal savior or Christ, the latter a Jungian symbol of the totality of the Self and, according to Edinger, a "paradigm of the individuating ego."[21] The *demonic* myth imbues the memories of Williams' characters with archetypal images of fragmentation and alienation--Blanche DuBois's exile from "Belle Reve"; Brick Pollitt's "broken up" (III, 135) condition; Alexandra del Lago's "fall" from fame; Shannon's psychic "crucifixion"; and the literal mutilation and dismemberment of Val Xavier, Sebastian Venable, and Chance Wayne. These images reflect the ego's resistance to estrangement from identification with the archetypes of primordial unity or wholeness, a painful but necessary stage in the process of healthy psychological development or individuation.[22] According to Jung, in order to achieve reconciliation between the ego (center of the conscious personality) and the Self (unifying center of the total psyche, conscious and unconscious)--which is the aim of individuation--the personality must "divest the self of the false wrappings of the persona on the one hand and of the suggestive power of primordial images on the other."[23]

Introduction

Just as Jung insists upon the relinquishing of the inflated ego in the process of individuation, so Williams divests his emotionally arrested characters of their dreams of regaining a paradise lost or of transcending an inherently flawed present by their confrontation with the existential reality of the isolated human condition. Though forced to recognize their human limitations, most of Williams' protagonists fail to achieve that psychic wholeness realized through individuation. According to Jung, "individuation, or becoming whole, is neither a *summum bonum* nor a *summum desideratum*, but the painful experience of the union of opposites," a process of becoming which is recurrent throughout one's lifetime.[24] Unable to reconcile their transcendent aspirations with existential limitations or to bear a world devoid of an ultimate resolution of conflict, such characters as Laura Wingfield, Blanche DuBois, Brick Pollitt, and Sebastian Venable sink into neurosis, psychosis, or achieve what Jung calls a pathological "identification with the archetype" (a devouring or swallowing-up of the conscious ego by the contents of the unconscious),[25] symbolized by their psychic or sacrificial deaths. Exceptions to these doomed romantics include Stella in *A Streetcar Named Desire*, Serafina in *The Rose Tattoo*, Maggie in *Cat on a Hot Tin Roof*, Alexandra del Lago in *Sweet Bird of Youth*, and Hannah in *The Night of the Iguana*, all of whom achieve a measure of psychic integration by their willingness to accept a less-than-ideal existence and make the compromises necessary to survive, endure, and "go on" (I, 406).

In "Desire and the Black Masseur," Williams expresses both a realistic understanding of the imperfect human condition and a romantic empathy with those who attempt to transcend or transform their flawed psychic worlds:

> For the sins of the world are really only its partialities, its incompletions, and these are what sufferings must atone for. . . . The nature of man is full of . . . makeshift arrangements, devised by himself to cover his incompletion. He feels a part of himself to be like a missing wall or a room left unfurnished and he tries as well as he can to make up for it. The use of imagination, resorting to dreams or the loftier purpose of art, is a mask he devises to cover his incompletion. . . . Then there is still another compensation. This one is found in the principle of atonement, the surrender of self to violent treatment by others with the idea of thereby clearing one's self of his guilt.[26]

10

This struggle to attain wholeness informs all of Williams' characterizations: his protagonists are representatives of a modern suffering humanity, victimized by their own conflicting drives and
desires and existentially alienated in a world become a metaphysical "heap of broken images."[27] They are at the same time testimony
to an essentially religious impulse to transcend such a "broken
world"[28] and to gain ultimate reconciliation with a universal
order: be it the *idyllic* unity of self, other, and a deity sought
through the mythic imagination or a *demonic* at-one-ment achieved by
physical surrender to the naturalistic laws of primal violence and
its consequent annihilation of all disparates.

Williams' psychologically fragmented and metaphysically isolated characters, guilty of a deep division between what they are
and what they would be, have their source in modern existentialist
philosophy and its basic concern with the human condition of isolation in a world rendered absurd by its lack of inherent meaning and
shattered religious beliefs. Williams is keenly aware that the
unique nature of each individual consciousness serves as a barrier
separating the experience of the self from the other, to the extent
that "We're all of us sentenced to solitary confinement inside our
own skins" (III, 3), the existential premise of all his work.
Thus, in his 1973 *Playboy* interview, Williams identified loneliness
as his major and recurrent theme.[29]

Not content simply to dramatize this fundamental human condition, however, Williams offers his theater as a kind of corrective
for it. He attests to a "highly personal, even intimate relationship with people who go to see plays" (III, 5) and conceives of his
plays as vehicles through which he works toward an "embrace" with
the audience: a dramatic experience which is largely affective
rather than intellectual, for Williams describes himself as a
playwright "permitted only to feel" (II, 423). His artistic ethos
is expressed in terms which reveal the sympathy toward his characters he attempts to evoke in his audience:

> Every artist has a basic premise pervading
> his whole life . . . and that premise can provide
> the impulse to everything he creates. For me the
> dominating premise has been the need for under-
> standing and tenderness and fortitude among
> individuals trapped by circumstances.[30]

Describing his dramatic mode as "personal lyricism," Williams seeks
to release through his plays that "outcry of prisoner to prisoner

from the cell in solitary where each is confined for the duration of his life" (III, 3): a *cri de coeur* intended to ameliorate existential isolation by participation in the suffering of a fellow "isolato."

The fundamental dramatic and theatrical concern of Williams, then, is to transform personal emotions, as they are embodied in the particular and sometimes peculiar maladies, neuroses, and compulsions of his characters, into universal human experience. Through the communal associations provided by archetypal images, mythical allusions, and ritual patterns, Williams attempts to create in his audience an empathetic response to his characterizations of the lonely, the alienated, the perverse, and the persecuted, thereby evoking that shock of recognition by which the audience acknowledges as familiar the characters' psychic conflicts. As Williams defines this artistic goal,

> In all human experience, there are parallels which
> permit common understanding in the telling and
> hearing, and it is the frightening responsibility
> of an artist to make what is directly or allu-
> sively close to his own being communicable and
> understandable, however disturbingly, to the
> hearts and minds of all whom he addresses. (V,
> 220)

To this end, Williams enlarges his characters to archetypal stature and invests their collective fall with the symbolic significance of a communal *rite de passage*.

CHAPTER ONE

THE GLASS MENAGERIE

Like some archetype of the universal
unconscious, the image of the gentleman
caller haunted our small apartment. . . .

I. A "Memory Play"

Memory structures both the form and content of *The Glass Menagerie* (1944-45), Williams' earliest successful play. Consisting of seven memory scenes framed by the present-time monologues of Tom Wingfield, "the narrator of the play, and also a character in it" (I, 145), the play focuses on Tom's remembered experience of the single momentous event in the drab life of his mother Amanda and his sister Laura: the arrival of a gentleman caller, Jim O'Connor. Within the "memory play" (p. 145) recalled by Tom, Amanda's reminiscences of a happier past mythicize its main event, imbuing both the ordinary social occasion and its caller with portentous symbolic significance.[1]

Amanda's memory-stories of her Southern girlhood and, especially, of her courtship by numerous "gentlemen callers" (p. 148) transport the play's events beyond the commonplace to evoke what Northrop Frye calls "the idyllic world" of romance: "a world associated with happiness, security, and peace; the emphasis is often thrown on childhood or on an 'innocent' or pre-genital period of youth, and the images are those of spring and summer, flowers and sunshine."[2] Implicit in Amanda's romantic recollections of courtship, however, is their inevitably disappointing outcome, evoking the equally unforgettable memory of her last caller--the husband who left her--and the "demonic" images of "separation, loneliness, humiliation, [and] pain."[3] From idealized beginning to realized end, Amanda's memories form a paradigm of experience that underlies the structure of the entire play--an ironic pattern of romantic expectations, momentary fulfillment, and ultimate loss.

It is, specifically, Amanda's mythicized memory of "One Sunday afternoon in Blue Mountain" when she received "*seventeen*!--gentlemen callers!" (p. 148) that is reenacted in a demythicized version by Laura and Jim. Their ironic romance thus merges the illusion of fulfilling romantic dreams with the reality of reenacting their loss. In the process of the memory's reenactment, Amanda is divested of her hopes of recapturing an idyllic past or of transforming existential reality. The juxtaposition of Amanda's memory of idyllic romance to its ironic reenactment by Laura and Jim ultimately gives the play its nostalgic mood, deepens the meaning of its mundane events, and defines its archetypal pattern: the inevitable fall of romantic aspirations to existential limitations.

Not only the meeting between Laura and Jim but every other event in the play also reflects this pattern of disillusionment. A similar pattern of great expectations and subsequent despair informs the experience of Tom, the aspiring poet ("Shakespeare" [p. 190]) whose dreams of life as a meaningful voyage (or "sea-change") end only in aimless drifting. Although Jim O'Connor's ability to compromise with a diminished reality distinguishes him from the members of the Wingfield family, the pattern also informs his experience, for he is the high-school hero--"The Pirate of Penzance" (p. 156)--who is reduced to a clerk in a warehouse, his romantic libretto exchanged for a paean to capitalistic enterprise. The pattern of initial anticipation and ultimate loss is capsulized at the very beginning of the play in the sardonic message contained in the father's picture postcard: "Hello--Goodbye!" (p. 145), a microcosmic image of the play's fleeting dreams.

The cumulative effect of the pattern's recurrence is to render life itself a series of losses, beginning with inflated expectations of its infinite possibilities and ending in confrontation with its inherent limitations. At the play's end, both Amanda's and Tom's romantic aspirations converge as understood experience: Amanda's failure to recapture a romantic past for Laura coincides with Tom's futile efforts to escape an inescapable reality, circumstances to which all three Wingfields respond with a mixture of bitterness, compassion, and "everlasting regret" (p. 185).

II. "The Glass Menagerie" as Symbol

Like the play's pattern, its symbols and images evoke a world that is at once metaphorically expansive and existentially constrictive. Even as archetypal images inflate the characters to mythic dimensions, concrete symbols define their human limitations. The principal concrete symbol in the play is, as the title suggests, the glass menagerie. It is, specifically, Laura's symbol,

IV. Amanda: Archetype of The Great Mother

The diverse imagery and mythic symbolism invested in Amanda render her an embodiment of "The Great Mother," psychic configuration of the "Archetypal Feminine" in all its complex aspects: the Good Mother, the Terrible Mother, the seductive young witch, and the innocent virgin.[5] Thus, Amanda's character and monologues are infused with a nostalgia which taps an emotional memory far beyond her "*Gone with the Wind*" (p. 160) account of her Southern girlhood. In her first monologue of the seventeen gentlemen callers, the very exaggeration of the number of her beaux recalls fairy tale and legends of romance in which the princess is beleaguered by suitors until the ideal knight or prince appears. The pastoral idyll she weaves in which the suitors are depicted as "planters and sons of planters" (p. 148) evokes both the Edenic Garden and the ancient myths of gods and goddesses of fertility, elevating Amanda to an Aphrodite called on by multiple analogues of Adonis, even as she recalls an Eve exiled from that first orchard.

Amanda's story always begins the same, on a "Sunday afternoon in Blue Mountain" (p. 148), combining the Christian religious day with overtones of Olympus, an archetypal point of epiphany.[6] It always ends at Moon Lake, recurrent site in Williams' plays of a fall from chastity or innocence. At the demonic level of Moon Lake, the pastoral scene evoked by her story turns into a graveyard, the uprooted or unweeded garden, most of Amanda's admirers having "turned up their toes to the daisies" (p. 149) after meeting violent ends. Success or survival in this fallen world depends on transplantation, the exchange of those genteel values of the fertile Delta of Greene County where Amanda spent her girlhood for those of the cold North, where at least one of her former suitors is transformed from gentleman planter to a lone "Wolf of Wall Street" (p. 149), a modern Midas whose touch turns all sustenance to unregenerative gold. The significance of the allusive imagery and fatalistic pattern of Amanda's story, then, extends beyond that of a paradigm for the historical collapse of the Plantation South in civil strife, beyond the corruption of the New World through mercenary exploitation. It evokes the Biblical myth of the Fall itself: humankind's expulsion from Eden, the subsequent violence of brother against brother, and the perversion of all attempts to cultivate "a paradise within" by reason of humankind's inherently defective nature.

In anticipation of the new gentleman caller, Jim, Amanda recounts to Laura in Scene vi another memory of her girlhood: a memory of spring and courtship, enacted in a kind of Dionysian meadow where the sexual and the spiritual are mythically reconciled. In Amanda's memory, fever, flowers, the heat of passion, and a sympathetically sensuous nature are all intertwined:

> I had malaria fever all that Spring. . . . I took quinine but kept on going, going! Evenings, dances! Afternoons, long, long rides! Picnics-- lovely! So lovely, that country in May--all lacy with dogwood, literally flooded with jonquils! (pp. 193-94)

Amanda's description of that momentous spring when she met her husband is perhaps one of the most lyrical passages in all of Williams' plays: "And then I--met your father! Malaria fever and jonquils and then - this - boy" (p. 194). At a breathless pace, Amanda more nearly sings than speaks her story, repeating the word *jonquils* until its sensuous and lyrical syllables assume incantatory power, invoking a flood of memories of rebirth and rejuvenation.

Amanda is herein endowed with the archetypal attributes of May Queen, the spirit of vegetation and fertility crowned with flowers who, amidst gaiety and dancing, enacts the ritual of spring, the mating rite. Because the "boy" she meets is also the husband who abandons her to the dark tenement in an impoverished reality, the story of Amanda also recalls the myth of Persephone, the goddess of spring whom Pluto snatched from her flower-gathering to his dark underworld. Like Persephone, Amanda has lost her springtime innocence and bitterly mourns the transitory nature of youth, beauty, and love; thus, "After the lord of the dark world carried her away she was never again the gay young creature who had played in the flowery meadow without a thought of care or trouble."[7] Her experience has taught her that beauty and charm may be enticements of seduction, and love itself an instrument of exploitation.

Thus, the youthful Amanda who triggers collective images of Aphrodite, Eve, May Queen, and Persephone also reveals the darker side of the feminine archetype, of woman as entrapment and danger. To Laura she speaks as *femme fatale*, advising her that "All pretty girls are a trap" (p. 192). To Tom, she is the Terrible Mother, the womb of the earth become the devouring maw of the underworld,[8] to which the fairy-tale analogue is the "ugly--babbling old--*witch*"

18

(p. 164), as Tom calls her. The anticipation of a gentleman caller, however, not only permits Amanda to assume the attributes of May Queen again for a brief time, but also allows her to play the benevolent role of fairy godmother, as she attempts the major transformation of the crippled Laura into a Cinderella, urging her to wish on a "little silver slipper of a moon" (p. 189).

V. Laura: The Anachronistic Ideal

The symbolism woven around Laura is composed largely of religious and ascetic images connoting the innocent otherworldliness of the saint, the cloistered nun, and the chaste virgin. In the play's "Production Notes," Williams directs that the light upon Laura should have "a peculiar pristine clarity such as light used in early religious portraits of female saints or madonnas" (pp. 133-34). Appropriately, candlelight, the halo of illumination set before shrines, is her milieu. Thus, Jim's attentions light her inwardly "with altar candles" (p. 219), suggesting the warmth of religious devotion, while her final disappointment is revealed as if the "holy candles on the altar of Laura's face have been snuffed out" (p. 230), signifying a loss of faith. In reinforcement of her saintly aspect, she is referred to by Amanda, Jim, and Tom as "sister," the traditional address for a nun, and calls herself "an old maid" (p. 150), the eternal virgin. Accordingly, her favorite animal in the glass menagerie is the mythical unicorn, "emblem of chastity and the lover of virgins."[9]

The recurrent music of "The Glass Menagerie," which may be imagined as the distant sound of a calliope on a merry-go-round, serves to evoke all the other images and qualities which characterize Laura's inner world: the tiny stationary glass animals, her childlike nature, and her uniqueness--in circus terms called freakish; in religious terms, miraculous; in temporal terms, anachronistic. Her symbolic name of "Blue Roses" further reinforces her unnatural or extraterrestrial nature, as does her favorite retreat, "the Jewel Box, that big glass house where they raise the tropical flowers" (p. 155), a metaphor for Laura's inner world, herself the *rara avis* or exotic flower that cannot survive transplantation to the outside world. Finally, it is perhaps no coincidence that Laura's name phonetically resembles *laurel*, the name of the flowering tree into which the mythic Daphne was transformed after evading the sexual pursuit of Apollo, thereby refusing the call to sexual maturity.[10]

VI. Tom: The Poète Maudit

Images of existential man dominate Tom's symbolic characterization: demonic images of fragmentation, suffocation, and alienation. It is he who identifies both the urban tenement and the warehouse as modern analogues of hell, himself sealed in a coffin, an ironic "*czar* of the *underworld*" or "*El Diablo!*" (p. 164), his deepest instincts and aspirations smoldering in frustration. Driven by the oppressive and repressive circumstances of his life and seduced by the illusory images of the movie screen to believe in a rainbow at the end of the journey, Tom attempts the sea-voyage which represents not only his personal search for self-realization but also the collective quest of twentieth-century humanity to restore to wholeness the fragmented self, threatened by dehumanization and disintegration. In Tom's struggle to integrate the primal instincts of "a lover, a hunter, a fighter" (p. 174) with the creative impulse of the poet may be recognized the attempt of modern man to heal that deep split between body and soul, flesh and spirit, which characterizes the modern malaise. Liberated from his Hades, however, Tom finds himself an aimless drifter in its modern equivalent, the Waste Land, self-exiled among the ruins of a nihilistic landscape, his dreams become "a heap of broken images." In Tom's final monologue, then, all the symbols of hope through which the characters have expressed their private visions of transcendence--Amanda's colorful jonquils, Laura's iridescent glass figures, Tom's flickering screen images and "shimmering . . . magic scarf" (p. 167), and the large glass sphere in the Paradise Dance Hall--are ultimately revealed as fragments of broken dreams: "bits of a shattered rainbow" (p. 237). Haunted by his abandonment of family in his futile quest for self-transcendence, Tom joins the ranks of other guilt-haunted wanderers--Cain, the Wandering Jew, the Flying Dutchman, the Ancient Mariner--archetypes of psychic alienation. Like the Ancient Mariner, Tom becomes the *poète maudit*, cursed with existential knowledge of the human condition and compelled to retell endlessly his story, herein, a modern fable of the failure of love and of modern man's inability to transcend his essential solitude in a world devoid of transcendent goals.

VII. Jim O'Connor: Ironic Savior

Jim O'Connor is at once the most symbolic character in the play and the most realistic. Accordingly, the allusive imagery from which he is constructed is multiple and paradoxical, romantic and ironic. As a reincarnation of the gentleman caller, he evokes both the infinite possibilities suggested by all seventeen suitors and the limited reality defined by the last caller, the father who abandoned wife and family. Thus, Jim represents both that "long-delayed but always expected something that we live for" (p. 145) and, ironically, "a nice, ordinary, young man" (p. 129), both the ideal and the real. "Like some archetype of the universal unconscious" (p. 159), Jim is invested with multiple heroic images. As the reborn gentleman caller, he is identified with a fertility god, the regenerative "planter"; his "Annunciation" (p. 178) signals the rebirth or second coming of Christ as the Savior; Amanda's wish upon "the little silver slipper of a moon" (p. 189) casts Jim in the role of Prince Charming to Laura's Cinderella; and in Scene vii, he plays the prince who awakens her Sleeping Beauty. He is the singing Pirate who will charm the Lady, and he is "Superman" (p. 210) who never fails to rescue Lois Lane. All of these symbols of expectation are ironically invested in a character who is the apotheosis of the All-American boy--extroverted, dynamic, and optimistic --thoroughly acculturated to the popular equation of happiness with technological progress and material success.

VIII. The Story Reenacted: A Demythicized Version

The enlargement of the characters through allusive imagery in the first part of the play is designed to heighten the emotional intensity of its climax in Scene vii: the reenactment of Amanda's story of her gentlemen callers in the meeting between Laura and Jim. The mythicization of the characters combined with the symbolic value invested in the images and props of the scene--Laura's physical transformation, the suggestion of rain, the circle of candlelight from the miraculously fire-salvaged candelabrum, and the glass of dandelion wine--all function to elevate the significance of that meeting beyond mere social ceremony to suggest a pagan rite of fertility or initiation, the Christian sacrament of Holy Communion, and the romantic ritual of courtship. Here, however, symbol is divorced from substance, the mythical is distinguished from the actual, and the bubbles of subjective reality in which the characters have insulated themselves are broken. At the same time, the infusion of symbolic meaning into ordinary human experience serves to evoke an emotional response appropriate to an event of momentous import, thereby deepening the significance of the failure of union between Laura and Jim.

The process of demythicization begins in Scene vii with Jim's breaking of the unicorn, medieval symbol of chastity and innocence, which signals the beginning of Laura's healthy sexual and emotional development and the divestment of her symbolic dimensions as virgin, saint, and child. As the unicorn divested of its horn is now "just like all the other horses" (p. 226), so Laura no longer feels freakish and estranged from vital human experience. In that respect her demythicization represents a *felix culpa*, a fortunate fall, or "blessing in disguise" (p. 226) as Laura refers to the "normalizing" of the unicorn. Laura's emergence into Jim's world of dynamic optimism is dramatically expressed by her cavalier reaction to the broken unicorn, her private world of imaginary animals having become less important than the real one of human relationships. Thus, Laura's response to Jim's breaking the unicorn is phrased in popular slang that parallels Jim's own idiomatic diction: "It's no tragedy, Freckles. Glass breaks so easily" (p. 226). Just as Laura's sexuality is awakened by Jim's natural exuberance, so his finer sensibilities are aroused by Laura's vulnerability and virginal beauty. Thus, for the brief moment of their kiss, the symbolic fusion of experience and innocence, flesh and spirit, or reality and dream is achieved. Jim's subsequent revelation of his engagement to another girl and the finality of his departure, however, not only abandon Laura to her shattered dreams but also deflate the entire matrix of mythical, romantic, and religious symbols evoked in the play.

Mocked by their symbols of transcendence, the characters are at the play's end identified starkly in terms of their human failings: "a mother deserted, an unmarried sister who's crippled," and a son who's a "selfish dreamer" (p. 236). The deflation of all the mythicized images and symbols previously developed in the play elicits an overwhelming sense of their loss. The failure of Jim to save Laura is made analogous to the failure of the fertlity god to achieve rebirth, the failure of Christ's second coming, and the failures of Prince Charming, the Pirate, and Superman to rescue the maiden in distress. Because Williams has so extended the symbolic meaning of Jim, the loss becomes one of "infinite desolation" (p. 230). It is the loss of all heroes, the death of all gods, the disillusionment of all transcendent hopes and dreams. Thus,

22

through a profusion of universal symbols and a recurrent tragic pattern, the meaning of the play is enlarged. It is not simply the story of one shy crippled girl, a neurotic mother, and a dreamer of a son, not the story of just one more broken family, but an analogue of modern man's alienation from God and his existential isolation from his fellow man.

IX. An Existential Tragedy

The Glass Menagerie embodies Williams' vision of the fundamental human situation as one of solitude in a universe indifferent to our fate and inimical to our transcendent aspirations. By the infusion of symbol, myth, and ritual into a naturalistic drama, Williams evokes a painful awareness of the central paradox of modern existence: that the transcendent imagination remains undiminished in a world empty of transcendent value. Yet, only by the divestment of deceptive illusions and romantic dreams of transcending the existentially limited human condition is the meaningful communcation of self with other possible. Human love itself, however, is shown as ultimately inadequate compensation for our epiphanic desires. Fleeting, incomplete, and too easily betrayed, human love too often leads only to the recognition of mutual despair.

The play ends, then, in an ironic family portrait. The ritual of divestment and the shattering of illusions lead the members of the Wingfield family to a brief moment of communion in a symbolic embrace. No longer encased within private visions of transcendence, they are in the play's final scene ironically united in their mutual understanding of their inherent isolation in an unredemptive reality. The ironic embrace is achieved aesthetically in Scene vii by our simultaneous vision of Amanda, Laura, and the departed Tom. We see, in mime, Amanda's compassionate gesture of consoling Laura, as Laura "lifts her head to smile at her mother" (p. 236), and Tom pledges emotional fidelity to his sister whose memory continues to haunt him, having discovered the value of her fragile beauty in a world "lit by lightning" (p. 237) and dedicated to its destruction. Paradoxically, the symbolic tableau transcends for a moment its literal meaning of loss and despair, but only for a moment. The play closes in darkness, all three characters confined to the prisons of self once more in a reality unrelieved by dreams of deliverance.

CHAPTER TWO

A STREETCAR NAMED DESIRE

> I don't want realism. I want magic! . . .
> I don't tell truth, I tell what *ought*
> to be truth. And if that is sinful,
> then let me be damned for it!

I. The Descent of Blanche DuBois: Demonic Romance

A Streetcar Named Desire (1947) moves between polar modes--romance and realism, tragedy and comedy, the mythic and the ironic --in its structure, characterization, symbolism, and visual-aural imagery. Embedded in the play's naturalistic context is an ironic quest myth, an archetypal conflict between the soul and the body, and what Northrop Frye calls the "descent theme" of romance.[1] As a parable of the soul's heroic but futile quest to transcend the inescapable demands, desires, and inevitable degeneration of its physical incarnation, the play focuses on the internal drama of its protagonist, Blanche DuBois, from whose memory and imagination all of the play's romantic elements emanate.[2] As product of the protagonist's mind, then, the play's romance is wholly illusory: her descent, however, is not.

Against the soul's romantic dreams, illusions, and aspirations is set the intractable reality of the flesh, its "brutal desire[s]" (I, 321) acknowledged and embodied by the protagonist herself even as she attempts to transcend and transform them by the shaping spirit of her mythic imagination. The biological necessities of human nature are personified by the play's antagonist to the romantic sensibility, Stanley Kowalski. The play's conflict, then, is dual, enacted as much within the warring personas of the protagonist's "moth-tiger" psyche as between her transcendent aspirations and her antagonist's fundamental animalism.[3] The structural center of the play resides in the recurrent archetypal sequences of Blanche DuBois's "fall," as remembered in the past and reenacted in the present: a pattern which begins always with mythically elevated expectations, followed by inevitable disillusionment, and the physical corruption of the soul's transcendent dreams.

According to Frye, the action of romance, like that of *Street-*

car, "seems to move simultaneously on two levels, one of the foreground action, the other inside the heroine's mind" (*Secular Scripture*, p. 91). As with Blanche and Stanley, the "heroines" and "villains" of romance are polarized entities, existing primarily "to symbolize a contrast between two worlds, one above the level of ordinary experience, the other below it" (*Secular Scripture*, p. 53). The structure of romance is vertical, so that "the romancer, scrambling over a series of disconnected episodes, seems to be trying to get us to the top" of a story, unlike the realist, who, "with his sense of logical and horizontal continuity, leads us to the end" of it (*Secular Scripture*, p. 50). In *Streetcar*, the structures of romance and realism are combined: even as Blanche, the play's romancer, reveals in "a series of disconnected episodes" the memories of a past she attempts to escape or transcend, Stanley, the realist, pursues the corrupt facts of her stories with a relentless "sense of logical and horizontal continuity" to the end of their exposure and Blanche's degradation. As in *Streetcar*, the movement of romance ranges from the elevated idyllic world of pastoral innocence--the world evoked by Blanche's memories of her youthful discovery of love with Allan Grey and by the name of the family plantation, "Belle Reve"--to a demonic nightmare world--the corrupt world of experience, sexuality, and death from which Blanche fruitlessly seeks to escape. Thus, Blanche's perception of Stanley's naturalistic territory corresponds to the archetypal imagery of the demonic world of romance, "a dark and labyrinthine world of caves and shadows where the forest has turned subter-ranean . . . surrounded by the shapes of animals" (*Secular Scripture*, p. 111). Herein, images of "cards and dice are common," reinforcing a fatalistic sense to Blanche's descent and degradation (*Secular Scripture*, p. 124). Finally, the demonic world of romance is characterized by an "erotic intensity," like that embodied by the threatening sexuality of Stanley; and its adventures, like those experienced by Blanche, are marked by "separation, loneli-ness, humiliation, pain, and the threat of more pain" (*Secular Scripture*, pp. 104, 53).

Although traditional or sentimental romance is patterned by a cyclical movement of "descent into a night world and a return to the idyllic world," in *Streetcar*, the romantic heroine descends into the demonic night world and stays there; according to Frye, "It is possible never to get out of this lower world, and some may not even want to" (*Secular Scripture*, pp. 54, 123). Thus, Blanche descends to "the point of her lowest fortunes" in the demonic nightworld of human sacrifice, rape, or near death: she is stripped of her romantic dreams and pretenses, forcibly made to embrace her essentially animal nature, and exposed to "the horror of being totally known . . . an involuntarily acquired self-knowledge that [in romance] is more terrible than death itself" (*Secular Scripture*, pp. 80, 123). According to Frye, the only companion that accompanies the romantic heroine to the end of her descent to the underworld is "the demonic accuser, who takes the form of the accusing memory. . . . It conveys to us the darkest knowledge at the bottom of the world, the vision of the absurd, the realization that only death is certain, and that nothing before or after death makes sense" (*Secular Scripture*, pp. 124-25). It is finally this "accusing memory" and its accompanying "horror of being totally known" that proves fatally inimical to the romance-quest of Blanche DuBois, leading to her imprisonment in a psychological underworld.

At the very bottom of her descent into madness, however, Blanche is aesthetically elevated to mythic stature, to "the position of a goddess [imprisoned] in a lower world" (*Secular Scripture*, p. 86); for, at the moment of her final debasement, she conducts herself with the regal dignity of a queen, albeit psychologically, she is, like Persephone, only "Queen of the Dead." Nevertheless, perhaps the finest moment in the literature of romance lies in Blanche DuBois's existentially mad but romantically heroic response to the Doctor who will lead her to her living death: "Whoever you are--I have always depended on the kindness of strangers" (p. 418). Through the "magic" of the imagination, Blanche transforms her own degradation into a romantic courtship ritual of hope and promise; and by the dignity with which she confronts her end, she imaginatively restores to her shattered psyche and debased identity the romantic roles of "Queen" (p. 398), "Dame Blanche" (p. 361), and "cultivated woman" (p. 396) which had mocked her in reality. In so doing, she fulfills Williams' personal definition of the "monarch" and the "lady," for, according to the playwright's own romantic code, such "high station in life is earned by the gallantry with which appalling experiences are survived with grace."[4]

Although Blanche's romantic gesture is existentially ironic and affectively pathetic, it nevertheless affirms that the yearning for romantic transcendence is never altogether suppressed. The play ends, then, with the conflict between romance and realism resumed: the final line's cruel reminder--that in the naturalistic world of "brutal desire," the name of life's game is "seven-card stud" (p. 419)--is juxtaposed to an image of irrepressible romance:

Blanche DuBois's imaginative transformation of degrading experience into a symbolic "deliverance" from the confines of an inherently corrupt human nature. In symbol, if not in substance, Blanche escapes from the demonic night world and completes the cycle of romance.

II. The Archetypal Story: Blanche DuBois's "Accusing Memory"

The fall of Blanche DuBois begins not upon her arrival in the ironically-named "Elysian Fields" of the naturalistic underworld, but long before, in the mythicized past of her youth as a "tender and trusting" (p. 376) young girl of "Belle Reve" where the transgression takes place which dooms her to the guilt-haunted wanderer of the play's dramatic present. That story of the past which is reenacted in the present is Blanche DuBois's memory of the disastrous consequences of her youthful marriage to Allan Grey, which leads to her subsequent "intimacies with strangers" (p. 386). It is first told in full by Blanche to Mitch in Scene vi--the precise center of the play's eleven-scene structure--but its echoes of dialogue and of visual and aural imagery adumbrate throughout the play. In its archetypal elements, the story recalls the myth of a paradise lost, from its idyllic beginnings to its demonic end: the "original sin" of the body's betrayal of the innocent soul, the consequent exile of humankind from the Edenic paradise where flesh and spirit were once united in shameless love, and the subsequent division between God and man, soul and body, dream and reality. Testifying to the inherent duality of human nature, Blanche DuBois not only embodies the frail, delicate spirit of the "moth" (p. 245) or "butterfly" (p. 332)--traditional symbols of the mythical Psyche or soul--but she also represents the "wildcat" (p. 383) or "tiger" (p. 402), manifestations of the body's fundamental animal nature. Attempting the impossible transcendence of the soul's inherently corrupt incarnation, Blanche DuBois is destined only to reenact the "original sin" of the body's betrayal of the soul again and again.

The story of the past begins as romantic myth. Blanche describes her first encounter with Allan Grey in the mythic terms of the illumination of Eros by Psyche: "When I was sixteen, I made the discovery--love. . . . It was like you suddenly turned a blinding light on something that had always been half in shadow, that's how it struck the world for me" (p. 354). Accordingly, Blanche elevates Allan Grey to godlike dimensions. As Stella recalls, "He was extremely good-looking. I think Blanche didn't just love him but worshipped the ground he walked on! Adored him and thought him almost too fine to be human!" (p. 364). Like the mythic Psyche in search of the god of Love, Blanche projects her romantic lamp onto an ideal soul-mate, and "when she was young, very young, she married a boy who wrote poetry" (p. 364).

The romantic spirit of Poe is evoked in this first memory, as his darker aspect is recalled throughout the play. Appropriately, and not coincidentally perhaps, the name of Blanche's idealized lover is a fusion of two last names adopted by the Southern romantic poet whose own soul--like that of the youthful Blanche--yearned for transcendence from vulgar reality: Edgar *Allan* Poe, alias Edward S. T. *Grey*.[5] Furthermore, in Blanche's nostalgic elevation of herself and the youthful Allan Grey to Edenic innocence--"He was a boy, just a boy, when I was a very young girl" (p. 354)--we hear echoes of Poe's similarly nostalgic ode to his own deceased child-wife in "Annabel Lee": "*I* was a child and *she* was a child,/ In this kingdom by the sea." Indeed, Blanche's romantic striving to elevate her adolescent relationship with Allan Grey to mythic dimensions is not unlike that spiritual yearning or "immortal instinct" which Poe has metaphorically defined as the essence of the poetic or imaginative faculty: "It is the desire of the moth for the star . . . no mere appreciation of the Beauty before us-- but a wild effort to reach the Beauty above."[6]

In the archetypal pattern of the soul's journey from innocence to experience, however, the next step is disillusionment: "But then she found out--this beautiful and talented young man was a degenerate" (p. 364), or, in Blanche's own words, "But I was unlucky. Deluded" (p. 354). As Blanche recounts the story, having come upon her beloved young husband in the midst of a homosexual liaison with an older man, she at first "pretended that nothing had been discovered," and the three of them drive out to Moon Lake Casino (recurrent site in Williams' plays of a tragic fall), "very drunk and laughing all the way." However, in the middle of dancing the polka to the tune of the Varsouviana, Blanche, "unable to stop myself," blurts out, "I saw! I know! You disgust me. . . ." and "the boy I had married broke away from me and ran out of the casino. A few moments later--a shot! . . . He'd stuck the revolver into his mouth, and fired--so that the back of his head had been-- blown away!" (p. 355).

This memory of sexual transgression, the harsh exposure of

corrupt human nature, and the violent destruction of romantic dreams is recalled and reenacted in its every aspect throughout the play, thereby evoking the "arrest of time" (II, 259) for the play's protagonist and emphasizing the inescapability of her guilt, "regrets--recriminations" (p. 388). Blanche's destructive exposure and rejection of Allan Grey corresponds mythically to Cain's "crime against human relationship,"[7] for which she receives his primal curse--"a fugitive and a vagabond shalt thou be in the earth"--and the existential knowledge that "we are a long way from being made in God's image" (p. 323). Although Blanche is later to claim that "Deliberate cruelty . . . the one unforgivable thing . . . is the one thing of which I have never, never been guilty" (p. 397), it is precisely this act of impulsive cruelty which haunts the guilt-ridden Blanche in the form of the "accusing memory." Its spontaneous nature ("unable to stop myself") serves only to reveal the depth of the transcendent soul's "disgust" with its own sexual incarnation. Thus, Blanche's condemnation of Allan Grey for the violation of her soul's romantic dreams and transcendent aspirations leads only to the realization of herself as inheritor of the crime with which she charges him, damned to the same all-too-human carnality.

Allan's betrayal of Blanche is thus reenacted as self-betrayal: a *psychomachia* of the eternally unresolved conflict between the transcendent aspirations of the soul and the "brutal desire" (p. 321) of the body, played out within her own divided self. Divested of her youthful innocence and illusions, and damned to the self-knowledge of the soul's inherently corrupt incarnation, Blanche nevertheless continues the romantic striving to achieve an ideal union in a "broken world."[8] Her transcendent aspirations recall Plato's myth of the division of humankind's original wholeness into a divided self, each half of which spends its entire life searching for its soul-mate. In this existential version of the myth, however, the debased soul, seeking sanctuary or "hunting for some protection" (p. 386), finds not a soul-mate, but only promiscuous "intimacies with strangers" (p. 386): soldiers, salesmen, and, finally, a seventeen-year-old boy, each of whom metes out the fit retribution of exposure and exile to the guilt-haunted Blanche. As Stanley triumphantly discloses in Scene vii, the army camp labels Blanche "Out-of-Bounds" (p. 361) for her bacchic orgies with young soldiers; the manager of the Hotel Flamingo (become for Blanche the demonic "Tarantula Arms") requests her "to turn in her room key--for permanently!" (p. 360) for luring its traveling supplymen like flies to "a big spider!" (p. 386); and, for

V. Mitch: The Diminished Ideal

The story of Blanche's relationship with Allan Grey--from its romanticized beginnings to its cruel conclusion--is reenacted by Blanche with Mitch in a diminished, retributive version. Divested of her youthful innocence and romantic illusions, and damned to the self-knowledge of an inherently corrupt nature, Blanche nevertheless attempts to transform her guilt-ridden past into a romantic present through the "magic" of the imagination. As she confesses to Mitch at the disastrous climax of their relationship: "I don't want realism. I want magic! Yes, yes, magic! I try to give that to people. I misrepresent things to them. I don't tell truth, I tell what *ought* to be truth. And if that is sinful, then let me be damned for it" (p. 385). Blanche herein suggests the paradox of the *poète maudit*, cursed with an imaginative sensibility that damns her to alienation and isolation from the human community even as it offers the only hope of salvation from a corrupt fallen world. Like the Ancient Mariner who is compelled to tell again and again his story of crime and punishment, Blanche is condemned to reenact hers.

From the beginning of their relationship, Blanche attempts to elevate Mitch to the romanticized status of the idealized Allan Grey. As Allan's analogue, Mitch shares his "softness and tenderness which wasn't like a man's" (p. 354), or, as Blanche says to Stella at her first sight of Mitch: "That one seems--superior to the others. . . . I thought he had a sort of sensitive look" (p. 292). Allan's homosexuality becomes in Mitch an over-solicitous attachment to his sick mother. As Blanche's "soul-mate," Mitch shares with her the loss of a youthful romantic love: "The girl's dead now" (p. 298). Accordingly, the "poems a dead boy wrote" (p. 282), which Blanche keeps in her trunk in memory of her husband, become for Mitch an inscription on the lighter given to him by his own deceased beloved; the inscription appropriately consists of the last lines from Sonnet XLIII of Elizabeth Barrett Browning's *Sonnets to the Portuguese*: "And if God choose,/ I shall but love thee better--after--death!" (p. 297).

As the disillusioned idealist, no longer seeking romance but "*rest!*" (p. 335) from her guilt-haunted past, Blanche admits to Stella her desire to "deceive" Mitch, "enough to make him--want me" (p. 335). To that end, Blanche misrepresents herself to Mitch, even as she knows that this shy, ordinary, middle-aged suitor who has a job as a "spare-parts precision" worker and lifts weights at the New Orleans Athletic Club is but a mere shadow of her youthful dreams. Thus, even while dressed in the "red satin wrapper" of the courtesan, her "tongue . . . a little thick" from liquor, Blanche weaves a web of illusions about herself that elevates her debased nature to the mythicized stature of a lily-white Southern Belle. Pretending to Edenic purity and youthful innocence, she tells Mitch her name means "white woods. Like an orchard in spring" (p. 299); feigning a delicacy long ago corrupted, she asks him to put an "adorable little colored paper lantern" over the naked light bulb, just as Blanche herself masks her true nature by her romantic pretenses; affecting "old-fashioned ideals" (p. 348), she coyly commands Mitch to "unhand me, sir" (p. 348) when he tries to embrace her and she resists more than a "good-night kiss," for, as she bluntly tells Stella, "I'm not 'putting out'" (p. 335).

Similarly, she invests Mitch with the elevated attributes of romantic and mythical figures to whom she plays female counterpart. Thus, she is the frail and refined lady to his image of gentleman caller, "a natural gentleman, one of the very few that are left in the world" (p. 348); and she plays the operatic role of Richard Strauss's youthful "Sophie" (rather than the aging beauty, "Marschallin") with Mitch as "My Rosenkavalier" (p. 339). Ironically, the other roles which Blanche assigns to Mitch and herself nearly betray the true promiscuity or duplicity of her nature: she evokes the image of herself as the treacherous Delilah by her reference to Mitch as "Samson!" (p. 347), and depicts herself as the courtesan "Dame aux Camellias" to his "Armand" (p. 344). As her last hope for sanctuary and salvation from a fallen world, however, Mitch is finally elevated to the apotheosis of transcendent love. To his simple offer of marriage, Blanche confers on him the highest accolade in a world where human love must take the place of divine redemption: "Sometimes--there's God--so quickly!" (p. 356).

As in the original story of Blanche and Allan, however, romantic inflation is to be followed by disillusionment and despair. "Wised up" by Stanley about Blanche's sexually promiscuous past, Mitch reenacts the retributive punishment of cruel exposure and fatal rejection to which Blanche had subjected Allan. Thus, at the beginning of Scene ix, in foreboding anticipation of the "disaster closing in on her" (p. 379), the "rapid, feverish polka tune" of the Varsouviana rises up in Blanche's memory. When Mitch appears-- her hope of redemption--"the polka tune stops" (p. 379), but it soon resumes as she realizes by his blue-denim work clothes and unshaven face that he no longer represents the image of romance, but the "utterly uncavalier" (p. 379) intrusion of harsh, unvarnished reality. As Blanche senses "something's the matter" (p. 381), she resorts to the tactic of pretending that "nothing had been discovered" (p. 355) as she had on finding Allan Grey with his lover; thus, she tells Mitch, "I'll just pretend I don't notice anything different about you!" (p. 381). But the haunting music--"The 'Varsouviana!' The polka tune they were playing when Allan . . ." (p. 381)--increases in intensity, as do Blanche's fears, anxieties, and guilt, until she hears "the shot!" (p. 381), and with the death of the accusing memory, the polka tune dies out again: "It always stops after that" (p. 381).

As the memory ends, however, its reenactment begins. Just as Blanche had exposed Allan Grey's true sexual nature, so Mitch exposes the "total ruin" (p. 254) beneath Blanche's idealized persona. Tearing the rose-colored Chinese lantern from the naked light-bulb, "So I can take a look at you good and plain!" (p. 384), Mitch not only strips Blanche of her romantic pretensions of youth, refinement, and virginal innocence, but also symbolically divests her of all her illusions, hopes, and dreams of magically transcending the corrupt past. Just as Blanche was "deluded" about Allan, so Mitch feels like "a fool . . . to believe you was straight" (p. 385). His disdainful rejection of her--"You're not clean enough to bring in the house with my mother" (p. 390)--parallels precisely Blanche's own contemptuous rejection of Allan: "You disgust me . . . " (p. 355).

For Blanche, however, degradation is not to be followed by "a shot!"--the quiescence of the accusing memory. Instead, "the polka tune fades in" (p. 388) once more, as recollections of her sordid past are evoked by the cry of the Mexican woman selling "Flores para los muertos" (flowers for the dead). Her memory of the death of Allan Grey merges with that of the loss of Belle Reve and of the young soldiers with whom she reveled in Dionysian abandon, their being gathered up "like daisies" (p. 389) by the paddy wagon.[12] Burning with shame, "regrets, recriminations" (p. 388), Blanche loses her "cleft in the rock of the world that I could hide in!" (p. 387). Symbolically raped by Mitch, she is to be physically violated by Stanley in an infernal version of the same story.

VI. Interlude: The Fairy-Tale Version

Even in the midst of creating an idealized image of herself as
a "prim and proper" (p. 335) maiden and of Mitch as gallant cavalier, Blanche violates her own romanticized persona. In Scene v,
while waiting for Mitch, an inebriated Blanche reenacts the role of
the *femme fatale* who seduced the seventeen-year-old boy in Laurel.
This time, the "young man" is the paper boy, whom Blanche imaginatively transforms to a fairy-tale "Prince out of the Arabian
Nights" (p. 339) and symbolically compares to a "cherry soda" (p.
338), whose virginal innocence tempts Blanche's sexual appetite: as
she tells the boy, "You make my mouth water!" (p. 338). Recalling
the consequences of that original story, however, Blanche, after a
kiss, lets the boy go; like a reformed witch out of "Hansel and
Gretel," she tells him that "It would be nice to keep you, but
I've got to be good--and keep my hands off children" (p. 339).
An ironic Scheherazade, Blanche hopes for deliverance from her
destructive sexuality by reenacting as fairy tale the sordid reality of past experience, but no story she tells can save her from
herself.

VII. The Demonic Version: Stanley as Dionysus

The dramatic *agon* between Stanley Kowalski and Blanche DuBois
represents an externalization of her own inner conflict: the struggle between the brutal desires of the flesh and the transcendent
aspirations of the spirit or soul. In this psychodrama, Stanley
embodies the Dionysian antithesis to Blanche's romantic dreams and
moral pretensions, the personified projection of her own libidin-
ousx impulses. Thus, Blanche's animosity toward Stanley's "animal
force" (p. 319) and "bestial" (p. 322) sexuality is also self-
disgust with her own irrepressible carnality, for, in Jungian
terms, "That which one passionately hates is sure to represent an
aspect of his own fate."[13] As the incarnation of her own animal
passions, then, Stanley is psychologically destined to act as the
"executioner" of her romantic fantasies and idealized persona: "The
first time I laid eyes on him I thought to myself, that man is my
executioner! That man will destroy me, unless . . ." (p. 351).
Mitch had represented the wish-fulfillment to which Blanche's "unless" refers, but with his rejection of her, she is left without
protection from her guilt-ridden memories and frustrated desires.
Like the moth, her symbol, Blanche is irresistibly drawn into the
flame of passion that destroys her. As her nemesis, the vengeful

slayer of her romantic illusions, Stanley is to reenact once again the retributive exposure, humiliation, and final degradation of Blanche DuBois in a demonic, rapacious version of her condemnation of Allan Grey and her subsequent "intimacies with strangers."

Stanley Kowalski is endowed with the multi-faceted attributes of the mythic Dionysus, the primitive Asian fertility god become the Greek god of wine, liberation, and sexual ecstasy, who represents the amoral force of nature, irresistible in its attraction. Like Dionysus, Stanley is described by Williams as the apotheosis of phallic fertility--"the gaudy seed-bearer" (p. 265)--in whom "animal joy . . . is implicit in all his movements and attitudes" (p. 264). Appropriately, Stanley's astrological sign is Capricorn--"the Goat!" (p. 328)--animal incarnation of Dionysus and symbol of unbridled lust,[14] while Blanche's sign is ironically "Virgo . . . the Virgin" (p. 329). Just as Dionysus is best known for the orgiastic rites he inspired among his female worshippers, the Maenads or Bacchae, so the center of Stanley's life is said to have been "pleasure with women" (p. 265). The Dionysian bliss he inspires in Stella is reflected by her attitude of "narcotized tranquility" (p. 310) after a night of their lovemaking, itself elevated to a mystery rite as described by Stella--"there are things that happen between a man and a woman in the dark" (p. 321)--and orgiastic as recalled by Stanley: "God, honey, it's gonna be sweet when we can make noise in the night . . . and get the colored lights going" (p. 373). As the "most terrible yet most gentle of gods,"[15] an amoral animal force, Dionysus sometimes exploded with the ferocity of a lion, and at other times embodied the perfect attunement with nature represented by a suckling fawn with its mother. So, too, Stanley is depicted as "a powder-keg" (p. 312) one moment--hurling cards onto a poker table, plates onto the floor, the radio out the window, or Stella across the room--and "good as a lamb" (p. 312) in the next. Finally, as the sociable leader of the pack who spends his time with the boys playing poker, bowling, and drinking beer, Stanley represents the Dionysian spirit of "unthinking physical enjoyment, of the instinctive group-personality, of anti-intellectual energy."[16]

Dionysus is not only known as the "gay reveler," however, but also as "the cruel hunter."[17] His vengeful spirit and savage brutality are reflected in Stanley as he tracks down Blanche's corrupt past and cruelly destroys her with its exposure. His very first appearance in Scene i when he throws Stella the "red-stained package from the butcher's" (p. 244) evokes not only the image of a "survivor of the Stone Age! Bearing the raw meat home from the kill" (p. 323), but also that of the savage Dionysus, "eater of raw flesh," whose orgiastic rites often concluded with the slaughtering and consuming of one of his several animal incarnations (lion, goat, bull) in the belief that by so ingesting the Dionysian spirit, his worshippers might rejuvenate their own life-blood.[18] Significantly, when Blanche discovers Stella is pregnant, she concedes that Stanley's "blood" might prove invigorating to their dying lineage: "maybe he's what we need to mix with our blood now that we've lost Belle Reve" (p. 285). In her final confrontation with Stanley, Blanche herself is to undergo an orgiastic rite of communion with the same Dionysian spirit.

VIII. *The Bacchae:* A Structural Analogue

In its structure and archetypal theme, the conflict between Stanley and Blanche parallels Dionysus' vengeful pursuit of Pentheus in Euripides' *The Bacchae*.[19] Both Pentheus and Blanche attempt to deny the necessity of embracing their own animal passions, personified by their antagonists. Blanche, like the Greek tragic hero, is guilty of *hubris* or overweening arrogance, in her attempt to transcend the human limitations defined by her inherent sexuality. Just as Pentheus scorns the incarnated god as a "foreigner" whose sexual excesses and animal nature are a corrupting and salacious influence on the Theban women and culture, so Blanche snobbishly demeans Stanley as a "Polack" (p. 262), as "common!" (p. 322), and as an atavistic threat to civilization's humanistic aspirations:

> There's something downright--bestial--about him.
> . . . He acts like an animal, has an animal's
> habits! Eats like one, moves like one, talks like
> one! There's even something--sub-human--something
> not quite to the stage of humanity yet! (p. 323)

Both Dionysus and Stanley revenge themselves of such slander and hypocritical self-righteousness, by divesting their victims of their superior moral pretensions, humiliating them in turn, and exposing their victims' own inherent animal natures through acts of violent retribution.

In *The Bacchae*, the conflict between Dionysus and Pentheus is structured as a hunt in which the roles of hunter and hunted are reversed midway through the play, in accordance with the classical dramatic convention of a peripety: that reversal of fortune which signals the protagonist's tragic fall. Thus, although the destruction of Pentheus is fated from the beginning, he initially assumes the role of the hunter who appears successful in capturing and conquering his animalistic opponent. However, Dionysus proves futile Pentheus' attempts to enchain his powerful life-force, and the tables turn: Dionysus, as the cruel hunter, corners his humiliator and vengefully drives him to madness and dismemberment.

In *Streetcar*, a similar contest, pursuit, and reversal of fortune and roles takes place between Stanley and Blanche. Here, however, the imagery of the hunt is supplemented by the metaphor of the poker game, in which Stanley's fluctuating fortune at cards reflects his changing status in the existential game of survival played between him and Blanche. Leonard Quirino brillantly summarizes the structural correspondences between the two contests:

> Pitting Stanley Kowalski, the powerful master of Elysian Fields against Blanche DuBois, the ineffectual ex-mistress of Belle Reve, Williams makes the former the inevitable winner of the game whose stakes are survival in the kind of world the play posits. For the first four of the eleven scenes of Streetcar, Blanche, by reason of her affectation of gentility and respectability, manages to bluff a good hand in her game with Stanley; thus, in the third scene Stanley is continually losing, principally to Mitch the potential ally of Blanche, in the poker game played onstage. However, generally suspicious of Blanche's behavior and her past, and made aware at the end of the fourth scene that she considers him an ape and a brute, Stanley pursues an investigation of the real identity of her cards. As, little by little, he finds proof of what he considers her own apishness and brutality, he continually discredits her gambits until, in the penultimate scene, he caps his winnings by raping her. In the last scene of the play, Stanley is not only winning every card being played onstage, but he has also won the game he played with Blanche.[20]

The device of the poker game, then, contributes to the fatalistic sense that Blanche is tragically destined to lose in her final bid to escape her corrupt past and transcend her inherent animal nature. Characterizing herself as "unlucky" (p. 354) and "played out" (p. 387) even before her arrival in Stanley's terri-

41

tory, Blanche, like Pentheus, is fated to destruction by the Dionysian life-force. But, in the first part of the play, she bluffs her way into the appearance of winning away from Stanley both Stella and Mitch, her two last chances for escape or sanctuary from her corrupt past.

IX. Stanley vs. Blanche: The *Agon*

That Stanley will reenact the story of Allan Grey in a retributive version is clear to Blanche from their very first encounter in Scene i. Recognizing in Stanley the same raw sexuality that has violated all her romantic dreams and fearful of its exposure in herself, Blanche, "drawing involuntarily back from his stare" (p. 265), senses his ability to "size women up at a glance, with sexual classifications" (p. 265). Thus, Stanley's question of "What happened?" to her marriage evokes immediately Blanche's memory of her cruel exposure of Allan Grey. As the music of the Varsouviana rises up, aural symbol of her guilty conscience, Blanche replies, "The boy--the boy died. . . . I'm afraid I'm--going to be sick" (p. 268).

Simultaneously attracted to and repelled by Stanley's sexuality, Blanche, in Scene ii, attempts to win Stanley over. Adopting the successive roles of helpless female, seductive "witch" (p. 279), and innocent naif, Blanche, like a good poker player, changes her strategy as quickly as Stanley exposes each deceptive tactic in her attempts to charm, flatter, or otherwise win him to her side. Rejecting all her ploys, Stanley bluntly expresses his suspicions of her promiscuity--"If I didn't know that you was my wife's sister I'd get ideas about you" (p. 281)--demanding that Blanche stop playing "so dumb," and "Lay . . . her cards on the table" (p. 279). Thus, when Stanley, in symbolic anticipation of the literal rape, roughly shoves open her trunk and desecrates the "poems a dead boy wrote" (p. 282), Blanche drops all her pretensions, frankly identifying Stanley as her dreaded adversary, that nemesis capable of destroying her as she had destroyed Allan Grey, by subjecting her to his contempt, cruelty, and the humiliating exposure of her own sexual transgressions: "I hurt him the way that you would like to hurt me" (p. 282). By the end of Scene ii, then, Blanche realizes that she has met her "match" in Stanley; but she still pretends to Stella that she has won Stanley over, disguising her attempt to seduce him as innocent flirtation: "I feel a bit shaky but I think I handled it nicely, . . . I called him a little boy and laughed and flirted" (p. 285).

As Quirino points out, at the beginning of Scene iii, Stanley is losing in the poker game, reflecting Blanche's upper hand in their existential contest, while Blanche appears to continue winning allies to her side by successfully bluffing her way into Mitch's admiration and respect. Exploding with frustration and rage at losing both Stella and Mitch to Blanche's deceptive tactics, Stanley hurls the radio playing romantic waltz music out the window, strikes Stella, and battles with his poker buddies. However, by the end of that scene, the reversal of fortune has begun. Unable to resist Stanley's Dionysian animal nature--reflected by his "howling . . . like a baying hound" (p. 306)--Stella is reconciled with him and "they come together with low, animal moans" (p. 307). Blanche, in turn, is forced to reenact the shocking discovery of Allan Grey with his lover, when, searching for Stella, she comes upon her making love with Stanley: "She stops before the dark entrance of her sister's flat. Then catches her breath as if struck" (p. 307). Just as she had fled into the arms of strangers after the loss of Allan, so now, having lost Stella to the same "brutal desire," she rushes out of the house searching for "sanctuary" (p. 307) and finds Mitch, whose "kindness" temporarily affords her a shelter from harsh reality.

In Scene iv, however, unable to persuade Stella to leave Stanley and flee with her, Blanche launches the vituperative attack on Stanley that extends the conflict between her transcendent aspirations and his fundamental carnality to a struggle for the preservation of civilization itself. Characterizing Stanley as the incarnation of barbaric bestiality--"animal," "sub-human," "a survivor of the Stone Age"--and his poker group as "this party of apes," Blanche depicts Stanley as the annihilator of all humanistic aspirations: "Such things as art--as poetry and music . . . some tenderer feelings . . . That we have got to make *grow*!" (p. 323). In imagery suggestive of Yeats's "The Second Coming," Blanche warns Stella that "In this dark march toward whatever it is we're approaching . . . *Don't--don't hang back with the brutes*!" (p. 323).

During this tirade Stanley enters and, like an invisible god, "stands unseen by the women" (p. 322) to overhear Blanche's attack on his "animal" nature. From this point on, Stanley's tactics change from defensive outbursts of childish resentment at Blanche's deceptions to aggressive revenge. As in *The Bacchae* where Dionysus returns point for point the insults, outrages, and humiliations

that Pentheus had heaped upon him, so Stanley retaliates by under-
taking the investigation of Blanche's past which is to expose her
own "animal" nature and brutish sexuality beneath her morally
superior pretensions: "Hoity-toity, describing me as an ape" (p.
378). Thus, by the end of Scene iv, Stanley has the upper hand; he
reveals to Blanche the irresistible force of her "animal" opponent,
as Stella embraces him "fiercely" and he "grins through the curtains at Blanche" (p. 324).

From Scene v to the end of the play, Stanley assumes the
Dionysian role of "cruel hunter" relentlessly stalking his prey.
Even as the dramatic action in Scenes v and vi focuses on Blanche's
apparent success in winning Mitch to her side, behind the scenes
Stanley plays the stealthy hunter ferreting out the facts of her
corrupt past. Ironically, even in that scene in which Blanche
believes she has finally found salvation in Mitch, her fate is
symbolically written in the stars. At the beginning of Scene vi,
having returned with Mitch from a night of "carnival games of
chance," Blanche searches the sky for "the Pleiades, the Seven
Sisters" and finally finds them, "God bless them, all in a bunch
going home from their little bridge party" (p. 342). According to
Edith Hamilton, the seven "daughters of Atlas" were placed in the
heavens as stars to protect them from seizure by Orion, the mighty
hunter who pursued them, "but it was said that even there Orion
persistently continued his pursuit."[21] Leonard Quirino points out
the significance of Blanche's reference to the Pleiades as bridge
ladies:

> It not only aligns them with the imagery of
> existence as a game of chance, but the famil-
> iarity with which Blanche treats the seven
> nymphs who, even as stars, must constantly flee
> the mighty, devastating hunter, Orion, suggests
> mythically and cosmically, a parallel to her own
> danger, pursued as she is by Stanley's vital
> lust for domination and destruction.[22]

In the myth, however, Orion never succeeds in capturing the
nymphs; in the play's demythicized version, Stanley traps Blanche.
Thus, in Scene vii, Stanley reveals to Stella the truth of
Blanche's corrupt past and sexually promiscuous nature, letting it
be known he has also "wised up" Mitch, even as the still unsus-
pecting Blanche ironically sings of transcendence by "Make-
Believe." In Scene viii, Stanley cruelly hands Blanche the bus
ticket back to Laurel, as the music of the Varsouviana rises up

again to remind her of her similarly cruel treatment of Allan Grey. Like Dionysus, the amoral and non-ethical spirit of nature, who in *The Bacchae* refuses to assume moral responsibility for his brutal revenge of his victim--"I am a god. I was blasphemed by you" (l. 1347)--so Stanley, when rebuked by Stella for his unnecessary cruelty to Blanche, responds in a similar spirit of vengeful justification and moral indifference: "Don't forget all that I took off her. . . . I done nothing to no one" (pp. 376-77).

In Scene x, the climactic confrontation between Stanley and Blanche, flesh and spirit, takes place, as Blanche, like the tragic victim in *The Bacchae*, learns too late the necessity of either embracing one's own animal passions or suffering the fate of being torn apart by them. The moment of demythicization is herein enacted as literal rape, as Blanche is physically as well as emotionally divested of her elevated roles of genteel Southern Belle, innocent "virgin" (p. 329), regal "empress" (p. 275), and "Queen of the Nile" (p. 398). As the scene opens, Blanche, drunken and dishevelled, sits before her vanity in reverie, speaking "as if to a group of spectral admirers" (p. 391). As she holds a hand mirror to her ravaged face, Stanley enters, the fantasy breaks, and the mirror shatters, evoking Blanche's analogy to Tennyson's Lady of Shalott, also destroyed by the intrusion of harsh reality. The broken mirror anticipates the imminent disintegration of Blanche's already fragile psyche; for, in Jungian terms, the schizophrenic personality is likened to "a mirror broken up into splinters," as the unified psyche is "shattered into fragments."[23]

Thus, as the music of the Varsouviana rises to remind Blanche once again of her guilt-ridden past, it is this time joined by "lurid reflections . . . of a grotesque and menacing form" (pp. 398-99) and by "inhuman voices like cries in a jungle" (p. 399): psychic symbols of her own repressed animal instincts that now threaten to destroy her already divided psyche. The internal sounds then shift to foreboding symbols of the immediate threat embodied by Stanley, as the "blues piano"--the music of a fallen world --merges with "the roar of an approaching locomotive" (p. 400), recurrent symbol of Stanley's phallic force.

Mocking her imaginative efforts to transform a corrupt reality, Stanley strips Blanche of all her romantic pretensions and reveals as "lies and conceit and tricks!" (p. 398) her attempts to disguise her true nature: "I've been on to you from the start! Not once did you pull any wool over this boy's eyes!" (p. 398).

45

"Caught in a trap" (p. 400), Blanche suffers the exposure of her own animal passions, as, on the eve of his child's birth, Stanley, in a celebratory mood, rapes her in a demonic version of a Dionysian orgy--the uninhibited celebration of the phallic impulse: "Tiger--tiger! Drop the bottle-top! . . . We've had this date with each other from the beginning!" (p. 402). As a consequence, Blanche undergoes the psychological equivalent of Pentheus' dismemberment, her psyche violently rent into the irretrievable fragments of schizophrenic madness. Thus, Blanche's destructive exposure of Allan Grey's sexual transgression, which drove him to suicide, is reenacted in Stanley's libidinous exposure of Blanche's own sexual promiscuity, driving her to a psychological death: for Blanche, a rapacious retribution.

X. The Rape: Demonic and Ironic Myth

The rape represents as well a demonic parody of marriage, as Stanley, in his "silk pyjamas I wore on my wedding night" (p. 395), and Blanche, in a "somewhat soiled and crumpled white satin evening gown . . . a pair of scuffed silver slippers" and "rhinestone tiara" (p. 391), reenact in a rapacious version the wedding night of Stanley and Stella, when he "pulled her down off them columns" (p. 377) of Belle Reve and smashed all the light bulbs with the heel of one of her slippers: a debased analogue of the fairy-tale romance of Cinderella and Prince Charming.

Other mythic parallels are similarly demythicized in the rape scene. Leonard Quirino finds the entire plot of *Streetcar* modeled ("in a way") on the Greek legend of Tereus, King of Thrace, his wife Procne, and her sister Philomela who plans to visit the married couple.[24] According to the legend, Philomela is deceived by Tereus into believing her sister has died, whereupon Tereus seduces Philomela into a "pretended marriage";[25] thus, "the rape of the visiting sister-in-law by her brother-in-law in the absence of his wife" has its naturalistic parallel in Stanley's rape of Blanche while Stella is at the hospital having their baby.[26] In the legend, Tereus afterwards cuts out Philomela's tongue so she cannot tell her sister of the incident, but Philomela weaves a tapestry depicting her seduction. In revenge, Procne kills Tereus' son and tricks him into a cannibalistic feast of their child, while the two sisters flee together from his wrath. In the play, however, although Blanche does tell Stella of Stanley's raping her, she may as well have been rendered tongueless, for Stella is unwilling or unable to believe her: "I couldn't believe her story and go on living with Stanley" (p. 405).

In the legend, also, Procne and Philomela are saved from Tereus' revenge by being turned into birds: Procne into a nightingale, Philomela into a swallow, "which, because her tongue was cut out, only twitters and can never sing," and Tereus into a hawk, a bird of prey.[27] However, according to Edith Hamilton, "the Roman writers who told the story somehow got the sisters confused and said that the tongueless Philomela was the nightingale," romantic symbol of exquisite melancholy, whose song was the "sweetest" and "saddest."[28] Bird images, Jungian symbols of psychological transcendence from "any confining pattern of existence,"[29] are also present in *Streetcar*, but their significance is ironic, testimony to the characters' earth-bound natures rather than symbols of liberation. Thus, the pregnant Stella is referred to as "plump as a little partridge" (p. 254), the non-flying bird in whom the nesting instinct is predominant. The allusion to Stella as a terrestrial bird symbolically anticipates the futility of Blanche's hopes and plans of "flight" with her. Likewise, Stanley calls Blanche a "canary-bird" (p. 359), but her bath-tub songs of transcendence by "Make-Believe" (p. 360) and of the liberation of a "captive maid" (p. 270) are not to be realized. Rather, she is herself exposed as "the parrot that cursed a blue streak" (p. 370) by her story about the old maid who, visited by the preacher, attempts to hide the bird's vulgarities, to no avail. Finally, Stanley, described as "a richly feathered male bird among hens" (p. 265), literally bases his phallic "power and pride" (p. 265) on his sexual equipment or "cock." Unlike the rooster in Steve's joke who, in the midst of chasing a young hen, starts pecking corn "and lets the hen get away" (p. 289), Stanley is singleminded in his pursuit of a goal, whether it be poker ("When I'm losing you want to eat!" [p. 287]) or the degradation of Blanche. Although never specifically identified as a "bird of prey," he aptly fulfills that role in the stalking and capture of Blanche.

Finally, in a psychological version of the rape of Persephone, Blanche, impersonating the virginal maiden, is trapped by her own sexuality and descends to the underworld of the unconscious; but, unlike the figure in the myth, her spring-like rebirth is illusory. According to Jung, the psychological descent to the underworld is a dangerous moment, the moment of decision between destruction and new life:

> If the libido [Jung's "psychic energy"] succeeds
> in tearing itself free and struggling up to the
> upper world again, then a miracle occurs, for
> this descent to the underworld has been a re-
> juvenation for the libido, and from its apparent
> death a new fruitfulness has awakened.

However, "If the libido remains caught in the wonderland of the inner world, the human being becomes a mere shadow in the upper world: he is no better than a dead man or a seriously ill one."[30] In her final attempt to escape an inherently corrupt reality, Blanche descends to the underworld of madness and stays there, finding only in the depths of her own unconscious the romantic "wonderland" she sought above.

XI. Shep Huntleigh: Ironic Savior

The antithesis of Stanley, Shep Huntleigh is first introduced in Scene iv as an "idea" (p. 315) or ideal of deliverance and rebirth, who Blanche imagines will rescue her and Stella from a "desperate situation" (p. 318) and help Blanche "Get hold of myself and make myself a new life!" (p. 313). Ostensibly "an old beau" (p. 393) from Blanche's college days become a Texas oil million-aire, Shep Huntleigh is invested with the mythicized attributes of a transcendent savior, whose symbolic significance is implicit in his very name: thus, Blanche, "hunting for some protection" (p. 386), seeks it finally in the Christ figure of the Good Shepherd. Accordingly, Blanche's rediscovery of him takes place on "Christmas Eve" (p. 316). His lack of reality, however, is affirmed from the beginning. Like the larger-than-life-size figure of the "tall tale," Shep is inflated to Midas-like proportions: "Texas is liter-ally spouting gold in his pockets" (p. 316), and he is said to drive a Cadillac "a block long!" (p. 316). His connection with Christmas, like Stanley's, proves to be ironic: just as Stanley, said to be born "just five minutes after Christmas" (p. 328), represents only an analogue of that "rough beast slouching toward Bethlehem," the bestial life-force of Yeats's "The Second Coming," so the "idea" of Shep Huntleigh as savior never materializes. Like the last of Amanda's gentlemen callers in *The Glass Menagerie*--her "long-distance" husband--Shep Huntleigh represents the Judeo-Christian God who remains incommunicado in the modern world of disbelief. Thus, Blanche's letters to him remain unwritten, her phone calls are never connected, and the frantic Western Union message she tries to send when finally cornered by Stanley--"In

48

desperate, desperate circumstances! Help me! Caught in a trap!" (p. 400)--cannot be delivered for lack of an "address." As ironic savior, Shep Huntleigh is realized only in the form of the Doctor who rescues Blanche from the world of harsh reality and delivers her to the sanctuary of the insane asylum. The recurrent sequence of initially romantic expectations, cruel betrayal, and ultimate disillusionment that patterns Blanche's experience with Allan Grey and all subsequent suitors is thus reenacted in a symbolic version with Shep Huntleigh, ironic archetype of redemption and rebirth; but it ends with Blanche's refusal to accept the existential "disappearance of God."

Thus, in the final scene of the play, Blanche, having retreated into the sanctuary of the imagination, packs for the mental institution which she has been told is a "rest in the country," but "She's got it mixed in her mind with Shep Huntleigh" (p. 405). Dressed in the "Della Robbia blue" (p. 409) of the Madonna, Blanche imagines herself reborn to virginal innocence and prepares for her reunion with Shep Huntleigh on "a cruise of the Caribbean!" (p. 393). The sea, however, is not only the original source of life, "the [primal] element that purifies everything because everything is reborn in it,"[31] but represents also dissolution and death. That Blanche's sea-voyage will become a passage on a psychological ship of death and Shep Huntleigh transformed into the Doctor who attends her psychic dissolution is anticipated in her romanticized reverie of her last rites: "I'm going to die on the sea . . . with my hand in the hand of some nice-looking ship's doctor" (p. 410).[32]

When Blanche finally encounters the Doctor and realizes he is not "the gentleman I was expecting" (p. 413), the violation of her romantic dreams is enacted once more. The memories of her guilt-ridden past are evoked by the haunting music of the Varsouviana and the "lurid reflections" of her psychic Furies, while "the cries and noises of the jungle" (p. 414) and the threatening figure of Stanley remind her of her inescapable animal nature and entrapment in an unredemptive present. As Stanley symbolically reenacts her exposure and rape by tearing the paper lantern from the light bulb, Blanche "cries out as if the lantern was herself" (p. 416). Psychologically stripped of the last vestige of her romantic illusions and physically pinned down like an animal by the "sinister" (p. 415) figure of the Matron, Blanche nevertheless makes a final imaginative attempt at transcendence. Because of his gentlemanly conduct, the Doctor--who respectfully addresses Blanche as "Miss DuBois" (p. 417), "draws her up gently" (p. 418), and gallantly offers his arm--ironically fulfills for her the role of protector and redeemer. At the same time, the language of Blanche's response --"Whoever you are--I have always depended on the kindness of strangers" (p. 418)--recalls the entire pattern of Blanche's "fall": the memories of all of Blanche's previous intimacies with "strangers," the devastating consequences following the "kindness" offered by Mitch, and her futile dreams of salvation by Shep Huntleigh, "the gentleman" who "respects me" (p. 396). For the moment, however, the sordid reality of her past and the pathos of her present circumstances are aesthetically transcended by Blanche's imaginative transformation of herself to a rescued maiden-in-distress and of the Doctor to her longed-for savior.

XII. *A Streetcar Named Desire* As Dark, Ironic Comedy

At the conclusion of *Streetcar*, the tragic symbols of isolation, madness, and death merge with the romantic images of rescue and redemption, as well as with the comic images of reunion and rebirth. As Blanche is led to her living death on the arm of the Doctor in a mock marriage procession, Stanley is reunited with Stella and their new-born son. Thus, Blanche's defeat is Stanley's victory.

The play is structured, then, not only as romantic tragedy, but also as a dark, ironic comedy: a mode in which, according to Frye, "the demonic world is never far away."[33] In this dark comic version, Blanche plays the role of impostor-intruder into the brawling, lusty, vulgar life of Stanley and Stella. In her impersonation of the puritanical prude who disdains and disrupts their raucous connubial and communal customs, Blanche fits the comic figure of "the churl"--the spoiler or refuser of festivity--described by Frye as "the killjoy who tries to stop the fun."[34] The brutal exposure of her true nature demonically parallels the comic *anagnorisis* or recognition scene, followed by the "scapegoat ritual . . . which gets rid of some irreconcilable character."[35] With the ousting of Blanche as *pharmakos* or scapegoat, however, neither the birth of a new society nor the reform of the old one concludes the plot. Rather, the original society embodied by Stanley and Stella is reestablished. The reestablishment of a society based on a fundamental animalism without transcendent meaning--a "party of apes" whose life's game is "seven-card stud"--corresponds to what Frye has designated the most ironic phase of comedy: "one in which a humorous society triumphs or remains undefeated. . . . This phase of comedy presents what Renaissance critics called . . . the way of the world, [or] 'cosi fan tutti.'"[36]

In the naturalistic world of *Streetcar*, the triumph of an inherently corrupt reality is, finally, "the way of the world," and its ultimate import is neither exclusively tragic nor comic but complexly tragicomic: in Chekhov's phrase, "life as it is."[37] Thus, at the end of the play, Stella's "comic" acceptance of life or embrace of reality is accompanied by her "luxurious sobbing" (p. 419); and the birth of her son, the miracle of new life, also ensures that Stanley's brutish nature will prevail. With the expulsion of Blanche--the end of illusion--the play's romance, myth, and tragedy are all rendered ironic, succumbing to a comic mode whose philosophy inheres in the pragmatic advice with which Eunice attempts to console Stella, a philosophy which posits as its basic tenets the acceptance of existential givens and the necessity of survival: "Life has got to go on. No matter what happens, you've got to keep on going" (p. 406). In a world devoid of romantic illusions and transcendent meaning, the existential choice is between "being" and "nothingness," for, in Williams' own words (an amalgam of lines from his poems and plays), "Nowadays is, indeed, lit by lightning, a plague has stricken the moths, and Blanche has been 'put away.'"[38] In its dual vision, the play balances a lament for the loss of illusions with a lusty embrace of being.

CHAPTER THREE

THE ROSE TATTOO

I remember my husband with a body
like a young boy and hair on his head
as thick and black as mine is and skin
on him smooth and sweet as a yellow rose petal.

I. Symbol and Structure

The structural imagery of *The Rose Tattoo* (1950-51) is more
cohesive, though no less evocative, than the fragmented images
drawn from diverse myths, legends, and fairy tales found in many
other Williams plays; for this play is concerned with union and
reconciliation rather than disintegration and alienation. Accordingly, the rose tattoo, central symbol of the play, is an emblem of
the union of spirit with flesh.

The rose, by itself, evokes a flood of collective images, both
secular and spiritual.   It is the conventional symbol of human
love, female sexuality, and natural beauty.   In its spiritual
aspect, the rose is the concrete universal of communion.[1] Its
wondrous aspect is illustrated by the medieval legend of the "miraculous" origin of the rose, which tells of the salvation of a
young martyred maiden from flames which, by her prayers and faith,
were transformed into "the first" roses.[2] Most significant to this
play, which dramatizes the struggle of its protagonist to reconcile
the traditions of Catholic morality with the fulfillment of her own
sexual nature, the rose is Dante's symbol for Mary, the miraculous
vehicle through whom divinity is humanized: "Here is the rose,
wherein the Word of God/ Made itself flesh" (*Paradiso* xxiii. 73-
74).[3] Finally, in its literal shape, the rose reflects the form of
the play's internal structure, a circle: Jungian archetype of
psychic wholeness or unity.[4]

The other half of the symbol, the tattoo, also suggests both
mundane and mystical meanings. Associated with the sailor and his
various wandering or adventurous counterparts, the tattoo is suggestive of both male virility and sentimentality. Its religious
connotations derive from its approximation both to *stigmata*, those
sympathetic scars resembling the wounds of the crucified Christ,

and to the brand of Cain, mark of infamy and disgrace.

In the course of the play, the symbol of the rose tattoo assumes all of these diverse meanings--the secular and miraculous, the corrupt and regenerative--as it reflects the unfolding awareness of life's ambiguities in the mind of the play's protagonist, Serafina delle Rose. Thus, at the play's beginning, the religious significance imparted by Serafina to the image of the rose etched on the chest of Rosario, her husband, indicates her need to create a reality suffused with transcendent meaning. The allegedly miraculous duplication of the rose tattoo on Serafina's own breast as an emblem prophetic of conception similarly represents her elevation of the sexual relations between herself and Rosario to the religious experience of mystical union. Accordingly, Serafina's description of the sensations accompanying the mysterious appearance of the rose on her breast suggests not only the process of tattooing but also the ecstatic suffering associated with the bearing of *stigmata*: "That night I woke up with a burning pain on me, here, on my left breast! A pain like a needle, quick, quick, hot little stitches" (II, 277). However, even as Serafina imbues her experience with miraculous import--elevating her husband to a Christ figure, herself to a devoted saint, and their sexual union to the level of religious ecstasy--the language she uses to describe the "miracle" derives from her mundane role as a lowly seamstress who creates fabrications from the raw material of experience. The linguistic analogy between Serafina's expressed religious experience and her familiar occupation of sewing serves to remind us that *stigmata* appear not only to the religiously ecstatic but also to the hysterically neurotic.[5] Herein, then, the sensation of "stitches" as from a "needle" which pricks Serafina ironically reveals the image of the rose on her breast to be psychosomatically self-inflicted.

The reduplication of the rose tattoo throughout the rest of the play parallels Serafina's struggle to acknowledge that the "glory" with which she has exalted Rosario and sanctified herself represents only gross invention. Thus, the symbol is corrupted to represent a mark of infidelity and adultery when duplicated on the chest of Estelle Hohengarten, Rosario's mistress. It is compromised in Serafina's eyes when reproduced on the chest of Alvaro Mangiacavallo, Rosario's clownish double. It reappears on the breast of Serafina as an emblem of birth and rebirth--the process of life itself--only after she has fully accepted all of its meanings and has herself transcended the need for ego inflation.

II. Rosario as Dionysus: The Mythic Story

Whereas fragmented myths reflect the disintegration of a tran-scendent mythos for Western civilization in many of Williams' plays, in *The Rose Tattoo* the pagan nature myth of Dionysus is offered in its entirety as a viable substitute for religious ro-manticism. The regenerative spirit of Dionysus as the seasonal demi-god of wine, fertility, and passionate inspiration informs characterization, structure, and atmosphere in this play.[6] Like the symbolic rose tattoo, the Dionysian myth represents a fusion of the sensual and the spiritual; its structural aspect is the cyc-lical pattern of a god who dies and is reborn. The integral rela-tionship between flesh and spirit implicit in both the symbol and the myth is metaphorically expressed by Williams in his remarks on the play:

> The Rose Tattoo is the Dionysian element in human life, its mystery, its beauty, its significance. . . . It is the lyric as well as the Bacchantic impulse. . . . It is the <u>rosa mystica</u>, the light on the bare golden flesh of a god whose back is turned to us. . . . It is the homely light of a kitchen candle burned in praise of a god.[7]

Rosario delle Rose embodies the play's initial representation of the archetypal Dionysian spirit. As Dionysus was known as a vegetation or "fruitful" god,[8] so Rosario represents the apotheosis of sexual prowess and fertility, reflected in his job as the driver of a ten-ton truck of bananas. As Dionysus was often represented as a floral god,[9] so Rosario is for Serafina "my rose of the world" (p. 345). Finally, like Dionysus, Rosario is to Serafina the god of love who suffers a violent death. He is idealized sexually as "the *first* best, the *only* best" (p. 311) and pictured as an eter-nally youthful god: "I remember my husband with a body like a young boy and hair on his head as thick and black as mine is and skin on him smooth and sweet as a yellow rose petal" (p. 311). Unable to acknowledge an unalloyed sexuality in human nature, however, Serafina attempts to imbue the Dionysian spirit with religious significance in her elevation of Rosario. Thus, Serafina makes her sexual union with her husband seem like an ecstatic ritual: "Each night for twelve years. Four thousand-three hundred-and eighty (p. 312) . . . To me the big bed was beautiful like a religion" (p. 342). The idealized Rosario is to Serafina what the romanticized gentleman caller is to Amanda in *The Glass Menagerie*, what Shep Huntleigh represents to Blanche in *A Streetcar Named Desire*, what Skipper is to Brick in *Cat on a Hot Tin Roof* and Heavenly is to Chance in *Sweet Bird of Youth*. Like Serafina, all are characters who must mythicize, romanticize, or civilize the expression of natural instincts to fulfill their longings for transcendent experience.

The Dionysian spirit, however, embodies not only the inspired passion of religious ecstasy to which Serafina would restrict it, but also sexuality at its most libidinous and indiscriminate. It is this orgiastic impulse of the Dionysian spirit which Serafina has attempted to confine to the monogamous relationship of the Christian marriage vow. The raw sexuality of Rosario is revealed through the discovery of his adulterous relationship with Estelle Hohengarten, who describes him as "wild like a Gypsy" (p. 283). Characteristically, Serafina not only refuses to acknowledge the truth of Rosario's betrayal but denies as well the very presence of an unsanctified sexuality in either Rosario or herself, or in their daughter Rosa: "I don't know nothing about wild men and wild women" (p. 283). Appropriately, it is the Strega's goat of which Serafina is most afraid, for Dionysus was often believed to be reincarnated in the form of the concupiscent goat, worshipped in ritual as "the one of the Black Goatskin."[10] As the objective correlative of the Dionysian spirit of unleashed lust, the black goat also symbolizes Serafina's own unconscious desires, her fear of it deriving from the repression of her own sexuality in its instinctual and unelevated form.

At the death of Rosario, Serafina is transfixed in the posture of looking backward to a memory of idealized and illusory perfection. Attempting to immortalize her elevated image of Rosario while denying his true nature, Serafina puts his ashes into a funeral urn and worships them before the shrine of the Madonna. To so Christianize the Dionysian spirit is to asceticize natural passion and attempt to fix its cyclical nature in a unique, definitive event. By so doing, Serafina attempts to deny the Dionysian impulse in herself, to enshrine her own body by refusing to participate in the regenerative process of life. As Alvaro tells her, "You have put your heart in the marble urn with the ashes" (p. 372).

III. Alvaro as Dionysus: The Demythicized Version

As in the other plays examined in this study, *The Rose Tattoo* is structured as a story told, then reenacted in a diminished version: here, Serafina's idealized relationship with Rosario is reenacted in a fully human version with Alvaro. Similarly, the "wild" or illicit relationship of natural passion between Estelle and Rosario is reenacted in an essentially innocent version by Rosario's daughter, "a twig off the old rosebush" (p. 281), and Jack Hunter, the sailor. Unlike many others of Williams' plays so structured, in this play the second version of these parallel stories ends more happily than the first. The two stories mesh as Rosa's defiance of moral conventions points the way to Serafina's own liberation from false idols and to her realization that human love needs no other consecration than its own expression.

The play turns from its tragic potential to its ultimate comic fulfillment with the appearance of Alvaro Mangiacavallo, an obvious parody of the exalted Rosario: "My *husband's body*, with the head of a *clown*!" (p. 354). Accordingly, Alvaro's social status is not that of the figure-head Baron, but that of "the grandson of the village idiot" (p. 366). A compromise of Rosario's idealized virility, Alvaro drives only an eight-ton truck of bananas. Whereas implications of mystery surrounded Rosario the contrabandist--"On top of the truck is bananas! But underneath--something else!" (p. 279)--nothing is mystifying about Alvaro. His identification with the unelevated sexuality of Dionysus is dramatized by his own resemblance to the goat, which he appropriately catches for Serafina. In Act III, Scene iii, when the drunken Alvaro spies the sleeping Rosa, his cries of "Che bella!" (p. 406) are echoed by the antiphonal responses of the goat's bleating "Baaa," in a love song to natural beauty inspired by natural passion. Finally, Alvaro's last name, Mangiacavallo, which means "Eat-a-horse" (p. 356), is a pun on the ritual custom of endowing a pagan god with a similar epithet in recognition of his animal reincarnation. Thus, Dionysus, who was believed reincarnated in one form as a bull, was known as "eater of bulls."[11] The name is here demythicized to the popular hyperbole, to be so hungry one could "eat a horse." Obviously, the ritual custom need not be known or consciously grasped in order to elicit humor. The animal epithet appears instantly ludicrous by contrast to the other names invested with religious and mystical connotations: Rosario delle Rose--the rosary of the rose; Serafina delle Rose--the seraph or archangel of the rose; and Rosa delle Rose--the rose of the rose.

Alvaro, then, is characterized not as half-mortal, half-divine, but as a fully humanized animal, his humanity elevating him from mindless bestiality even as his instincts lead him to offer Serafina "Love and affection!--in a world that is lonely--and cold!" (p. 366). Combining masculine strength with feminine tenderness, Alvaro's androgynous nature is presented as so sympathetic, sensitive, and passionate that his kindness and warmth make up for the loss of a god.

IV. The Ritual of Divestment: From Illusion to Reality

The divestment of Serafina's illusions is dramatized in this play, as in other Williams plays, through an act of breakage: Serafina shatters the urn filled with Rosario's ashes even as she perceives that the Madonna icon with whose image she had identified is but "a poor little doll with the paint peeling off" (p. 396). Serafina's deflated view of both Rosario and herself acts as prelude to the liberation of her own Dionysian spirit from all the constraints imposed by her adherence to the moral strictures and sexual taboos of organized religion and social convention. In this play, then, the moment of demythicization is followed not only by the protagonist's necessary confrontation with human limitations, but also by her embrace of that diminished reality. Just as the divestment of Serafina's mythicized image as Madonna releases her repressed sexual spirit, so her illicit act of passion with Alvaro frees her from the social proprieties and sexually constrictive roles of both "bride" and "widow" (p. 270), whose restrictive moral conventions had been objectified throughout the play by two inanimate and faceless dummies. Similarly, the relinquishment of her exalted social status as Baronessa restores Serafina to the community of Sicilian women. Finally, Rosa's exposure of the hypocritical disparity between Serafina's public image and her private desires, between her moral affectations and her sexual needs, not only frees Serafina from social pretense but also leads her to psychic wholeness and self-acceptance. Thus mitigated by Alvaro's love and sanctioned by Rosa's example, the divestment of Serafina's self-generated mythos and mysticism results neither in the existential loneliness of the Wingfield family in *The Glass Menagerie* nor in the psychic withdrawal of Blanche DuBois in *A Streetcar Named Desire*. Instead, Serafina's embrace of reality leads to the blossoming of love as a natural experience so full and rich that its expression simultaneously fulfills the imagination and the flesh. She is led to forgive the capricious sexual vitality of Rosario in the acceptance of her own animal nature and to understand life as a process of fulfilling instinctual and all-too-human needs and desires. Thus, as fervently as she had previously attempted to arrest time, Serafina is now able to follow Rosa's example and surrender to its flow. As Williams himself remarked, Serafina learns that the spirit of Dionysus "can not be confined to memory nor an urn, nor the conventions and proprieties of a plump little seamstress who wanted to fortify her happiness with the respect of the community," but that "the blood of the wild young daughter was better, as a memorial, than ashes kept in a crematory urn."[12]

V. The Dying and Reviving God: A Comic Celebration

The Rose Tattoo ends in a crescendo of color, motion, and music: a comic celebration. Serafina's embrace of inclusive experience--life's inherent passions as well as their corruption--permits the rose tattoo to assume the symbolic values of regeneration and rebirth. The apocalyptic finality with which Serafina had regarded the deified Rosario's death is exchanged for the regenerative cycle of the Dionysian spirit by her acceptance of Alvaro, Rosario's demythicized double. The play enacts, then, an existential version of the fertility rite of the dying and reviving god. Thus, at the play's end, the rose tattoo reproduced on Alvaro reappears on the breast of Serafina, once more a symbol of conception and of her own passionate rebirth, but also as the merely mortal imprint of flesh against flesh. The rose silk shirt, previously the symbol of Rosario's infidelity, is similarly invested with new meaning as it becomes Serafina's gift of love to Alvaro. The wind, symbol of life's transience as well as its vitality, assumes major metaphorical significance in the play's final scene. It is the wind that scatters the ashes of Rosario, thereby releasing the impregnating power of the Dionysian spirit rather than enshrining it. It is also the wind that carries the child's red kite, symbol of Serafina's uninhibited freedom. Finally, it is the wind-like motion of the Sicilian women that propels the rose-colored shirt "like a streak of flame shooting up a dry hill" (p. 413) to unite Serafina with Alvaro, with the community, and with her own passionate nature. The shirt is a banner joyfully spread in celebration of the dynamic process of life in all its human complexity, and testimony to the inherently transcendent function of passionate human communion. In *The Rose Tattoo*, the annual rebirth of the Dionysian spirit is a ritual successfully reenacted in a fully human version.

CHAPTER FOUR

CAT ON A HOT TIN ROOF

It was one of those beautiful, ideal
things they tell about in the Greek legends.

I. Story and Structure: Platonic Myth and its Existential Analogue

In *Cat on a Hot Tin Roof* (1955), the story which controls the dramatic structure of the play includes Brick Pollitt's idealized memory of a Platonic relationship with his college football teammate, Skipper; Brick's rejection of that relationship's existential reality; and the tragic consequences of his rejection for himself, his wife Maggie, and, not least, for Skipper who dies to disavow "the inadmissible thing" (III, 114) between them. Brick's story, from its mythicized beginning to its existential conclusion, is central to the play's themes of life's inherent corruption and "mendacity" (p. 106); to its archetypal conflicts of illusion *vs.* reality, sterility *vs.* fertility, death *vs.* life; and, finally, to the play's ironic reenactment of the myth of a dying and reviving god. At the center of these primal conflicts are the two surviving victims of Brick's story--Brick himself and "Maggie the Cat"--each of whom responds antithetically to its tragic outcome: whereas Brick passively withdraws to a psychological Death--pure, peaceful, "solid quiet" (p. 89), Maggie actively embraces Life--corrupt, chaotic, and tenaciously regenerative.

II. Brick and Skipper vs. Maggie and Brick

Brick's characterization encompasses mythic, mundane, and potentially regenerative dimensions. He is elevated to a "superior creature" (p. 56), a "godlike being" (p. 56), and a "conquerin' hero" (p. 196) in that mythicized past to which he remains in thrall; he is reduced to the anti-heroic roles of crippled athlete, alcoholic, disinterested husband, and "son of a bitch" (p. 56) in the dramatized present; and he is given the opportunity to assume the redemptive role of "Little Father" (p.165) in the play's projected future. Exiled from what he perceives as his rightful place and time--his laurel-crowned athletic youth --and, especially, from the "one great good true thing in his life . . . Not love with you, Maggie, but friendship with Skipper" (p. 58), Brick elevates his relationship with Skipper to the ideal embodiment of Platonic love, that exclusively male bond which at its highest level manifests itself purely as a "marriage of noble minds."[1] Like the Athenians of the fourth and fifth centuries B.C. who believed that homosexual love alone is capable of satisfying a man's highest and noblest aspirations, and, conversely, that heterosexual love is altogether inferior--a mere "physical impulse whose sole object is the pro-creation of children"[2]--Brick clearly regards his relationship with Skipper as vastly superior to the earthy love offered him by Maggie. Even the very adjectives used by Brick to describe that relationship--"the one," "good," "true"--suggest the moral and philosophical terms of the Platonic absolutes or Ideas of the Good, the Beautiful, and the True. Maggie's own analogy of Brick and Skipper's friendship to "one of those beautiful, ideal things they tell about in the Greek legends" (p. 57) testifies to Brick's idealization of it to the highest level of Platonic homosexuality.

Ironically, however, the male relationship which Brick elevates to a Platonic ideal is one that was thoroughly stigmatized in the United States of the 1950's which is the play's historical milieu; thus, as an existential reality, it was a "love that never could be carried through to anything satisfying or even talked about plainly" (p. 57). As the athlete-ideal of that society, Brick has thoroughly internalized its negative cultural attitudes toward realized homosexual love. Thus, even as Brick elevates his friendship with Skipper to the Platonic ideal, he denies and deni-grates its inherent implications of homosexuality, calling Maggie's attempts to so define the relationship as "naming it dirty" (p. 58). Accordingly, he expresses shock, outrage, and disgust with Big Daddy's parallel of him and Skipper to Jack Straw[3] and Peter Ochello, the overtly homosexual original owners of the Pollitt plantation, whom he disparages as "that pair of old sisters" (p. 115), "dirty old men," (p. 118), "a couple of ducking sissies" (p. 118), "Queers" (p. 118) and "*Fairies*" (p. 120). Although Brick admits to some physical contact with Skipper--"once in a while he put his hand on my shoulder or I'd put mine on his," and on tour in hotels "we'd reach across the space between the two beds and shake hands to say goodnight" (p. 121)--he vehemently denies any demon-stration of physical passion between them, maintaining that their relationship transcended gross physical desire, remaining "pure" (p. 121), "true," and "clean" (p. 120). The conflicts engendered in Brick by his longing to recapture his idealized past with

Skipper versus his inability to face the truth about the existential nature of that relationship render him sexually immobilized, psychologically arrested, and morally crippled. Unwilling to explore his own sexual nature, Brick is thereby unable to accept his animal, instinctual self, as represented by either a flesh-and-blood Skipper or "Maggie the Cat."

III. Brick's Mythic Analogues

One of the Greek legends suggested by Brick's idealization of his relationship with Skipper is the myth of Apollo and his "dearest companion," Hyacinthus, whom he accidentally kills while both are engaged in a game of quoits.[4] Apollo, like Brick, bitterly mourns his friend's death, wishing even to "give my life for yours, or die with you." Unlike Apollo (significantly, the God of Truth), Brick refuses to assume any responsibility for the death of Skipper, though he, too, surely had a part in "killing" his friend. In the myth, Hyacinthus is resurrected, in the form of "the wondrous flower that was to make the lad's name known forever."[5] In the play, Skipper remains only a haunting memory.

Brick's exaggerated mourning for the loss of Skipper is clearly both symptomatic and symbolic of grief engendered by a far greater loss, a loss of mythic proportion. Metaphysically, Brick's idealization of his relationship with Skipper may be said to reflect that desire for a restoration of primordial wholeness and original unity to the human condition which, according to Jungian psychology, is fundamental to the psyche, and is therefore mythicized in the literature of all ages and nations.[6] Plato's myth of the original round man who, split into two halves, must spend his life seeking the completion of his divided self is the archetypal image evoked by Brick's obsession with Skipper. According to the myth, recounted by Aristophanes in *The Symposium*, mortals are merely halves of original wholes, a unity destroyed by Zeus as punishment for their hubris. As a result of their bisection, each half is condemned to spend his entire life seeking to regain the lost happiness of being whole. To ameliorate that intolerable condition, Love came into being. Thus, love is defined by Aristophanes as "the desire and pursuit of the whole."[7] Furthermore, of the reunions of each half of the three mythical sexes with its other--male with male, female with female, and hermaphrodite with female--the most enduring love, according to Aristophanes, derives from the reuniting of those individuals who are halves of male wholes, or male homosexuals. They become not only sexual mates but also soul mates:

> Affection and kinship and love combined inspire in him [the lover of boys] an emotion which is quite overwhelming, and such a pair practically refuse ever to be separated even for a moment. . . . No one can suppose that it is mere physical enjoyment which causes the one to take such intense delight in the company of the other. It is clear that the soul of each has some other longing which it cannot express, but can only surmise and obscurely hint at.[8]

Unable to recapture that sense of primordial wholeness he knew with Skipper--"exceptional friendship, *real, real, deep, deep friendship*! between two men" (p.120)--and unwilling to compromise his ideal by accepting Maggie's offer of an inferior relationship, Brick remains incomplete, divided, or, in the words of Aristophanes, "the mere broken tally of a man."[9]

In his abstinence from sexual activity and his inability to love, Brick resembles several of those mythological figures who reject the call to sexual maturity and remain in thrall to an idealized and impossible concept: Hippolytus, the great athlete and hunter who scorned Aphrodite (goddess of Love) and worshipped only Artemis, the chaste goddess of the moon, mountains, and woods;[10] and Narcissus, the beautiful young boy who is cursed to love only himself, because he would not love others,[11] an image evoked by Brick's frequent trips to "Echo Spring"--the epithet for his liquor cabinet--which alludes to the Narcissan "spring" or pool where Brick recurrently drowns in his reflections of the golden past with his own mirror-image, or other half, Skipper. According to Jungian psychology, however, the myth of Narcissus implies a condition just the opposite of an excess of indulgent self-love. Narcissism is, instead, symptomatic of the alienated ego that cannot love, "a frustrated state of yearning for a self-possession which does not yet exist."[12] Before Narcissus can love another, he must learn to "love"--confront, accept, forgive--himself, with all his flaws and limitations. Brick's inability to acknowledge his own "shadow-side," reflected in his refusal to accept Skipper's homosexual love or to embrace the equally "corrupt" heterosexual union offered by Maggie, engenders in him a narcissism which drives him to "Echo Spring" in an attempt to escape the responsibilities of human love altogether and to recapture, instead, its mythicized ideal.

IV. Brick and Maggie: The "Dying and Reviving God" and His Consort

That past for which Brick yearns, and from which he feels exiled, extends beyond his own laurel-crowned athletic youth, beyond even the mythicized ideal of the Golden Age of Greece, to an archetypal psychic yearning for primordial wholeness. Emotionally arrested, morally paralyzed, and sexually impotent (or, at least, apathetic), Brick is symbolically and psychologically dead to either the delights or demands of existential reality. Indeed, in his godlike beauty, latent virility, and withdrawn state, Brick suggests no other archetypal figure so much as that of the "dying god," that mythic personification of winter's sterility which becomes spring's fertility and is thereby "reborn."

According to Sir James Frazer, archetypal figures of seasonal death and rebirth were worshipped in many forms by ancient cultures:

> Under the names of [the Egyptian god] Osiris,
> [the Babylonian god] Tammuz, [the Greek god]
> Adonis, and [the Phrygian god] Attis, the peoples
> of Egypt and Western Asia represented the yearly
> decay and revival of life . . . which they per-
> sonified as a god who annually died and rose
> again from the dead.[13]

Like them, Brick is depicted as a dismembered fertility god: his "broken ankle," the physical correlative of his psychological fragmentation; his crutch (an obvious Freudian phallic symbol), the objective correlative of his sexual, emotional, and moral paralysis; and his liquor bottles, the concrete means of his attempt to escape his conflicts by achieving oblivion or "solid quiet" (p. 89). Appropriately, Brick's gaze is directed to that dead planet, the moon, symbol of his chosen chastity and pure, impossible love. His reflective attitude suggests a philosophy of *contemptus mundi*: in Platonic terms, the rejection of participation in the world for a life spent in "the contemplation of absolute beauty."[14] Thus, Brick responds to the noisy, aggressive, sensual life around him "indifferently" (p. 29), "vaguely" (p. 52), "without interest" (p. 19), "absently" (p. 26), and with "that cool air of detachment that people have who have given up the struggle" (p. 19). Like the mythical dying gods, Brick needs to be restored to life, fertility, and wholeness.

65

Maggie is well qualified to represent the dying god's consort, that loving female goddess who effects the restoration or resurrection of the dead god through her magical or superhuman ministrations. Hers is the role mythically embodied by the Egyptian Isis, the Babylonian Ishtar, the Greek Aphrodite, and the Phrygian Cebele--all of whom combine the functions of wife, mother, and/ or sister.[15] Like them, Maggie acts as both loyal wife and maternal companion to Brick, her "Baby" (p. 21), "boy of mine" (p. 20); she is "determined" to restore life to Brick's emotionally broken spirit, physically crippled body, and morally paralyzed soul. Set against Brick's refusal to compromise his idyllic memory of a once-perfect relationship, or to acknowledge his own betrayal of that relationship, is Maggie's insistence that life is better than either death or dream: "life has got to be allowed to continue even after the *dream* of life--is--all over" (p. 57). The oversized matrimonial bed dominating the set is the symbol of that vital life force offered Brick by Maggie as the means to restore to wholeness his divided self.

V. Brick and Maggie: Osiris and Isis

The relationship and characterization of Brick and Maggie recall multiple analogues of figures and myths of death and resurrection, dismemberment and reunion. The Egyptian myth of the dying and reviving god Osiris most closely resembles in several particulars the relationship of Brick and Maggie, an analogy reinforced by Big Daddy's allusion to the fertile plains of Egypt in his description of the Pollitt plantation as "twenty-eight thousand acres of the richest land this side of the valley Nile" (p. 86). According to the myth, Osiris, one of the greatest fertility gods in the Egyptian pantheon, is dismembered by his jealous brother, Set, who aspires to his throne.[16] Brick also has been sexually "dismembered" (though not wholly through the machinations of his own jealous brother, Gooper), and he, too, is in danger of being cut out of the inheritance of his father's estate, due largely to Gooper and his wife Mae's prolific fertility (five "no-neck monsters" and another on the way), while Brick and Maggie remain "totally childless and therefore totally useless!" (p. 19). In the myth, it is Isis, the consort-sister of Osiris, revered in her own right as a "potent magician," who is said to have "reconstituted the body of Osiris, cunningly joining the fragments together."[17] Just so, Maggie, whose own name suggests magus or magician, is determined to use all her powers to heal the broken heart, mind, and body of Brick. Thus, just as Isis is said to have conceived a son, Horus, "by union with her husband's corpse, miraculously re-animated by her charms,"[18] so does Maggie attempt to conceive with the emotionally dead Brick, thereby casting herself in the Isis-role of life-restorer: "What you need is someone to take hold of you--gently, with love, and hand your life back to you . . . and I can!" (p. 215).

VI. Maggie the Cat: Ironic Artemis and Martyred "Saint"

Maggie's characterization is not confined to one mythological prototype; rather, it is complex, composite, and often contradictory. Allusions to her nature encompass the Christian, the pagan, and the bestial: she is variously dubbed a martyred saint ("Saint Maggie"), the Roman goddess "Diana" (p. 36), and a "cat on a hot tin roof" (p. 54). In short, she is as multi-dimensional as Brick is one-dimensional.

In Act I, Maggie characterizes herself as a saint in her dialogue with Brick: "I wish you *would* lose your looks. If you did it would make the martyrdom of Saint Maggie a little more bearable" (p. 30). According to Butler's *Lives of The Saints*, St. Margaret, virgin and martyr, was "one of the most famous and widely venerated saints" of the Roman Catholic Church, revered as "patroness of women in childbirth," until her acts were revealed to be "pure forgery."[19] Correspondingly, Maggie may be considered a "pat-roness . . . of childbirth," for it is Brick's child, an heir to the Pollitt estate, that she desires above all, and she indulges in a lie, or "act of forgery," to ensure its fulfillment. Whereas the original St. Margaret chose martyrdom rather than lose her chastity to a princely suitor, however, the sexual "martyrdom" of Maggie Pollitt is involuntary and her "sainthood" ironic.

Maggie's mythicized stature seems to derive from the confla-tion of several mythological female deities: the Egyptian goddess Bast, the Roman Diana, and the Greek goddess Artemis. Like the primitive divinity Bast, Maggie is represented as half-female, half-feline: "I am Maggie the Cat!" (p. 48).[20] In her dual attempt to revitalize Brick's sexual interest and to conceive a child by him, Maggie, like Bast, personifies "the fertilising [sic] warmth of the sun" in antithetical contrast to the "cool," sterile, moon-struck Brick. As the playful sex-kitten who shares Big Daddy's earthy enjoyment of sheer physicality, she is, like Bast, "the goddess of pleasure." Finally, as the healing and redemptive spirit of the play, Maggie shares Bast's benevolent office of a protector against "evil spirits." Significantly, the Greeks identified Bast with Artemis, another of Maggie's mythic analogues.

Maggie is explicitly identified in the play with the Archer-goddess, Diana--the Roman counterpart to the Greek Artemis--when she refers to the bow of her archery set as "my Diana Trophy" (p. 36). Like Diana-Artemis, "goddess of the chase and of forests,"[21] Maggie loves to "run with dogs through chilly woods, run, run, leap over obstructions" (p. 36), in contrast to Brick's inability to clear hurdles on the Glorious Hill high-school athletic field: an obvious indication of Maggie's determination "to win" (p. 31) versus Brick's passive "charm of the defeated" (p. 31). As the huntress, Maggie is relentless in stalking her prey, and in this play, her prey is Brick--her goal, a child and heir to the Pollitt estate. Thus, Maggie shares as well the maternal function of the Roman Diana, one of the Great Mother goddesses worshipped at Nemi.[22]

However, because Brick, in his sexual abstinence, refuses to grant Maggie the maternal role of Diana, she must ironically remain confined to the virginal office of Artemis,[23] stern protector of chastity: "She's childless because that big beautiful athlete husband of hers won't go to bed with her" (p. 151). Thus, just as the Roman Diana, "an Italian goddess of mountains and woods and of women and childbirth,"[24] historically assumed the additional characteristics of the Greek virgin huntress Artemis, one of the most multifaceted of the divinities--at times benevolent and merciful, at others "fierce and revengeful"[25]--so, too, Maggie testifies to being transformed from a loving, lusty, playful bride--"we were happy, weren't we, we were blissful, yes, hit heaven together ev'ry time that we loved" (p. 58)--to a harsh, jealous, sexually frustrated, vengeful shrew: "I've gone through this--*hideous!--transformation*, become--*hard*! *Frantic!--cruel!!*" (p. 27). Just as the mythological character of Diana-Artemis is said to be complex and contradictory, "in which, it would seem, different divinities are merged,"[26] so, too, Maggie is endowed with the animal sensuosity and instinctive tenacity of a cat, the athletic aggressiveness of the Roman Diana, and, ironically, the chastity of both the Greek Artemis and a martyred saint. She is, by turn, generous, kind, gentle, loyal, protective, and truly loving as well as mean, catty, vulgar, scheming, vengeful, and mendacious.

Like the androgynous Artemis, who, though female, holds the masculine office of "Huntsman-in-chief" to the gods, "odd office for a woman,"[27] Maggie must assume the actively aggressive male sexual role to Brick's passive, emasculate one. Significantly, Williams notes that Maggie's voice sometimes "drops low as a boy's" and asks us to imagine her "playing boy's games as a child" (p. 21).

As the Archer-goddess, armed with bow and arrow, Artemis was often depicted as "the deity of sudden death," slaying her detractors at times savagely, at other times mercifully.[28] Maggie evokes the image of the slayer-Artemis when she tells of her role in breaking up the relationship between Brick and Skipper, and in precipitating Skipper's subsequent dissolution: "I said, 'Skipper! Stop lovin' my husband or tell him he's got to let you admit it to him!' . . . *Who shot cock robin? I with my - - - merciful arrow!*" (p. 59). Maggie's role in the break-up of Brick and Skipper suggests the mythological story of the vengeance of Artemis on Otus and Ephialtes, the twin brothers who "cared only for each other. Theirs was a great devotion."[29] Both pursued Artemis, however, for "Ephialtes was in love with Artemis, or thought he was." In order to elude their pursuit, Artemis turned herself into a lovely white deer and lured them to hunt her. In the midst of the hunt, the transformed Artemis positioned herself between the two devoted brothers: "At the same moment each suddenly saw her . . . but neither saw . . . his brother. They threw their javelins and the hind vanished." Each had killed the other. Just so, Maggie thrusts herself between Brick and Skipper, forcing Skipper to confront his latent homosexuality: "In this way, I destroyed him. . . . From then on Skipper was nothing at all but a receptacle for liquor and drugs" (p. 59). But it is not Maggie's forced revelation that kills Skipper; she, like Artemis, simply acts as the agent which causes Brick and Skipper to destroy each other. At the end of Act II, Big Daddy forces Brick to face the truth of his betrayal of Skipper and the specific source of his self-disgust: "a long-distance call which I had from Skipper, in which he made a drunken confession to me and on which I hung up!--last time we spoke to each other in our lives" (p. 124). As Big Daddy climactically sums up: "*You!*--dug the grave of your friend and kicked him in it!--before you'd face truth with him" (p. 124). Thus, Brick kills Skipper with betrayal as Skipper "kills" Brick with truth.

VII. Brick: A Broken Apollo

If Maggie evokes, through allusion and analogy, a modern, vulgarized, ironic version of the mythical Diana-Artemis, then Brick is surely cast in the role of a similarly debased Apollo, twin brother to Artemis, to whom the laurel was sacred.[30] Apollo, like Artemis, is a hunter, "the Archer-god"; so, too, Brick and Maggie are depicted as twin hunters: "Brick and I still have our special archers' license. We're goin' deer-huntin' on Moon Lake as soon as the season starts" (p. 36). This Archer-god, however, has a broken ankle, hobbles on a crutch, and can no longer jump the hurdles he used to as a youth "crowned . . . with early laurel" (p. 120)--an aging, degenerate version of his prototype. Thus, whereas Apollo was known as a master musician, Brick merely hums, whistles, or intones a few bars of "By the light of the silvery moon" (p. 185) or "Show me the way to go home" (pp. 153-54)--pop tunes of the sentimental and the drunk. Whereas the mythical Apollo was often confused with and conflated with the Sun God, Helios, his diminished version worships the moon, dim reflection of the sun. Most important, however, Apollo is best known as the guardian and lover of Truth. Just so, Brick ironically casts himself as a lover of truth, claiming that the source of his withdrawal and disgust with life is its inherent "mendacity" (p. 106). In his climactic scene with Big Daddy in Act II, however, Brick is stripped of his self-righteous Apollonian stature and forced to realize that "This disgust with mendacity is disgust with yourself" (p. 124). In ignominious retaliation, Brick hurls the deadly truth of Big Daddy's cancerous condition at his self-deceived father, thus reducing the great Apollonian oracular power to a vindictive child's game: "You told *me*! I told *you*!" (p. 128). Appropriately, at this moment, "a child rushes into the room," screaming "Bang,bang,bang, bang,bang,bang,bang" (p. 128)--a dramatic analogy to the "shoot-'em-up" to which Brick has reduced Apollo's momentous prophecies of life and death.

VIII. The Story Told, Then Reenacted: Two Versions

As in the other plays concerned with the quest to recapture a romantic past, Brick's memory of his idealized Platonic relationship with Skipper is reenacted in a diminished and demythicized version. Here, however, the reenactment is not dramatized but is only anticipated in the form of the flesh-and-blood, and thus--to Brick--inferior, heterosexual union offered him by his wife,

70

Maggie. Two antithetical versions of the play's ending further complicate the dramatic significance of Brick's story and characterization. In Act III of both versions, Maggie seeks to resume sexual union with Brick, to achieve partial redemption for Big Daddy's dying, and, not least, to ensure the inheritance of the Pollitt estate, by her "mendacious" announcement that she is going to have Brick's child. Mae's truncated response, "You can't conceive a child by a man that won't sleep with you unless you think you're--" (p. 161), temporarily invests Maggie with the sanctity of an ironic Virgin Mary. However, Maggie's subsequent seduction of Brick in order to work the miracle that will "make that lie come true" (p. 214) leads to two entirely different outcomes of the play.

IX. The Broadway Conclusion: Love (Heterosexuality) Conquers All

In the concluding act as altered by Williams at the insistence of director Elia Kazan for the play's Broadway premiere, Brick is literally transformed and figuratively reborn. Apparently moved by his forced confrontation with the truth of his betrayal of Skipper in Act II, Brick is depicted in Act III as a willing accomplice of Maggie's plans for their reunion, suggesting that Brick chooses to replace an illusion fraught with deceit and self-delusion with the less pure, but wholly productive, flesh-and-blood relationship offered him by Maggie. To ensure his cooperation, Maggie breaks Brick's liquor bottles, thereby irreparably shattering his means of escaping reality.

Moreover, if, as Robert Heilman suggests, Brick's earlier refusal to sleep with Maggie is interpreted as his way of punishing her for causing Skipper's death, then Brick's resuming sexual relations with Maggie implies that he has stopped blaming her and makes possible "his acknowledgment and understanding of his own role--in Skipper's death and in his and Margaret's subsequent misery."[31] Although this interpretation substantially deepens the meaning of Brick's sudden conversion, there is little support in the light-hearted mood, tone, or content of Brick's speeches for the attribution of such a "heavy" or tragic significance to his changes in attitude and behavior. The mood of the Broadway conclusion is, rather, essentially comic: an ambience in which sudden conversions and "miraculous" transformations of character need no justification other than the *fact* of their happening, with little

regard to *how* they come about.[32] Brick merely utters an equivocal
and ambiguous admission of self-deception--"I've lied to nobody,
nobody but myself, just lied to myself" (p. 172)--for his psychological integration to be achieved, his moral "paralysis" lifted.
His admission contains no acknowledgment of his own tacit betrayal
of Skipper, and he implicitly denies having harmed anyone but
himself. Nevertheless, in the comic spirit of rebirth, Brick is
released from both dream and self-delusion, and willingly re-enters
life, accepting its corruptions, compromises, and compensations:
"An' now if you will stop actin' as if Brick Pollitt was dead an'
buried, invisible, not heard, an' go on back to your peeophole in
the wall--I'm drunk, and sleepy--not as alive as Maggie, but still
alive . . . " (p. 212).

The Broadway version concludes, then, in a celebratory climax
to all the rituals, myths, and mythical figures evoked throughout
the play. Brick and Maggie successfully reenact the roles of the
play's Apollo and Artemis. Just as Apollo and Artemis join forces
in Greek legend to strike down the prolific progeny of Niobe, the
mortal queen who had the audacity to boast of her six sons and six
daughters,[33] so do Brick and Maggie join forces to "kill" the
chances of Gooper and Mae ("that monster of fertility") to inherit
the Pollitt estate. By his admission of self-delusion--"I've lied
to . . . myself" (p. 172)--and by cooperating with Maggie to make
her announcement of incipient childbirth "come true," Brick fulfills the Apollonian function of God of Truth. Accordingly, Maggie
as Diana-Artemis, the huntress, captures her prey and prepares to
assume Diana's pre-Hellenistic role of Great Mother.

Brick and Maggie may also be said to reenact successfully the
archetypal fertility rite of Osiris and Isis. Brick, the modern
analogue of the dismembered god, is restored to health, wholeness,
and fertility through the loving ministrations of Maggie, who
fulfills the Isis-role of life-restorer. Thus, just as Isis, who
mythically represents the fertile plains of Egypt, is made fruitful
by the annual inundation of the Nile, personified by Osiris,[34] so,
too, by their anticipated sexual reunion, Maggie and Brick make
secure their own inheritance of the coveted "twenty-eight thousand
acres of the richest land this side of the valley Nile" (p. 86).

Finally, the birthday celebration, which forms the ritual core
of the play and which had become bitterly ironic in the face of
Big Daddy's imminent death, is fully redeemed through Brick's
symbolic rebirth as well as by Big Daddy's actual reappearance and

the promise of Brick's child to perpetuate Big Daddy's seed: "a grandson as much like his son as his son is like Big Daddy" (p. 202). Significantly, in this version, Maggie's announcement of her pregnancy assumes the intonation, syntax, and elevated diction of the Christian annunciation of the savior: "Announcement of life beginning! A child is coming, sired by Brick, and out of Maggie the Cat!" (p. 208). In this essentially comic conclusion, then, miracle, myth, and ritual are successfully reenacted. The play ends with the resurrection of a dismembered god, the anticipation of a successful fertility rite, and the redemptive miracle of new birth: "Big Daddy's dream come true!" (p. 208).

X. Williams' Original Conclusion: An "American Tragedy"

Although the 1955 Broadway version of *Cat on a Hot Tin Roof* was an enormous commercial and critical success, Williams retained ambivalent feelings about its dramatic integrity and, especially, about its lack of sufficient motivation for Brick's sudden conversion in Act III. According to Williams, Kazan had justified the Broadway conclusion on the grounds that the vitality of Big Daddy's personality necessitated his reappearance in Act III, that Maggie's sympathetic characterization should be more clearly projected, and, most important, that "the character of Brick should undergo some apparent mutation as a result of the virtual vivisection that he undergoes in his interview with his father in Act Two" (III, 168). However, Williams had rejected in his original ending just such a dramatic peripeteia which conventionally signals a decisive change in character. In his "Note of Explanation" appended to all published editions of the play that include both endings, Williams defends Brick's static characterization in the original conclusion:

> I felt that the moral paralysis of Brick was a root thing in his tragedy, and to show a dramatic progression would obscure the meaning of that tragedy in him and because I don't believe that a conversation, however revelatory, ever effects so immediate a change in the heart or even conduct of a person in Brick's state of spiritual disrepair. (III, 168)

Thus, no change takes place in Brick's character in Williams' original conclusion. Even though Big Daddy has forced Brick to confront the truth of his betrayal of Skipper by the end of Act II, Brick neither gains insight into his own condition nor asssumes of responsibility for Skipper's dissolution in Williams' Act III.

Although it is strongly implied that he will reluctantly yield physically to Maggie's seduction and plans for conception, Brick remains, as before, emotionally and spiritually disengaged from Maggie's desperate bid for love. In this version, Brick remains a passive personification of Plato's "divided self," condemned to spend his entire life remembering, rather than seeking to regain, the lost happiness of being whole--that idyllic condition he enjoyed with Skipper so long as it remained a mythicized ideal, but which he rejected when it was "named dirty" as culturally taboo experience.

Although Brick's condition is described as a "tragedy" in Williams' "Note" to his original ending, the moral stature of his protagonist as depicted in that conclusion is not tragic. While Brick resembles the more nearly tragic figure of Blanche DuBois both in his conflicts between the ideal and the real, spirit and flesh, and by his act of cruelty against a homosexual loved one, unlike Blanche, Brick neither asssumes responsibility for the devastating consequences of that act nor is he admittedly haunted by a sense of guilt. Brick's failure to explore the moral implications of his cruel rejection of Skipper or to express remorse for that cruelty precludes his rise to tragic stature. Instead, that guilt which is the personal burden of the tragic character is shifted in this play to the society which spawned it, for Brick's response to Skipper derives from his thorough internalization of the negative cultural attitudes toward homosexuality in America of the 1950's, which is the play's social context. In Act II, Williams himself confirms Brick's acculturated value judgment of homosexuality: "In his utterance of this word ["*Fairies*"], we gauge the wide and profound reach of the conventional mores he got from the world that crowned him with early laurel" (p. 120). Accordingly, by his refusal to feel guilty for rejecting a relationship which his society had declared "dirty," "unclean," and "disgusting," Brick remains innocent of both the tragic moral sense and of an individual moral core. Moreover, because throughout the play the conventional mores of this society are depicted as corrupt, hypocritical, and mendacious, so becomes our final perception of Brick, owing to his inability to divest himself of their authority and to accept an unconventional nature, whether Skipper's or his own. Thus, Brick emerges in Act III of Williams' original conclusion not as a tragic figure but as both victim and perpetrator of the cultural attitudes of a society that will not allow its members to admit to a homosexual nature with impunity. In its indictment of that society, the play reflects an "American tragedy" rather than a personal one.

Myth, miracle, and fairy tale, then, are defeated in this conclusion of the play by their collision with social reality: a reality in which homosexuality is stigmatized, and heterosexual union is depicted as breeding only mendacity, greed, lovelessness, and "no-neck monsters." Caught in this cultural double-bind, Brick is reduced to an ironic, demythicized analogue of the "dying and reviving god," who remains emotionally, spiritually, and morally dead. Deflated to an ironic Apollo (God of Truth), Brick refuses to explore, much less admit to the possiblity of, a socially unacceptable truth about his own nature or that of his friend. As an equally ironic analogue of the dismembered god Osiris, Brick remains "broken up" (p. 135), "gone t' pieces" (p. 181); accordingly, Maggie, reduced to a vulgarized Isis, fails to fulfill her role as the restorer of life-giving love and represents, instead, survival, at any cost. Thus, Brick's nominal acquiescence to Maggie's life-force makes a mockery of the successful fertility rite or rebirth ritual of the mythical dying and reviving gods. In this existential version of the myth, the dying god remains dead.

In anticipation of its existential ending, Maggie's mendacious announcement of her pregnancy lacks the mythicized overtones of her "annunciation" in the Broadway conclusion: it is stated in a flat, declarative prose which, while reflecting Maggie's indomitable will, suggests no rebirth of love even by its fulfillment: "Brick and I are going to--*have a child*!" (p. 158). Also, rather than irretrievably shattering Brick's liquor bottles, in this version, Maggie just locks up his liquor and threatens to make Brick "satisfy my desire before I unlock it!" (p. 164), suggesting their union represents only a temporary change in Brick's conduct rather than a true metamorphosis of his character. Similarly, she merely hurls Brick's crutch over the railing, where, we may imagine, it will be subsequently retrieved. In this sense, the play returns at its end to the conflicts with which it began, both within Brick and between him and Maggie.

At the very end of this conclusion to *Cat*, Maggie makes a final declaration of love to Brick--"I *do* love you, Brick, I *do*"-- to which Brick, "smiling with charming sadness," replies: "Wouldn't it be funny if that was true?" (p. 166). Significantly, this closing line of Williams' original conclusion to the play echoes the final words of another spiritually maimed figure in another major literary work concerned with the failure of love in the modern world. Jake Barnes in Hemingway's *The Sun Also Rises* is, like Brick, an existential analogue of a mythical fertility god-- both are ironic and impotent Fisher-Kings. In the similar conclusion to Hemingway's novel, Brett, in a moment of self-indulgent reminiscence, attempts to elicit a sense of bittersweet nostalgia from Jake: "'Oh, Jake . . . we could have had such a damned good time together.'" Jake, however, isn't having any. Believing that only realized, immediate experience has any significance, the anti-romantic Jake replies, "'Isn't it pretty to think so?'"[35]

On the surface, of course, Brick and Jake are antithetical figures. The irony of Jake's condition is his physical inability to fulfill his emotional manhood; the irony of Brick's, his inability to admit to a possible lack of emotional "manhood," even as he fulfills with reluctance the physically masculine sexual role. Accordingly, whereas Jake's "'Isn't it pretty to think so?'" adds the cutting edge of stoical self-knowledge to the "irony and pity" of his thorough disillusionment, Brick's "'Wouldn't it be funny if that was true?'" leaves characteristically ambiguous its import, lending to its evocation of irony and pity a sense of romantic nostalgia (memories of Maggie? or of Skipper?), a whiff of mendacity (recognition of his duplicity to Maggie? to Skipper? or to self?), and a barely supportable hope for Brick's future self-examination (will this question lead to tragic self-knowledge or is it merely rhetorical?). Ultimately, however, the last lines of both works reflect the same theme: a deep disillusionment with the power of heterosexual love to redeem the divided self from its existential isolation, *angst*, and despair in the demythicized modern world.

XI. Williams' Existential Theme: The Failure of Love (Heterosexuality) in the Modern World

Rather than reenacting the mythical events of love's rebirth and resurrection, then, Maggie and Brick remain in Williams' original conclusion the personifications of divorce and alienation. Their personal plight is symptomatic of a generalized failure of heterosexual love to provide a redemptive humanism for its participants. Brick's "mendacious" ability to resume sexual relations with Maggie while withholding from her his love and affection is anticipated by Big Daddy's description of his similar loveless, hypocritical relationship with Big Mama throughout their marriage: "I haven't been able to stand the sight, sound, or smell of that woman for forty years now!--even when I *laid* her!--regular as a piston" (p. 108). Significantly, Maggie's final, desperate declaration of love for her husband--"I *do* love you, Brick, I *do*!" (p. 166)--echoes Big Mama's expression of a similar passion for her own spouse in the past--"*And I did, I did so much, I did love you!*--I even loved your hate and your hardness, Big Daddy!" (p. 78). As a further parallel, Brick's response to Maggie's declaration of love reiterates exactly his father's musing reply to Big Mama's passionate outburst: "Wouldn't it be funny if that was true" (pp. 78 and 166).[36] The cumulative effect of these duplications of speech and manner in both the elder Pollitts and the younger couple is to suggest that the union of Brick and Maggie, even if fruitful, will ultimately bear nothing more positive than the perpetuation by another generation of Pollitts of the loveless, mendacious, and exploitative sexual attitudes which mark not only the relationship of Big Daddy and Big Mama but also the marriage of Mae and Gooper, whose prolific reproduction of "no-neck monsters" is inspired only by greed. In this conclusion, then, the family perpetuated by heterosexual love represents but the microcosm of a corrupt society and culture.

XII.   The Homosexual Alternative: An Exemplum of Self-Integrity

In conspicuous contrast to the overwhelming dramatic evidence attesting to the lovelessness of heterosexual relationships are brief, favorable references in the play to Jack Straw and Peter Ochello, the "pair of old bachelors who shared this room [the "bed-sitting-room" of the Pollitt plantation-home] all their lives together," and whose "ghosts" are said by Williams in his prefatory "Notes for the Designer" to impart a "gently and poetically haunted" ambience to the play's environs (p. 15). Of the Straw-Ochello relationship, Williams notes that it "must have involved a tenderness which was uncommon" (p. 15), an accolade similar to Brick's description of his idealized Platonic relationship with Skipper as "exceptional" (p. 120) and "too rare to be normal" (p. 121). Unlike Brick's Platonic friendship with Skipper, however, the play suggests that the relationship between Straw and Ochello was an openly declared and fully realized homosexual love: a relationship which, it is hinted, once might have included Big Daddy, who, "leaving a lot unspoken" (p. 116), attempts to convince Brick of the importance of understanding and "tolerance!" (p. 120) toward the unconventional couple. Finally, in distinct contrast to

Brick's betrayal of Skipper's friendship, the Straw-Ochello relationship is invested with the mythic love, loyalty, and brotherly devotion embodied by Castor and Pollux, as suggested by Big Daddy's account of Ochello's behavior when Straw died: "When Jack Straw died--why, old Peter Ochello quit eatin' like a dog does when its master's dead, and died, too!" (p. 117).

Given William's original conclusion, the fully realized homosexual relationship exemplified by Straw and Ochello represents the only alternative in the play to either loveless heterosexual couplings or tragically suppressed homosexual longings. An exemplum of self-integrity, the admitted and embraced homosexual relationship between Straw and Ochello affords the existential fulfillment of love. Like the existentialist view of life, the homosexual relationship is self-sufficient, exists for no other purpose than its own fulfillment, and is "fruitless" (though not futile) as opposed to reproductive or self-perpetuating. However, the play presents with such subtlety its favorable attitudes toward the Straw-Ochello relationship that they are easily dismissed as irrelevant--an aside, a footnote--to the play's central theme. The play's failure to establish fully its sympathetic portrayal of the Straw-Ochello relationship thus obscures its significance as a viable alternative to the corruption depicted as inherent in heterosexual love, in American society, and, by extension, in modern Western culture, all of which are presented as spawning only continuing cycles of greed, lovelessness, and mendacity.

Just as the play fails to make clear the significance of the Straw-Ochello relationship, so it also leaves ambiguous Brick's true sexual nature. The question of Brick's sexuality is deliberately left undetermined, for, according to Williams, "Some mystery should be left in the revelation of character in a play, just as a great deal of mystery is always left in the revelation of character in life, even in one's own character to himself" (pp. 114-15). Williams implies that it would be reductive to the complexity of Brick's character to identify him as homosexual, thereby resolving "one man's psychological problem" through "'pat' conclusions, facile definitions which make a play just a play, not a snare for the truth of human experience" (pp. 114-15). While these ideas are existentially valid, they become in this play dramatically problematic; for, ultimately, Brick's failure to explore his own psychological nature leads first to his internalization of society's attitudes rather than the development of his own, and hence to his cruelty to Skipper, his punishment of Maggie, his childish vindictiveness toward Big Daddy, and, at least in Williams' original conclusion, to his inability to love at all, either himself or another: all of which comprise that "moral paralysis" which Williams in his "Note of Explanation" terms Brick's "tragedy" (p. 168). If, however, Brick remains a mystery even to himself, then he is not tragic but simply pathetic, the victim of self-ignorance.

Rather than being woven into the very fabric of the drama, then, both the positive value accorded the Straw-Ochello relationship and the question of Brick's homosexuality are largely confined to the author's explanatory notes and stage directions, which are themselves far too often ambiguous or contradictory to the play's expressed dramatic attitudes. In the same "Note" in which Williams insists on leaving undetermined Brick's sexual nature, he also verifies that Brick's arrested psychological and emotional condition is due to his being so fully acculturated to the conventions of his society that even if he *were* homosexual he could not admit it--to Skipper, to Maggie, to Big Daddy, or to himself--and therefore is doomed to the existential condition of "bad faith" and to the divided, incomplete self. Williams tells us as much in his interpolative commentary about Brick in the midst of Act II:

> The thing they're discussing [the homosexual implications of Brick's relationship with Skipper], timidly and painfully on the side of Big Daddy, fiercely, violently on Brick's side, is the inadmissible thing that Skipper died to disavow between them. The fact that if it existed it had to be disavowed to "keep face" in the world they lived in, may be at the heart of the "mendacity" that Brick drinks to kill his disgust with. (p. 114)

However, Williams' positive depiction of Straw and Ochello, as well as Big Daddy's acceptance and defense of their relationship, belies the idea that the existence of a homosexual relationship between Brick and Skipper *had* "to be disavowed to 'keep face' in the world they lived in." That Brick *feels* it "had to be disavowed" serves to reveal only how thoroughly his attitudes match those of the society with which he claims disgust. In this sense, whether or not Brick is homosexual is, indeed, beside the point: the intolerance and moral hollowness he reflects by his betrayal of a homosexual friend because of his unconventional nature, in order to "keep face" in a society which is exposed in the play as thoroughly corrupt, become the larger moral issues of Brick's psychological conflict. Although Brick does not change, then, in Williams' original conclusion, our perception of him does: in this larger context, his pathetic condition, whether that of disillusioned romantic or frustrated homosexual, is darkened to the ignominious one of moral coward.

XIII. "A Play of Evasions"

As Robert Heilman suggests, Williams was of "two minds" regarding the dramatic focus, development, and outcome of *Cat on a Hot Tin Roof*: "one toward the portrait of the strong competitive woman [Maggie] . . . the other toward inner conflict that has tragic potential [Brick]."[37] To these two perspectives may be added several other directions the play takes: one toward exposing the corruption inherent in heterosexual love, in American materialism, and in the existential process of living; another expressing admiration for life's irrepressibility, no matter how corrupt; a third, revealing sympathy for the romantic yearning for transcendence; and a fourth, though muted, suggesting a viable alternative to the others in the "uncommon tenderness" and self-integrity afforded by realized homosexual love. As a result, Williams sacrifices the tragic development of the internal conflicts or "psychological problem" of Brick, from whose memory and divided self the play's structure and focus originally derive, in order to encompass all points of view by attempting to capture "the true quality of experience in a group of people . . . [the] interplay of live human beings in the thundercloud of a common crisis" (p. 114).

In the process, the play becomes dominated instead by the forceful, dynamic, and essentially "whole" personalities of two characters who assert their wills over the chaos of "live" experience: Maggie and Big Daddy. Maggie's is the dynamic personality which threatens to overwhelm Brick's passive characterization in the play's very first act (a force which is shifted to Big Daddy in Act II) and which literally saves the thematic and structural coherence of the play in Act III by her "announcement" of her pregnancy by Brick, the crucial lie which promises the reenactment of Brick's mythicized memory of his idealized relationship with Skipper in its diminished existential version with Maggie (a union rendered miraculous in the Broadway ending, mendacious in Williams' original conclusion).[38]

Thus, *Cat on a Hot Tin Roof* is aptly named, for "Maggie the Cat" emerges as the literal *tour de force* and figurative *dea ex machina* by whose vitality and tenacious personality the play is dramatically resolved and its structural pattern of recollection and reenactment fulfilled. Maggie's intervention leads to a kind of romantic comedy in the play's original Broadway version, to a more realistic outcome in its original version. Williams' declared intention to create "a snare for the truth of human experience" in all its "cloudy, flickering, evanescent" (pp. 114-15) interplay makes for exhilarating theater. At the same time, by its broadening of experience and its diffusion of focus, the play fails to elevate in either version Brick's "psychological problem" and "moral paralysis" to the stature of tragedy, and evades, finally, "the meaning of that tragedy in him" (p. 168).[39] In more than one sense, then, the play merits Walter Kerr's review of its 1955 Broadway production as "a beautifully written, perfectly directed, stunningly acted play of evasions."[40]

CHAPTER FIVE

ORPHEUS DESCENDING

And you must learn, even you, what we have learned,
the passion there is for declivity in this world,
the impulse to fall that follows a rising fountain.

from "Orpheus Descending" in In The Winter of Cities

I. Orphic Myth and Idyllic Memory: Two Stories

In *Orpheus Descending* (1957), a revised version of Williams' first professional production *Battle of Angels* (1940), the symbolic structure--based on a mythicized story which is reenacted in a demythicized version--is complicated. Not one, but several stories structure the events of this play. Furthermore, one of the two major stories dramatized by the play is not told in the play by its protagonist--Val Xavier--nor does it derive from a past event in his life, but has its reference in the title: the Greek myth of Orpheus and Eurydice. The other major story, which is organic to the human drama, derives from the idyllic memory of young love and subsequent tragedy of its protagonist, Lady Torrance; it is first recounted in the Prologue to the first act by Dolly and Beulah (the play's parodic Greek chorus) and is later retold by Lady herself before it is reenacted. The play's dramatic tension results largely from the clash between its two central protagonists who pursue antithetical goals in the reenactment of their separate stories, a structural pattern Williams repeats in *Sweet Bird of Youth*. Thus, even as Val Xavier attempts an Orphic quest to *escape* his corrupt past, Lady Torrance engages him in her equally tran-scendent efforts to *recapture* an idyllic memory.

However, because the presence of the Orphic myth is made known by extrinsic rather than organic means, the determinants of the myth's original plot too often seem superimposed onto the human conflicts integral to the drama. At the same time, the implicit reference in the title to the play's main characters, Val Xavier and Lady Torrance, as modern analogues of Orpheus and Eurydice raises expectations of a strict allegorical correlation between the mythological figures and their dramatic counterparts, which the play does not fulfill. Instead, Lady's story expands the play's plot beyond the confines of the original myth, while Val is in-

vested with multiple symbolic images that extend his characterization further than a single identification with Orpheus, to include
his analogy to Dionysus, Christ, and his name-saint, St. Valentine.
(Evocations of both Christian and pagan mythic figures inform the
other characters as well.) As Benjamin Nelson points out, the
attempted fusion of these two major stories --the Orphic myth with
the personal memory of Lady Torrance --creates confusion in both
plot and characterization, for each story vies with the other for
clarity and focus.[1] Throughout much of the play, then, the focus
alternates between the two stories, each with its separate protagonist; when they do merge, however, the reenactment of Lady's
personal past adds complications that deepen and darken the significance of both the myth and her memory.

II. The Myth of Orpheus and Eurydice Reenacted: A Modern Existential Version

The myth of Orpheus and Eurydice not only informs structure
and characterization in the play but is itself reenacted in a
modern existential version. In the original myth, Orpheus descends
into the underworld in an attempt to rescue his bride, Eurydice,
after she has been bitten by a snake and abducted by Pluto. His
music so charms the guardians of Hades that Eurydice's return is
promised him on the condition that he not look back at her as she
follows him out of the underworld. But Orpheus disobeys and by
looking back loses Eurydice to the underworld forever.

In the play, Val Xavier is given the mythical attributes of
Orpheus, archetypal embodiment of inspired poetic or musical expression; Lady Torrance represents his Eurydice; and Jabe Torrance,
Lady's dying husband, is Pluto's equivalent--"Death's self" (III,
338). Like Orpheus, Val is a wandering minstrel, his guitar correlative to the Orphic lyre, although his "charm" resides more in
his inherent sexuality than in his music. As analogue to the lyre
of Orpheus which was placed among the constellations after his
death, Val's guitar is inscribed with the autographs of immortalized black musicians and singers--Leadbelly, King Oliver, Bessie
Smith, and Fats Waller--whose names are "written in the stars" (p.
261). The correspondence, however, is ultimately ironic; for,
whereas the Orphic lyre represents the ideal of harmony,[2] the
"blues" and jazz expressed by these noted musicians reflects the
essential discord in the history of black people in a predominately
white America, even as their music also represents a means to rise

above it. His calling as a bohemian-musician serves, finally, to link Val--himself stigmatized as an undesirable outcast and alien in this oppressive Southern town--with Carol Cutrere, a disillusioned civil rights reformer; with Lady's murdered father, Papa Romano, a "foreign" egalitarian; with the feared Negro Conjureman exiled to Blue Mountain (recurrent site in Williams' plays of an ideal locus of primordial unity); and with the black "runaway convict" who is torn to pieces by the sheriff's dogs and whom Val calls "brother" (p. 294) in acknowledgment of their shared identity and fate. Val's guitar thus links him with all those collectively known in the play as "the fugitive kind" (p. 341), whose lives foreshadow Val's own violent victimization by and martyrdom to the forces of hatred, oppression, and bigotry. Nevertheless, Val, at the play's beginning, attempts to dissociate himself from the nonconformist nature of the fugitive kind; his ideal is to attain the Orphic qualities of asceticism and peace, through the sublimation of his Dionysian energies and sexuality. As he tells Carol Cutrere, who identifies herself with his wild, passionate youth which he now attempts to transcend, "Heavy drinking and smoking the weed and shacking with strangers is okay for kids in their twenties but this is my thirtieth birthday and I'm all through with that route" (p. 246). He vows, instead, to be "steady and honest and hardworking" (p. 267).

The underworld of the provincial Southern town into which this Orpheus descends combines the demonic atmosphere of a Christian Hell with the savage and brutal pagan upper world inhabited by the Dionysian Maenads, those female embodiments of passion-gone-mad who tore the mythic Orpheus to pieces. In this analogous subterranean world of "Beatings! . . . Lynchings! . . . Runaway convicts torn to pieces by hounds!" (p. 291), Val finds not only a Eurydice in Lady Torrance, but also a Cassandra in Carol Cutrere[3] (to whose repeated prophetic warnings of danger Val pays no heed), and a Saint Veronica in Vee Talbott[4] (through whose eyes Val is elevated to a Lawrentian phallic Christ-figure). All three are sexually repressed or frustrated women who either tacitly or verbally implore Val to "take me out of this hell!" (p. 333). Just as Orpheus was unsuccessful in liberating Eurydice from her underworld, so Val's rescue efforts fail.

Williams' attempt to parallel Val's failure to rescue Lady with the Orphic act of "looking back" is complicated, however, by the intrusion of elements from Lady's own story, the fusion of which is effected by a certain amount of histrionics and theatrical fireworks that create dramatic confusion at the conclusion of the play. In Act III, Scene iii, Val, "threatened with violence if I stay here" (p. 330), tells Lady that he is leaving, but that he loves her, and indicates that she is to follow him: "I'll wait for you out of this country" (p. 331). However, after a series of frenzied outbursts by Lady--first, pleading with Val to stay; then, threatening to withhold his pay and destroy his guitar if he leaves; and, finally, urging him to "Go, go" (p. 337)--she, unlike Eurydice, not only refuses to follow Val out of her underworld but also prevents his own leaving until it is too late. Lady's refusal to leave derives from complications in her own story--in particular, her attempt to re-create her father's wine garden in the confectionery of the mercantile store and her discovery of her husband's part in the destruction of both the original wine garden and her father--which motivate her to revenge: "Death has got to die before we can go" (p. 333). When, in turn, Val discovers that he has made Lady pregnant --in reenactment of another event in Lady's past--he puts aside all thoughts of escape, and, shortly thereafter, both he and Lady lose their chance to flee, as she is lost forever to the play's Pluto, her husband who kills her. Val's act of "looking back" leads not only to Lady's destruction but also to his own violent analogue of Orphic dismemberment: immolation by blowtorch, administered by the play's male counterparts to the Maenads, the savage and mad "Dawgs" of this infernal Southern town, its hounds of hell. At the same time, by altering Val's motivation to "look back" from its Orphic parallel of disobedience to its significance as a gesture of love and selflessness, Williams invests Val with an elevated moral stature which has its analogue in Christian rather than pagan myth. As Hugh Dickinson points out, Val's decision to stay with Lady exemplifies "the most Christ-like action he performs in the play"; it constitutes "a tragic choice with tragic consequences . . . that cleanses him of whatever guilt he bears."[5] Lady's subsequent death and Val's crucifixion, however, rob both her pregnancy and his self-sacrifice of existentially redemptive value.

III. Analogues to Orpheus: Archetype of the Ironic Savior

In the course of the play, the mythic symbols elevating Val proliferate, their sacred and supernatural connotations tempered by reminders of his innately profane and earth-bound nature: his transcendent aspirations qualified by his instinctive sexuality as a "Male at Stud" (p. 258). Attempting to repudiate his former life of corrupt sensuality as well as his inherently Dionysian nature, Val assumes the roles of erotic saint, neophyte shaman, and ironic Christ.

His very name, Valentine Xavier,[6] evokes his Christianized role as archetypal "Savior," combining as it does the image of love with that of salvation, even as it suggests his violent death by the invocation of his martyred namesake, Saint Valentine.[7] To Vee Talbott, a Christian fanatic in whom sexual repression emerges as religious sublimation, Val is perceived as both saint and Christ, sent to redeem her from the corruption and violence she has witnessed in the world. Like St. Valentine, "a priest of Rome . . . imprisoned for succoring persecuted Christians" who is said to have "restored the sight of his jailer's blind daughter,"[8] Val offers sympathetic consolation to the persecuted Vee, wife of the town's sheriff; and he similarly restores her sight when she is "*struck blind!*" (p. 314) by her vision of "the eyes of my Savior!" (p. 315), which she subsequently "sees" are the eyes of Val. As Nancy Traubitz suggests, Vee Talbott also represents in this instance an analogue of Saint Veronica, who gave Christ her veil to wipe his forehead on the road to Calvary and received it back with the lasting impression of Christ's face upon it.[9] Herein, Vee--primitive painter and self-proclaimed visionary "born with a caul! A sort of thing like a veil" (p. 290)--projects her own vision (or "vera-icon") of Christ "Crucified and then Risen!" (p. 316) onto Val in a psychological parallel to the Veronica legend.

At the same time, Val is identified with the Negro Conjureman, a kind of shaman "bedizened with . . . good-luck charms of shell and bone and feather . . . [and] daubed with cryptic signs in white paint" (p. 239), whose Choctaw cry--"a series of barking sounds that rise to a high sustained note of wild intensity" (p. 240)-- twice invokes Val's sudden appearance, "as though the cry had brought him" (pp. 240, 327). Through his mystical affinity with the Conjureman, Val is cast in the role of neophyte shaman. Like the shamans of primitive religions--"mediators of the sacred"--who, according to Mircea Eliade, "exhibit powers of . . . self-control well above the average," Val claims qualities which may be considered superhuman.[10] In parody of the epic vaunt or boast by which the exemplary model of a culture states his heroic qualifications, Val asserts that his temperature is "always a couple degrees above normal the same as a dog's" (p. 259), and he has mastered his normal biological functions to the extent that, "I can sleep on a concrete floor or go without sleeping . . . for forty-eight hours.

87

And I can hold my breath three minutes without blacking out. . . .
And I can go a whole day without passing water" (p. 264). He adds,
ominously, that he can "burn down . . . Any two-footed woman" (p.
264). Despite Val's obvious exaggeration of his abilities, just
such qualities as the tolerance of heat and heightened temperature,
respiratory control, and the imitation of the behavior (and cries)
of animals are, according to Eliade, universal techniques used by
shamans in all primitive cultures to enable them "to rise above the
present condition of man--that of *man corrupted*--and to re-enter
the state of the primordial man described to us in the paradisiac
myths."[11]

Val, too, expresses the archetypal desire to transcend his
human limitations in the form of the mythical bird of Paradise,
which he describes as a species that "don't have no legs at all and
they live their whole lives on the wing, and they sleep on the
wind . . . and never light on this earth but one time when they
die!"; so, they are "never . . . corrupted!" (pp. 265-66). Val
thus aspires to the transcendent power of the shaman, which resides
in "his supposed ability to leave his body and fly about the universe as a bird";[12] he thereby recaptures "a beatitude, a sponta-
neity and freedom . . . lost in consequence of the fall."[13] The
bird who never lands on earth and so can "never be--corrupted" (p.
266) is commemorated by Coleridge in "The Eolian Harp," which
compares the ethereal music of the harp to "Melodies . . . Foot-
less and wild, like the birds of Paradise,/ Nor pause, nor perch,
hovering on untam'd wing!" (ll. 23-25). Val's desire for incorrup-
tibility is also put to music played on his guitar; as analogue to
the transcendent Orphic lyre, it is the instrument which "washes me
clean like water when anything unclean has touched me" (p. 261).
The ballad of "Heavenly Grass" which Val plays throughout the play
refers to a Williams poem,[14] whose lyrics suggest not only Val's
desire for transcendence from the corruption of earthly life, but
also nostalgia for the paradise of a Platonic-Wordsworthian pre-
existence from which humankind is painfully exiled at birth:

> My feet took a walk in heavenly grass.
> All day while the sky shone clear as glass.
> My feet took a walk in heavenly grass.
> All night while the lonesome stars rolled past.
> Then my feet come down to walk on earth,
> And my mother cried when she give me birth.
> Now my feet walk far and my feet walk fast,
> . . . .
> But they still got an itch for heavenly grass.

Interestingly enough, the triadic image of Val as Dionysus-Orpheus-Christ as well as its evolution in his personal history parallels the historical development of the mythic figures in the Greco-Roman and Christian religions. According to Joseph L. Henderson in "Ancient Myths and Modern Man," as the rites of Dionysus became too wildly orgiastic, they lost their emotive religious power: "There emerged an almost oriental longing for liberation from their exclusive preoccupation with the purely natural symbols of life and love. . . . These [more ascetic souls] came to experience their religious ecstasies inwardly, in the worship of Orpheus."[15] Just as the religion of Dionysus gave way to that of Orpheus, so too "the early Christian Church saw in Orpheus the prototype of Christ." Thus, the Dionysian process of seasonal rebirth and the Christian hope of a final and ultimate resurrection "somehow fuse in the figure of Orpheus, the god who remembers Dionysus but looks foward to Christ."[16] Just so, Val attempts to rise above his Dionysian nature and orgiastic past, becoming the Orphic figure who longs for "a life of the spirit that might triumph over the primitive animal passions of man and . . . give him peace."[17] He embodies an archetypal duality between spirit and flesh, a conflict between the Orphic sublime and Dionysian sexuality.

Like Orpheus, both Dionysus and Christ meet violent deaths by dismemberment and make a descent into the underworld: Dionysus to save his mother Semele and Christ to liberate the pre-Christian faithful. Christian doctrine places the time of Christ's descent into Hell on Holy Saturday, the day which falls between his Crucifixion on Good Friday and his Resurrection on Easter Sunday. Appropriately, Val's downfall takes place on "the Saturday before Easter" (p. 306). As ironic savior, however, Val descends into death's underworld and remains there; no resurrection occurs. His immolation by blowtorch renders his demythicization literal and complete; only his snakeskin jacket survives.

IV. The Snakeskin Jacket: Symbol of Ironic Rebirth

In the Orphic myth, the rebirth of the demi-god is symbolized by the Muses' salvaging of his severed head, which continues, even after his death, to sing, testifying to the irrepressibility of the transcendent spirit. In the play, not Val's head, but his snakeskin jacket is saved (by the Conjureman) and passed on to Carol Cutrere, the disillusioned idealist become the town's promiscuous pariah.

   As symbol, the snakeskin evokes multiple associations relevant to Val's characterization and roles. Mythically, it brings to mind the snake whose bite kills Eurydice. It also suggests the sepentine guise of Satan whose seduction of Eve brings about the loss of Eden and the fall from innocence. Its stunning appearance and phallic connotations evoke the ambivalence with which fallen man regards his sexual nature: his simultaneous attraction to it and repulsion from it. Finally, although in primitive and pagan religions, the shedding of the snakeskin each spring connotes renewal and regeneration, in fact, its divestment simply heralds the growth of another similar covering. While all of these allusions identify Val, himself called "Snakeskin" (p. 258), as an embodiment of natural or fallen man, his attraction to the mythical bird of Paradise, which spends its life in empyrean purity, reveals his Orphic yearnings to transcend his corporeal and earthbound condition. Attempting to mitigate Lady's loneliness, however, Val betrays his own quest for transcendence and becomes a victim of his intrinsic sexuality as well as of the world's inherent corruption. The failure of Val's efforts to reconcile spirit and flesh--to become, as it were, a winged serpent, mediator between heaven and earth--reveals only how tightly wrapped around him is the snakeskin, concrete symbol of his own earthbound nature of tainted sexuality. As if in recognition of the futility of his transcendent quest, it is Val who says, "We're all of us sentenced to solitary confinement inside our own skins, for life!" (p. 271).

   Unlike the head of Orpheus, then, Val's snakeskin jacket does not symbolize the rebirth of man's transcendent spirit or spiritual nature. Its reappearance after Val's death represents only a futile and unregenerative martyrdom, the sacrificial death of its wearer a testimony to man's inability to rise above his own flawed nature, to escape his own skin. Assumed by Carol Cutrere, embittered liberal reformer, the snakeskin becomes the emblem of "the fugitive kind" (p. 341), idealistic purveyors of love, freedom, and brotherhood, who would deliver humankind from lives filled with frustration, alienation, and oppression, but who are perpetually doomed to persecution by the forces of hatred, bigotry, and violence, or betrayed by their own carnal needs.

   In his poem also entitled "Orpheus Descending,"[18] Williams attests to the unredemptive condition of twentieth-century man and to the futility of Val's transcendent quest:

And you must learn, even you, what we have learned,
the passion there is for declivity in this world,
the impulse to fall that follows a rising fountain.
Now Orpheus, crawl, O shamefaced fugitive, crawl
back under the crumbling broken wall of yourself,
for you are not stars, sky-set in the shape of a lyre,
but the dust of those who have been dismembered by Furies!

The conflict dramatized both within Val and between him and the native inhabitants of this modern inferno represents the on-going psychic and societal battle between the anarchic energy of the Dionysian spirit and the Orphic impulse to reform and redirect that energy toward compassionate and humane ends. The "rebirth" of Val's snakeskin jacket and its inheritance by Carol Cutrere signifies only that this "battle of angels" between the archetypal forces of darkness and light will continue; for, as Leonard Quirino points out, although the forces of light--"the fugitive kind"--are "cruelly defeated (often by mutiny within their own ranks)" and "appear never destined to win," they are also "never totally destroyed."[19] As a symbol of rebirth, then, Val's snakeskin jacket represents a tragicomic emblem of humanity's endurance, a totem "passed from one to another, so that the fugitive kind can always follow their kind" (p. 341).

V. The Second Story: A Paradise Lost

The second major story told and reenacted in the play is a human drama whose protagonist is Lady Torrance. Its theme is the youthful love affair between Lady and David Cutrere, recalled as an idyllic moment of passionate fulfillment in the wine garden built by Lady's immigrant father in the orchard on Moon Lake, Williams' recurrent analogue for the fallen world. In the midst of this fallen world, Papa Romano attempts to create an earthly paradise; its "grapevines and fruit trees" (p. 231), its white-latticed arbors, and couples making love evoke the combined image of Adam and Eve's Edenic bower and the Dionysian wine grove. Both the inspirational and savage aspects of the Dionysian spirit--"sometimes man's blessing, sometimes his ruin"[20]--inform this story. The ecstatic passion of David and Lady bears fruit in Lady's conceiving, while the savage side of the Dionysian spirit is embodied by the "Mystic Crew" (p. 232) who burn up the wine garden because Papa Romano "sold liquor to niggers" (p. 232). Thus, Papa Romano represents one of "the fugitive kind," who is himself burned alive by those envious of his efforts to realize an Edenic unity. The result is both a moral and psychic Wasteland: Lady has an abortion and David is "bought" by a rich society girl. In despair, Lady "sells" herself to Jabe Torrance, unaware that he is one of the "Mystic Crew" who burned up the wine garden, her father, and her dreams.

Lady Torrance is one of Williams' transfixed or frozen characters, her emotional life arrested by the memory of her youthful love with David Cutrere and the idyllic vision of the wine garden, her lost Eden. She dreams of re-creating the wine garden in the confectionary of the "Torrance Mercantile Store," but "looking back" is to be her destruction as well as Val's. Val's arrival not only concurs with her reconstruction of the wine garden but also brings about the reenactment of her entire story, from its passionate beginnings to its tragic end.

The love affair of Lady and David in the orchard is reenacted by Lady and Val in the store behind a faded Oriental curtain imprinted with the design of "a gold tree with scarlet fruit and fantastic birds" (p. 227), the mere facade of the former Edenic paradise. Their passion also leads to fertility and conception, but ends in the permanent sterility of their deaths. Although Val professes love to Lady, it is implied that he, like David Cutrere, is leaving her for a "rich society girl"; the girl is, ironically, David's sister, Carol. At his discovery of Lady's pregnancy, Jabe fulfills his role as Death personified once more, this time killing Lady as he had previously killed her father. As a final parallel to the original story, Val, like Papa Romano, is burned alive.

In this reenactment of Lady's story, the attempt to restore fertility and love to the underworld is undermined not only by the savage brutality of mob action, but also by an individual betrayal of love. Lady Torrance, in her loneliness and despair, exploits Val as a means to her own rejuvenation and rebirth, even as her heart remains with David and his with her. She seduces Val in the surrogate orchard, thereby corrupting his Orphic attempts to rise above his sexual appetites. She subsequently betrays the love he professes for her by summarily dismissing him after he has rendered his sexual service of impregnating her: "You've given me life, you can go!" (p. 337). The mythic dimensions of Val as Orpheus, Dionysus, and Christ the Redeemer are thus reduced to the status of "Male at Stud" (p. 258). It is this story of loneliness, passion, betrayal, and revenge which is organic to the play, but which is obscured by a welter of frenzied actions that confuse rather than clarify its integration with the Orphic myth, the Dionysian duality, and an ironic Christ.

VI. Two Concluding Tales: Their Demonic Reenactment

The frenzied see-saw of anticipation and loss, of expectation and disappointment, of hope and ultimate despair which characterizes the action of the play is exacerbated in its final act by the introduction of two additional stories, both told by Lady Torrance and quickly reenacted. Lady's story of the barren fig tree in her father's garden which miraculously bears fruit and which she adorns with Christmas ornaments as a symbol of her own rebirth invests Lady with the Christian symbolism already surrounding Val.[21] Her story is a kind of apocryphal conclusion to the New Testament parable of the fig tree, wherein the possibility of rebirth is tentative at best. In the Gospel, the story is told of a landowner who, consulted about the fate of a barren fig tree, orders it cut down. But his gardener counsels him otherwise: "Let it alone, sir, this year also, till I dig about it and put on manure. And if it bears fruit next year, well and good; but if not, you can cut it down" (Luke 13. 6-9). In another version of the parable, however, the barren fig tree receives no second chance; instead, it is given Christ's curse: "In the morning . . . he was hungry. And seeing a fig tree . . . he went to it, and found nothing on it but leaves only. And he said to it, 'May no fruit ever come from you again!' And the fig tree withered at once" (Matthew 21. 18-22). Lady, identified with the fig tree, is first blessed with a second chance for fertility--"I've won, I've won, Mr. Death, I'm going to bear!" (p. 338)--and then is cursed with total and everlasting sterility.

The other story is also introduced in the last act and is reenacted almost immediately. It is, perhaps, the real story of the play: its theme, the divestment of illusion, the futility of rejuvenation, and the finality of death. The story is told by Lady about a monkey sold to her father by a man who claimed it was young, "but he was a liar, it was a very old monkey, it was on its last legs, ha, ha, ha!" (p. 325). The monkey was dressed up in a "green velvet suit and a little red cap that it tipped and [it held] a tambourine that it passed around for money" (p. 325), while the organ grinder played and the monkey danced in the sun. But, as Lady recalls, "One day, the monkey danced too much in the sun and it was a very old monkey and it dropped dead. . . . My Papa, he turned to the people, he made them a bow and he said, 'The show is over, the monkey is dead.' Ha Ha!'" (p. 325).

The image of the monkey and the organ grinder recalls Beulah's description of Lady Torrance and her father in the wine garden, where "The Wop and his daughter would sing and play Dago songs" (p. 232). Like the monkey, Lady is an aging woman who attempts to revive her youthful image and recapture her days of wine and roses. She attempts rejuvenation by going to the beauty parlor and getting all dressed up on the night of her opening of the re-created wine garden. But it is all artifice, only the illusion of passionate life: "Electric moon, cutout silver-paper stars and artificial vines" (p. 324). Lady, too, attempts to "dance in the sun," to infuse life and vitality into her sterile existence. But her final frenzied and grotesque dance in celebration of her fertility and freedom becomes a *danse macabre* as Jabe descends the stairs and kills her. Thus, Lady's last words, echoing the grim punch line of her father's story, are an admission of ultimate despair, confirming the futility of dreams, the sterility of life, and the finality of death without redemption: "The show is over. The monkey is dead" (p. 339).

Beneath the mythic stories of Orpheus, Dionysus, and Christ, and beyond the human story of loneliness, love, and betrayal lies Williams' darkest tale of humankind's fundamental nature: the story of a monkey and a stud. It is the vision of man as an animal, bought and sold, a slave to his own base instincts and abused by those more brutal than he. As Benjamin Nelson has remarked, "In *Orpheus Descending*, there is the strong sense of disgust with reality. Whatever is human, whatever is of the earth, is prey to corruption."[22] Neither the aesthetic reconciliation which ameliorates the existential tragedy of *The Glass Menagerie* nor the essential faith in human instincts celebrated in *The Rose Tattoo* redeems Williams' vision in *Orpheus* of the inevitable corruption inherent in human nature. Human sexuality, which Williams elsewhere suggests is man's only salvation from psychic and metaphysical loneliness, is here presented as the fundamental source of his damnation: Val and Lady are martyred victims of their own inescapably fallen natures. As Leonard Quirino suggests, the "hell" to which this play's Orpheus descends is "a metaphor for existence."[23]

VII. Critique

In *Orpheus Descending*, Williams attempts to fuse a depiction of humankind's capacity for senseless hatred and violent destruction with symbols of stoic survival and hope, and thereby to infuse a story of personal tragedy with a mythic sense of its timelessness. The result, however, is dramatic action that lacks sufficient motivation and thematic unity, and that ultimately fails to achieve the complete integration of the play's extrinsic myth with the dramatic reenactment of its organic story. Rather than achieving the "*arrest of time* . . . that gives to certain plays their feeling of depth and significance," *Orpheus Descending* approximates the "continual rush of time, so violent that it appears to be screaming, that deprives our actual lives of so much dignity and meaning" (II, 259). Furthermore, in this play, Williams does not so much tap a collective unconscious or trigger emotional memory as he tests our intellectual background in mythology, Christian doctrine, and Biblical parable. Because many of his symbols or symbolic references are not organically evocative but intellectual and often esoteric, they can be apprehended only as puzzling or extraneous in performance. Thus, although first-night reviews of the play in 1957 were somewhat mixed (*New York Times* critic Brooks Atkinson oddly described it as "one of Mr. Williams' pleasantest plays"[24]), most critics found its meaning obscured by a deluge of symbolism.[25] John Chapman of the *Daily News* concluded that "the curtain falls on a scene of brutality and disillusionment because Williams hasn't been able to think of a better way out of the mess he has created for himself."[26] Analysis of the profusion of symbols and allusions invested in this play indicates, however, not that Williams thought too little during seventeen years of revising *Battle of Angels*, the play's original version, but that perhaps he thought too much.

VIII. The Original Version: *Battle of Angels*

Despite its flaws, *Orpheus Descending* represents a more controlled and far less melodramatic treatment of themes first presented in *Battle of Angels* (1940): the eternal struggle between the forces of light and darkness, liberation and oppression, Eros and Thanatos. Dubbed an artistic and commercial failure from its very first performance, *Battle of Angels* suffers even more than its revised version from excessive symbolism, extraneous anecdotes, and theatrical pyrotechnics, which lead to a frenetic climax "with everything happening at once," including "a Wagnerian conflagration."[27] Nevertheless, this early play is important as a repository of images, symbols, themes, place-names, character types, and even bits of dialogue that Williams was to draw upon and develop more expertly throughout his dramatic career. Structurally, it is important also, for, as Williams' first professional production, it initiates the pattern based on the memory-story and its dramatic reenactment which becomes the fundamental structural organization of Williams' subsequent plays.

As in its revised version, *Battle of Angels* is structured by the existential reenactment of the mythicized stories told about its two main protagonists: Myra Torrance ("Lady" in *Orpheus*) and Valentine Xavier (also given the symbolically fatalistic name of "Jonathan West" in this play). The clarity of the play's architectonics, however, is obscured by an excess of doubling devices, contrived parallels between events, a "proliferation of the circumstances contributing to the catastrophe," and the labored foreshadowing of Val's and Myra's fates.[28] In addition, the clarity of both structure and theme is blurred by the use of a present-time Prologue and Epilogue in which the flashback events of the play are introduced and explained by two minor characters, the Temple Sisters. Ironically, as representatives of the forces of sexual repression and religious hypocrisy against which the play inveighs, the Temple Sisters are least qualified to interpret those events accurately. Acting as museum guides who charge admission for the public viewing of the "relics" of the tragedy preserved in the Torrance Mercantile store, the Temple Sisters transform the play's tragic events into a tourist attraction and reduce their significance to lurid sensationalism. Thus, the tragic events of the drama are, at beginning and end, literally "framed" by a satirical depiction of society's continued misunderstanding and crass exploitation of them.

Within the dramaticized flashback, two memory-stories structure the action, the one idyllic, the other demonic. As in *Orpheus*, Myra's story of an Edenic romance with her youthful lover, David (here named Anderson, not Cutrere), is reenacted by Myra and Val in the back room of the store's confectionery, which she has redecorated to re-create the springtime "orchard across from Moon Lake" (I, 65), the scene of her youthful passion. Unlike the revised version, however, no mention is here made of Lady's father, Papa Romano; of his wine-garden; or of the fiery destruction of both by her husband and his Klan-like "Mystic Crew." *Battle of*

Angels thus omits the important parallels developed in *Orpheus* between Papa Romano and Val (both exempla of "the fugitive kind") which prepare us for Val's similar death by fire at the hands of racist and repressive forces. The lack of development of Myra's memory-story beyond her re-creation of the Moon Lake orchard and the reenactment of her youthful romance tends to relegate its structural significance to secondary importance, for it plays no part in the drama's final outcome.

Instead, Val's story assumes major structural importance. In this original version, Val is cast in the role of a vagrant writer rather than an Orphic minstrel, to whom "The Book" (p. 50), not the guitar, is his passion. Accordingly, the parallels to the myth of Orpheus and Eurydice which inform Val's characterization and his relationship with Lady in the later play are in the original version made less specific and are symbolically conflated with similar myths of Persephone and Pluto, Adonis and Aphrodite, and the Biblical "Fall," as well as with the passion and death of Christ.[29] Instead of explicitly reenacting the Orphic myth, then, in this version Val tells a personal story which foreshadows his fate and which is reenacted in the play's catastrophic finale by him and Myra. Thus, the later problem of superimposing a myth onto the play's organic drama does not exist in its original version. Unfortunately, however, the melodramatic nature of Val's personal story, as well as that of its reenactment, lends itself too easily to the sensational interpretation given it by the Temple Sisters at the play's conclusion.

In Act II, Scene iii, Val tells Myra the story of his drunken sexual encounter with a married woman from Waco, Texas, who afterwards begs Val to stay and, when he insists on leaving alone, charges him with rape. In the throes of a "terrible, hopeless, twisted kind of love" (p. 104), the woman from Waco threatens to track Val down and trap him, like a Lawrentian "fox that's chased by hounds."[30] At the play's conclusion, not only does the woman from Waco reappear to fulfill her threat, but her entire relationship with Val is suddenly reenacted by Myra. Pregnant with Val's child, Myra also begs Val to stay, and, when he insists once again on leaving alone, she, too, turns on him; in a similar display of "twisted" love, Myra accuses Val of robbing the store's cash register (a symbolic parallel to rape). This act precipitates Val's frantic flight from both the Sheriff and the woman from Waco into the hands of "the stave-mill workers" (p. 120) who take him to "the lynching tree" (p. 120)--foreshadowed in Vee Talbott's vision (p.

94)--where, it is implied, he is both hanged and immolated (pre-saged by Val's pyrophobia and Cassandra's "warning"). The destruction of lives is increased in *Battle*: not only is Myra shot by Jabe and Val crucified as a martyred victim, but to Vee Talbott's madness and Jabe's death by cancer is added the drowning of Cassandra Whiteside who, as Carol Cutrere, in *Orpheus* becomes a symbol of survival. As in *Orpheus*, however, Val's snakeskin jacket survives, saved by the Conjureman; but its symbolic significance as the irrepressible spirit of sexual vitality is made ironic by its enshrinement (or entrapment) in the Temple Sisters' museum as "A shameless, flaunting symbol of the Beast Untamed!" (p. 120). In this version, the human drama of two romantic idealists who attempt to realize the "religious purity and beauty of the sexual relation-ship"[31] is reduced in the Epilogue to a lurid Gothic romance of five lives "Tied together in one fatal knot of passion" (p. 121). Because the events of the drama are themselves so melodramatic, the satire of the Temple Sisters' meretricious commentary is lost, and theirs remains the final impression of the play.

CHAPTER SIX

SUDDENLY LAST SUMMER

I know it's a hideous story
but it's a true story of our time
and the world we live in.

I. Demonic Myth

The symbolic story which structures *Suddenly Last Summer* (1958)[1] conflates the legend of a Christian saint's martyrdom with a Greek myth of death and rebirth and an allegorical struggle between good and evil. In its modern existential version, however, legend, myth, and morality play are debased to a dark, naturalistic tale of a rapacious appetite which pervades a Darwinian universe in all its aspects--animal, plant, and human--and underlies all its relationships: biological, theological, psychological, and sociological. As a parody of the romantic and apocalyptic worlds, its imagery is what Northrop Frye terms *demonic*: "the world of the nightmare and the scapegoat, of bondage and pain and confusion . . . of perverted or wasted work, ruins and catacombs, instruments of torture and monuments of folly," a world which suggests "an existential hell."[2] In demonic myth, the symbols of transcendence are inverted and made ironic: thus, the romantic image of marriage, signifying "the union of two souls in one flesh," is inverted to forms of "hermaphroditism, incest . . . or homosexuality"; the sacrificial crucifixion is rendered as unregenerate *sparagmos*; and the Eucharistic Feast is debased to its demonic parody, cannibalism.[3] Correspondingly, the play's mythical and archetypal figures are rendered ironic and demonic counterparts of their former Christian, pagan, and fairy-tale prototypes, each enacting the dual role of victim and victimizer, predator and prey, engaged in a struggle for survival rather than salvation.

II. Story and Structure

The play's narrative centers on the major events leading to and culminating in the cannibalism of Sebastian Venable, the telling of whose story encompasses the entire duration of the play. Sebastian's story is begun by his mother and traveling companion,

Violet Venable, who elevates Sebastian's character to the status of devoted son, poet-priest, and visionary saint. It is completed by his cousin and final companion, Catharine Holly,[4] whose antithetical characterization of Sebastian deflates Mrs. Venable's sanctification of her son, exposing it as ironic and demonic.

While the narrative focuses on Sebastian, however, the drama itself centers on Catharine, who is herself threatened with an analogous version of Sebastian's savage fate. In an attempt to discredit Catharine's "hideous" story of Sebastian's character and death, Mrs. Venable has her declared insane and means to have "cut out" of Catharine's brain her debasing memories of Sebastian through the neurosurgery of lobotomy: a once medically-sanctioned and ostensibly civilized form of Sebastian's cannibalization. Thus, even as Mrs. Venable and Catharine narrate their antithetical memory-stories of Sebastian's life and death, they act as the major antagonists in his story's dramatic reenactment. As dramatically realized, then, the play is structured not in the sequential pattern of a story told, then reenacted, but by the *simultaneous* revelations of the fate of Sebastian and the fate of Catharine-- thereby heightening the suspense of each revelation and creating emotional tension by withholding the full understanding of their analogical significance until the play's very end.

As a further complication, the outcomes of drama and story are antithetical--Sebastian is destroyed, Catharine survives--largely due to the intervention of an additional character, absent from Sebastian's story but crucial to Catharine's reenactment: Dr. Cukrowicz, chief surgeon of the state asylum, ultimate judge of the truth of both women's stories, and final arbiter of Catharine's fate. By refusing to submit Catharine to the "cannibalization" of lobotomy, Dr. Cukrowicz assumes at the end of play the structural function of the classical *deus ex machina*, but the play's resolution remains existentially ambiguous. It is only because of the doctor's recognition of Sebastian's cannibalism as an analogue for the savagery inherent in all relationships--human, natural, and "divine"--that Catharine is redeemed from its reenactment. The play ends, then, as tragic parody: from its ironic *anagnorisis* derives the traditional sense of a gain and a loss, which is, however, in this case unbalanced--for it is achieved by setting off the survival of one individual against the dark knowledge and overwhelming evidence of man's essential helplessness in the jaws of a universally rapacious appetite. From this truth, the play offers no catharsis.

100

III. A Story Told, Then Reenacted

Although the play dramatically realizes its major story and its reenactment simultaneously, the paradigmatic sequence of a story told, then reenacted is retained in the narrative itself. Two major events, representing a recollection and its reenactment, structure the story of Sebastian Venable; the respective accounts are neatly divided between the two narrators, Mrs. Venable and Catharine, both of whom tell their versions to the same listener, Dr. Cukrowicz.

In the first half of the play, Mrs. Venable tells Dr. Cukrowicz of her son's "poetic" occupation, his "religious" nature, and his "devotion" as her filial companion in their many trips around the world. In so doing, Mrs. Venable invests Sebastian with the collective attributes of priest, saint, and Christ-figure, and appoints herself his acolyte, dedicated to the task of sanctifying his work and memory. As poet-priest, Sebastian is described as the charming but "chaste" center of an elite group of young disciples; and his annual poetic work, "Poem of Summer," is revered by Mrs. Venable as his sacred embodiment, to partake of which is likened to the sacrament of holy communion--"She lifts a thin gilt-edged volume from the patio table as if elevating the Host before the altar" (III, 353). Accordingly, Sebastian has remained celibate, "As strictly as if he'd *vowed* to!" (p. 362); and his reclusive life is devoted to a religious quest for a "clear image" (p. 357) of God.

The major event which structures Sebastian's story as told by Mrs. Venable is the result of just such a pilgrimage to the Galapagos Islands, undertaken by Sebastian and his mother after he reads Herman Melville's description of them as sterile wastelands in his ironically titled "The Encantadas or Enchanted Isles." There, Sebastian witnesses the devouring of the newly-hatched sea turtles by flesh-eating birds, an annual naturalistic rite which Sebastian concludes reflects the image of God. According to Mrs. Venable, "when he [Sebastian] came back down the rigging [from the crow's nest of the schooner], he said, Well, now I've seen Him!-- and he meant God" (p. 357).[5] Having envisioned this demonic image of God, Sebastian falls into feverish delirium and retreats to a Buddhist monastery, declaring his renunciation of the world and all his material possessions; but he is thrust back into the "cruel" world by Mrs. Venable, resuming his travels with her and indulging

101

in a perverse reenactment of the predatory spectacle witnessed on the Encantadas.

In the last half of the play, Catharine, as his final summer's companion, adds her version of Sebastian's story under interrogation by Dr. Cukrowicz, who injects her with truth serum. Catharine exposes the underside of Sebastian's nature: his homosexual victimization of young boys, for which Catharine is made to act as lure or bait; his previous exploitation of his mother in a similar way; and his self-consuming quest to sacrifice his own corrupt flesh to the rapacious life-force he had envisioned in the Encantadas: to complete "a sort of!--*image!*--he had of himself as a sort of!--*sacrifice* to a!--*terrible* sort of a . . . God" (p. 397). Thus, in the play's climactic finale, Catharine recounts Sebastian's ultimate reenactment of that grisly scene, as Sebastian, cast in the role of the victimized sea turtle, undergoes the fit retribution of being dismembered and devoured by the young boys of Cabeza de Lobo ("Head of the Wolf") whom he had previously victimized in a sexually analogous way.

To reinforce the analogy between the devouring of the turtles by the flesh-eating birds and the cannibalizing of Sebastian, each narrator employs similar imagery describing the separate events. Thus, Mrs. Venable describes the scene in the Encantadas as occurring on a "blazing sand-beach" (p. 355) made black with the motion of the flesh-eating birds, whose harsh cries signal their slaughter of the vulnerable sea turtles by "tearing the undersides open and rending and eating their flesh" (p. 356). In analogous terms, Catharine describes the cannibalizing of Sebastian, also enacted on the "blazing white hot" street of a beach darkened by Sebastian's attackers. The "band of frightfully thin and dark naked children" who attack Sebastian is depicted as looking like "a flock of black plucked little birds," who "screamed . . . and seemed to fly in the air" in pursuit of him; and who, finally, like the flesh-eating birds in destroying the turtles, tore "bits of him away and stuffed them into those gobbling fierce little empty black mouths of theirs" (pp. 421-22).

IV. An Ironic Saint Sebastian

In the course of the play, Sebastian Venable is first elevated to the status of saint, then debased to its ironic and demonic counterpart. Williams first explicitly identifies Sebastian's religious prototype by reference to the name of the beach where he lures the young boys of Cabeza de Lobo and on which he is subsequently martyred: "a beach that's named for Sebastian's name saint --La Playa San Sebastian" (p. 410). Like St. Sebastian, the Roman martyr who, according to Gilbert Debusscher, was "traditionally considered the lover of Emperor Diocletian," Sebastian Venable is also depicted as homosexual.[6] As recounted in Butler's *Lives of the Saints*, upon St. Sebastian's conversion to Christianity, he was ordered by the Emperor to be "delivered . . . over to certain archers of Mauritania, to be shot to death."[7] Thus, "His body was pierced through with arrows and he was left for dead"; although St. Sebastian survived this ordeal, he was subsequently beaten to death. As Tatsumi Funatsi points out, the description of Sebastian Venable's assailants "reminds us not only of the carnivorous birds over the Encantadas, but [also] of the arrows with which St. Sebastian was struck to [near] death."[8] Thus, the description of Sebastian's attackers is carefully worded so as to evoke the image of arrows that "would come *darting up* to the barbed wire fence as if blown there by the wind" (p. 415) and, at the moment of attack, "seemed to fly in the air" (p. 421). According to Jung, such arrows as those said to pierce the flesh of Sebastian have a sexual significance: "the arrow is a libido-symbol, the meaning of [which] 'piercing' is . . . the act of union with oneself, a sort of self-fertilization, and also a self-violation, a self-murder."[9] In a psychological sense, then, Sebastian Venable is a self-willed martyr, having courted his own destruction.

As a further parallel between Sebastian and his patron saint, the martyred body of St. Sebastian is secretly interred and thus preserved for memorial by "a lady called Lucinda";[10] in a similar way, Mrs. Venable seeks to enshrine the memory of her son. Significantly, however, the legend of St. Sebastian's exemplary martyrdom is, according to Butler, "now generally admitted by scholars to be no more than a pious fable."[11] So, too, is Sebastian Venable's reputed sainthood rendered spurious; the climax of his demythicization (or, decanonization) from "chaste" saint to "chased" debaucher is depicted as a literal stripping away of his own corrupt flesh and blood.

As a final irony, the saint's martyrdom, an act of *caritas* and self-sacrifice in imitation of and atonement for the sufferings of the crucified Christ, is in the play inverted, perverted, and degraded to an act of retributive violence without redemptive significance. The devouring of the sea turtles by flesh-eating birds is reenacted initially as the loveless sexual "communion" between Sebastian and the young boys he exploits for that purpose, a parallel in which Sebastian assumes the role of the "cruel" (p. 397) God he sees reflected in that predatory spectacle--the incarnation of a demonic "Son of God." The subsequent cannibalizing of Sebastian by the young boys represents his own ironic martyrdom. Cast in the role of the victimized sea turtle, Sebastian is forced to undergo a parodic imitation of Christ's crucifixion--or its profane analogue, Dionysian *sparagmos*--in symbolic retaliation for his own selfish abuse of others, epitomized by his acts of sexual exploitation. Accordingly, the language Williams uses to describe the process by which the turtles are attacked also suggests violent versions of the sexual acts of sodomy and fellatio: the birds "diving down on the hatched sea turtles, turning them over to expose their soft undersides, tearing the undersides open and rending and eating their flesh" (p. 356). Thus, Sebastian's ironic martyrdom is (as Williams himself has expressed it) to be "eaten up by those whom he had eaten"--victimizer become victim, predator become prey--in fit retribution.[12] At the same time, because Sebastian is symbolically consumed by his own acts of obeisance to a God perceived as "terrible" and "cruel," his cannibalization is invested with the significance of an authentic religious martyrdom--albeit, a black mass, a demonic crucifixion, and a sexual parody of the Eucharistic Feast. By his forced submission to the primal violence he perceives as universal order, Sebastian Venable achieves ironic atonement (at-one-ment) or ultimate reconciliation with "God" in a demonic epiphany.

In his 1948 poem "San Sebastiano de Sodoma,"[13] Williams similarly equates the martyrdom of St. Sebastian with the sexual acts of fellatio and sodomy. The poem's St. Sebastian is also pierced with phallic arrows in "throat and thigh," as Mary plays the role of voyeur, raising "a corner/ of a cloud through which to spy." In the poem's climax, the Eucharistic chalice becomes the desecrated anal "cup," which, when pierced in an erotic act, releases its "sweet, intemperate wine," a profane analogue to the communal rite. In "Erotic Mythology in the Poetry of Tennessee Williams," John Ower suggests that by such intermingling of erotic and religious imagery, of carnal passions with Christ's Passion, Williams intends to emphasize the suffering experienced by man because of his dual nature; neither the desires of his flesh nor the transcendent longings of his spirit are ever reconciled, because "carnal pleasure is spiritual suffering, whereas the salvation of the soul involves painful physical mortification."[14] Thus, in the poem, as in the play, the saint's "homosexual servitude . . . is symbolic of the soul's defilement by a corporeal existence."[15]

Analogies between homosexual acts and cannibalism, carnal passion and the Passion (suffering of Christ), are also made metaphors for achieving an ironic atonement in Williams' short story "Desire and the Black Masseur."[16] In that story, Williams offers cannibalism as a metaphor for achieving a nihilistic "communion" by a literal *kenosis* (emptying out) of man's corrupt flesh and blood: a demonic version of the spiritual purgation of sin achieved by "the surrender of self to violent treatment by others with the idea of thereby clearing one's self of his guilt.[17] Thus, in a world bereft of those religious myths, symbols, and rituals which once permitted hope of reconciliation between body and soul, flesh and spirit, human nature and a transcendent God, man is rendered a divided self: the soul still longs for transcendence but knows itself damned to an inherently corrupt corporeal existence. In such an existential "hell," carnal passion is elevated to an unholy communion, and cannibalism is its consummate redemption.

V. A Vision of Universal Savagery: Reflections of Darwin and Melville

Charles Darwin in *The Voyage of the Beagle* (1840), his seminal work on evolution derived from his observations of the process of natural selection on the Galapagos Islands, recorded the annual naturalistic rite witnessed by Sebastian Venable:

> They [the giant tortoises] were at this time
> (October) laying their eggs. The female, where
> the soil is sandy, deposits them together, and
> covers them up with sand; but where the ground is
> rocky she drops them indiscriminately in any hole.
> . . . The young tortoises, as soon as they are
> hatched, fall a prey in great numbers to the
> carrion-feeding buzzard.[18]

From these observations of a "constantly-recurrent Struggle for Existence," Darwin was to deduce his major evolutionary theories based on "one general law leading to the advancement of all organic beings,--namely, multiply, vary, let the strongest live and the weakest die."[19] In this law of nature, Sebastian Venable sees reflected a "clear image" (p. 357) of God and, by extension, of that creation conceived in His image, humankind.

Several critics of *Suddenly Last Summer* advance the thesis that Sebastian Venable's interpretation of this naturalistic predatory spectacle as a *reflection* of a "terrible" and "cruel" (p. 397) God is rather a *projection* of Sebastian's own introverted, perverted, exploitative, and morally-diseased nature. Falling prey to his own vision of evil, Sebastian is ultimately consumed by it. Thus, Paul J. Hurley in "*Suddenly Last Summer* as 'Morality Play'" suggests that Sebastian's demonic vision of a cruel God is *not* to be equated with Williams' own vision of the contemporary world, which, through Sebastian's eyes, is "a vile, hideous place where men, as well as birds and animals, attack and devour their fellow creatures."[20] Because the play demonstrates that "Sebastian Venable's vision of God was a reflection of the image he held of man and nature" (and thus is a projection of his own "warped ideals and distorted values"), Hurley concludes that the sole thematic idea of the play is represented by its presentation of Sebastian as a negative exemplum of self-consuming evil:

> What his [Williams'] drama proclaims is that recognition of evil, if carried to the point of a consuming obsession, may be the worst form of evil. To look about oneself for manifestations of sinfulness and to become so overwhelmed by the viciousness of humanity that one begins to see cruelty and vulgarity as the only truths about human nature is, for Williams, as it was for Hawthorne, a fearful sin. A daemonic vision of human nature may irredeemably corrupt the one who possesses that vision.[21]

To affirm the play's presentation of Sebastian's vision of a savage or "terrible" God as an inflated projection of his own corrupt psyche, however, is not to deny the play's confirmation of just such a savagery inherent in the more mundane realms of plant, animal, and human nature.

Not Hawthorne, but his contemporary and admirer, Melville, is explicitly invoked by the play's literary allusions. *Moby Dick* presents Meville's portrayal of a similarly obsessed figure, Ahab, who saw incarnated in a white whale the collective evil and malignity of the entire universe, thus creating by his very thoughts both his own inflated self-image as a Prometheus and the "vulture [which] feeds upon that heart forever."[22] In the novel, Pip's "crazy-witty" conjugation--"I look, you look, he looks; we look, ye look, they look"--represents Melville's recognition that multiple perceptions of a single objective phenomenon yield equally multiple interpretations or versions of that reality.[23]   However, the depiction of Ahab as a madman who projects onto an essentially ambiguous nature his own vengeful motives does not invalidate Melville's own dark vision of the "horrible vulturism of earth" or its sharkish equivalent in all human nature: "Who is not a cannibal?" asks Ishmael[24]--a question that surely could be asked of the characters in Williams' play.   Williams' play, like Melville's novel, ultimately presents savagery as both within and without the human capacity to engender it, though its origin remains unknowable.

In at least one instance, however, Williams' depiction of nature is ostensibly darker than Melville's; as Mrs. Venable expresses it, "We saw the Encantadas, but on the Encantadas we saw something Melville *hadn't* written about" (p. 355).   In Melville's tale of "The Encantadas," whose wasteland description of a fallen world motivates Sebastian's visit there, Melville stresses that there are *two* sides to its native tortoise: its back is black, but, turned onto that back, it exposes a bright underbelly.   Melville's moral:

> Enjoy the bright, keep it turned up perpetually if you can, but be honest, and don't deny the black. Neither should he, who cannot turn the tortoise from its natural position so as to hide the darker and expose his livelier aspect, like a great October pumpkin in the sun, for that cause declare the creature to be one total inky blot. The tortoise is both black and bright.[25]

In Williams' version, it is precisely that bright, soft, golden underbelly that provides the culinary delicacy for the flesh-eating birds.   What Sebastian sees that Melville didn't describe is the birds' violent assault on the newly-hatched sea turtles by "turning them over to expose their soft undersides" in order to more easily eat "their flesh" (p. 356).   Melville, however, also recognized the irony in his image of the tortoise's "bright side" being exposed only when it lies on its back in an unnatural, vulnerable, and helpless position, and of his comparison of its golden underbelly to "a great October pumpkin in the sun"--thus ripe for eating.   His darker vision is demonstrated by the ending to his essay on the tortoises which testifies to the predatory instinct not only in animals but in men, whose own "merry repast" consists of turning the Galapagos tortoises into soup and the bright, golden calipees attached to the undersides of their shells into "three gorgeous salvers."[26]

Like Melville, Williams also presents an embodiment of nature's "bright side" in his play--the "blond, young Doctor" Cukrowicz. However, it is just such bright light youths that Sebastian Venable had planned to make "next on the menu. . . . Cousin Sebastian said he was famished for blonds, he was fed up with the dark ones and was famished for blonds" (p. 375). Although Dr. Cukrowicz is spared such explicit victimization as would extinguish completely the bright side he stands for, his mythic aura is, as shall be demonstrated, considerably dimmed by his own understanding of the undeniable darkness in human nature, by the end of the play.

Another image which Williams shares with Melville is that of whiteness as a symbolic hue. James R. Hurt in his comparative essay "*Suddenly Last Summer*: Williams and Melville" offers his interpretation of Wiiliams' use of that whiteness which in *Moby Dick* represents the terrifying mystery of the universe--its "dumb blankness, full of meaning"--although to Ahab, its incarnation in the whale signifies only nature's malevolence.[27] Hurt quotes (in its entirety) only the passage from *Suddenly Last Summer* in which Catharine describes the scene as she and Sebastian leave the cafe on the day of his savage murder:

> It was all white outside. White hot, a blazing white hot, hot blazing white, at five o'clock in the afternoon in the city of--Cabeza de Lobo. It looked as if . . . a huge white bone had caught on fire in the sky and blazed so bright it was white and turned the sky and everything under the sky white with it! (pp. 419-20).

From this passage, Hurt draws the following conclusion about the symbolic significance of whiteness:

> This whiteness is the same ambivalent color in which man, as Melville notes, has seen beneficence and malevolence all through history, but which is, in fact, completely neutral. Only a man like Ahab (or Sebastian) can turn this symbol of mindless energy against himself and, by his own choice, destroy himself, paradoxically, with the evil which he himself imagined in this neutrality.[28]

Although Hurt's interpretation of Melville's concept of whiteness as neutrality is accurate, what he doesn't explain is that the idea of its neutrality or "blankness" was, to Melville, appalling, evoking as it does only a sense of "the heartless voids and immensities of the universe."[29] Furthermore, the scene Hurt cites as exemplary of *Sebastian's* distorted psychological perceptions is not described by Sebastian at all, but by *Catharine*. It is not Sebastian who imagines "evil" in the sky's "completely neutral" whiteness, but Catharine who perceives the sky's white heat as apocalyptic, if not infernal, in its unredeeming illumination of the savagery to be committed beneath its fiery expanse. Indeed, Catharine's image of the "blazing white hot sky" as "a great white bone of a giant beast that had caught on fire" (p. 421) corresponds precisely to the imagery used to describe Sebastian's subsequent cannibalization, thus foreshadowing the realization of his naked flesh and bones illuminated against a "blazing white wall" (p. 422), a demonic vision of sacramental communion. The "hot blazing white" of the sky, the sun, the street, the wall against which lies the mutilated and dismembered Sebastian in a demonic version of the Christian martyr's auto-da-fé and sacrificial atonement combines to suggest a symbol of ultimate purgation--the elimination of divine meaning itself from both the heavens and earth, and its replacement by a fiery illumination and "dreadful heat" (p. 421) that turns the whole world into an existential purgatory from which there is no appeal and no expiation but unredemptive death. If such "blazing white" can be a called "mindless energy," then surely the metaphysical neutrality of its unremitting glare on such savagery is intended to be as fully appalling in Williams' play as in Melville's novel. Indeed, the addition of "heat" to the image of whiteness evokes Melville's description of "the tryworks"; and Williams' scene of infernal savagery is reminiscent of Melville's image of the microcosmic world of the Pequod "freighted with savages, and laden with fire, and burning a corpse, and plunging into that blackness of darkness, [which] seemed the material counterpart of her monomaniac commander's soul."[30] That such a dark picture of the world is to Melville not solely the private vision of a single deranged mind, however, is suggested by his novel's comprehensive documentation of the world's savage nature, which daylight serves only to better illuminate:

> "the sun hides not Virginia's Dismal Swamp, nor Rome's accursed Campagna, nor wide Sahara, nor all the millions of miles of deserts and of griefs beneath the moon. . . . So, therefore, that mortal man who hath more of joy than sorrow in him, that mortal man cannot be true--not true, or undeveloped."[31]

In Williams' play, also, the world's savagery is a shared, not

109

a solipsistic, vision; both the *black* sky observed by Sebastian and Mrs. Venable and the *white* sky observed by Catharine are similarly perceived as savage. Indeed, Catharine's fiery vision of the blazing, hot, white sky of Cabeza de Lobo suggests a demonic "catherine's wheel."[32] Furthermore, her description of the white sky's being darkened by the the young cannibals in pursuit of Sebastian, themselves looking like a "flock of black . . . birds," serves to confirm Sebastian's interpretation of the predatory spectacle he witnessed in the Encantadas; for Mrs. Venable also describes both a beach and sky turned black "with savage, devouring birds" (p. 367), on those islands which Melville himself is said to have imagined as "looking much as the world at large might look-- after a last conflagration" (pp. 354-55). Both ultimately describe a blazing, white sky become a dark, ashen wasteland. In *Suddenly Last Summer*, then, the sky--once a transcendent symbol of a loving God's presence--reflects in the modern world only the existential acts of savagery committed within and beneath its expanse: both its blackness and its whiteness reveal a heaven become an existential hell.

Throughout Williams' play, then, whiteness serves only to disguise the darkness behind its "colorless, all-color" surface.[33] Thus, on his last afternoon, Sebastian himself is dressed "white as the weather." As Catharine recalls, "He had on a spotless white silk Shantung suit and a white silk tie and a white panama and white shoes, white--white lizard skin--pumps! He . . . kept touching his face and his throat here and there with a white silk handkerchief and popping little white pills in his mouth" (p. 414), ironically signifying his preparation for the demonic version of sacrificial communion in which he is to play the role of "Host." The sky's image of whiteness corresponds not only to Sebastian's garb as sacrificial victim but also to the light appearance of those blond Nordic youths Sebastian had planned next to victimize. As "bait" for the fulfillment of Sebastian's dark motives, Catharine also dresses in white, in a "one-piece [bathing] suit made of white lisle" (p. 412) that becomes transparent in the water. Finally, the blond Dr. Cukrowicz, like Sebastian, is dressed "all in white" (p. 350); described as "glacially brilliant" and as having an "icy charm," he is called "Doctor Sugar" (pp. 350- 51). Ironically, the doctor's ultimate enlightenment--his crucial recognition that Catharine's story of human savagery "could be true" (p. 423)--is also an admission of the dark impulses in the universe at large, even beneath his own "skillful surgeon's" hand. Only the tone of speculation conveyed by the qualifiers embedded in

110

Dr. Cukrowicz's final utterance--"I *think* we ought *at least* to *consider* the *possibility* that the girl's story *could* be true [emphasis mine]" (p. 423)--suggests any ambiguity about that savage truth which the play's substance and symbols present in otherwise unrelenting clarity. Whether conscious or unconscious, willed or instinctual, deliberate or unintentional, the savagery without and within the human psyche is presented as a complex web in which all the play's human characters are enmeshed as both victims and victimizers, thereby eliciting at once the tragic emotions of deepest pity and primal terror.

Williams' play implies, then, that Sebastian's demonic vision --at least, of a savagery inherent in all creation, if not in an unknowable creator--is not shaped solely by his perception of it. That Sebastian's perception of the universe as rapacious and exploitative is *not* wholly a solipsistic, deranged, and morbid self-projection is supported by the multiple analogues of that savage nature throughout the play, in all its events, relationships, allusions, and imagery--concrete, symbolic, visual, auditory. Sebastian's equation of that instinctual predatory impulse in nature with a divine source of all creation represents but an inflated, exaggerated version of a universal truth given ample confirmation in the play. Finally, not Sebastian's vision of God as savage, but his own deliberate, godlike enactment of that savagery is what differentiates him from the other characters; and even for those loveless acts of exploitation, Sebastian is not held solely responsible, for (as shall be demonstrated in Section VIII) he is himself revealed to be the victim of an equally exploitative, though largely unconscious, devouring "mother-love."

VI. Analogues of Archetypal Violence

Both by concrete reference and symbolic allusion, the play's historical scope is extended from its immediate setting to encompass an epic vision of the savagery existing in Western civilization from its primeval beginnings to its fascist-threatened present of 1936.[34] As Leonard Quirino has pointed out, by the telescoping of history through a montage of references to a pre-historic past, a "Victorian-Gothic" decor, and a Nazi-dominated present, the play evokes the universality and archetypal timelessness of violence, whether it be labelled primitive savagery, Gothic barbarism, Victorian imperialism, or the Holocaust.[35]

The play's expressionistic survey of universal violence ironically culminates in the posh "Garden District of New Orleans" (p.
349), the prinicipal setting of which is Sebastian's garden--
concrete symbol of predatory nature. As such, the garden, "more
like a tropical jungle, or forest," is, according to Williams'
stage directions, so designed as to evoke "the prehistoric age of
giant fern-forests when living creatures had flippers turning to
limbs and scales to skin" (p. 349)--an organic testimony to the
Darwinian usurpation of the Biblical Eden. As Eden's demonic
inversion, the garden's "massive" flowers are made to suggest
"organs of a body, torn out, still glistening with undried blood"
(p. 349), thus serving as immediate visual analogues to the several
instances of animal and human dismemberment recounted throughout
the play: to the vulnerable turtles torn apart by the carnivorous
birds; to the remains of Sebastian's similarly rent body, described
by Catharine as resembling just such flowers, "a bunch of red
roses . . . *torn, thrown, crushed*!" (p. 422); and to the imagined
mutilation of Catharine's proposed lobotomy, which would "bore a
hole in my skull and turn a knife in my brain" (p. 389).

From the garden can be heard "harsh cries and sibilant hiss-
ings and thrashing sounds . . . as if it were inhabited by beasts,
serpents and birds, all of a savage nature" (p. 349). This "jungle
music" is surrealistically interpolated throughout the play to
reinforce the parallels between a primal savagery, the predatory
spectacle on the Galapagos Islands, and the play's instances of
human savagery; and culminates in the similarly "harsh cries,"
discordant playing, and "gobbling noises" (p. 415) of the "flock of
plucked birds" that cannibalize Sebastian. The "prize specimen" of
that garden is the "Venus's-flytrap," the insectivorous flower
which Sebastian feeds with living fruit flies obtained, significantly, from a scientific laboratory engaged in genetic ex-
periments--suggesting a further parallel between the predatory
instincts of both the plant and human species, the primeval past
and the ostensibly civilized present.

VII. Violet Venable as Venus Flytrap

A chief embodiment of this Darwinian nature is Violet Venable
herself, beneath whose civilized veneer is revealed the rapaciousness of the flesh-eating birds and the seductive deadliness of the
Venus Flytrap.[36] Her very name--Venable--evokes a plethora of
associations, such as venal, venomous, and, ironically, Venus--

Roman goddess of love--which here, however, suggests only her affinity to the carnivorous flower in Sebastian's jungle-garden and her symbolic identity as a *femme fatale* or psychological *vagina dentata*, the role she assumes as mother-emasculator and consort of the homosexual Sebastian. Venable also suggests "venerable," the accolade she wishes to bestow upon Sebastian and herself; more significant, however, as the name shared by both Sebastian and his mother, Venable made "venerable" suggests the archetypal agelessness of their mutual savagery, the historical longevity of their rapacious attitudes and actions, as well as their mythic aura.[37]

Mrs. Venable's first name, Violet, not only connotes her frail, delicate, and thus flower-like state of ill-health; but the violet is also a common symbol of mourning and suffering, of death and resurrection, in literature and mythology, thus related to Violet Venable's mourning for and attempt to resurrect an unsullied memory of her son.[38] Phonetically, however, Violet resembles "violent." Significant in this regard is Freud's interpretation of the sexual symbolism evoked by the name, for he notes that the word "violet" resembles both the French term *viol*, or rape, and the English *violate*.[39] Whether or not Williams intended to suggest Violet Venable's venal violence through her name, it is clearly indigenous to her character, as shown through her relationships with Catharine, the Holly family, Dr. Cukrowicz, and Sebastian himself. Like the other characters in the play, however, Mrs. Venable is ultimately depicted as "vulnerable" also: both victimizer and victim, predator and prey, sacrificer and sacrificed.[40]

To Catharine, who insists that her narrative of Sebastian's cannibalization represents but "a true story of our time and the world we live in" (p. 382), Violet Venable acts as the flesh-rending victimizer, seeking to "*cut this hideous story out of her brain!*" (p. 423). The analogy between the projected fate of Catharine and the savage mutilation of Sebastian is further reinforced by the phonological similarity between *lobotomy* and Cabeza de *Lobo*, or "Wolf's Head," the name of the site of Sebastian's cannibalization. The association between both terms serves to emphasize the inherent savagery beneath Mrs. Venable's (and, by extension, humankind's) ostensibly civilized behavior, reminding us that often "man is a wolf to man."

Mrs. Venable correspondingly attempts to violate Dr. Cukrowicz's ethical and moral integrity by bribing him to perform the lobotomy on Catharine in exchange for her subsidizing his medical research; and she similarly preys on the economic hunger of the members of Catharine Holly's own family, by threatening to cut them out of Sebastian's inheritance unless they succeed in persuading Catharine to "forget that story" (p. 380). In turn, Catharine's mother and her brother George confirm Mrs. Venable's cynical belief in the predatory essence of human nature by showing their eager willingness to sacrifice both Catharine and truth to satisfy their selfish ambitions and greed. Finally, in the dog-eat-dog world she inhabits, Violet Venable is herself exploited in her role of wealthy benefactor, the sacrificial victim of others' avaricious natures, of all those who "want your blood on the altar steps of their *outraged, outrageous* egos" (p. 364).

VIII. "Sebastian and Violet, Violet and Sebastian"--The Psychological Version[41]

The relationship between Mrs. Venable and her son is also revealed to be of a mutually exploitative nature. Explicitly revealed is Sebastian's victimization of his mother, who, before her disfiguring stroke, served the same function of solicitor or pimp subsequently assumed by Catharine: "*Not consciously!* She didn't *know* that she was procuring for him. . . . [but] We both did the same thing for him, made contacts for him" (p. 412).

Implicit and, the play suggests, also unconscious is Mrs. Venable's far more extensive, and more damaging, psychological exploitation of her son, starting, as Catharine speculates, on "the day he was born in this house" (p. 405). On that "day," according to modern psychological theory, begins the emotionally incestuous relationship between mother and child which is neurotically overextended by Mrs. Venable to Sebastian's fortieth year: a relationship which is evidenced by Mrs. Venable's unnatural enthusiasm for their acknowledgment as a "famous couple," of whom people spoke not as mother and son, but as "Sebastian and Violet, Violet and Sebastian" (p. 362). This relationship accounts for Mrs. Venable's preference to stay with her son during his Buddhist retreat to the Himalayas over returning to her critically-ill husband, thereby (according to Freud) abnormally gratifying the Oedipal wish of every male child to take the place of his own father; and it culminates in Sebastian's characterized personality as a self-absorbed, homosexual snob, whose arrested emotional and social development corresponds to the psychologically-defined "uroboric state": that original state of ego-inflation in which the infant believes himself still the womb-like center and narcissistic hub of his universe.[42]

Like the Venus Flytrap, that displaced tropical flower which, in order to survive in a hostile environment, "has to be kept under glass from early fall to late spring" (p. 350), Sebastian is similarly incubated in the over-protective womb of Mrs. Venable for "nine months of the year" (p. 354), preparing for the birth of his annual "Poem of Summer." Significantly, his poem is delivered only during the summer months in the company of and under the dominating influence of his mother, thus keeping Sebastian "in the morally poisonous atmosphere of infancy."[43] Raised in such a "well-groomed jungle" (p. 351), Sebastian develops an attitude toward life which is at once decadent, elitist, and savage--"An attitude toward life that's hardly been known in the world since the great Renaissance princes were crowded out of their palaces and gardens by successful shopkeepers!" (p. 362). This attitude--the fascistic, dehumanizing attitude of the Medicis, Borgias, and Niccolo Machievelli--which represents the exploitation of the weak by the strong, of the poor by the wealthy and powerful, is ironically given a demonic rebirth at the very moment of Mrs. Venable's lament for its passing, by the fascist powers of Hitler and Mussolini, whose atrocities and crimes against humanity derive precisely from the same inflated sense of exclusiveness and superiority which she and her son revere and embody. Sebastian's egocentric elitism also makes decadent his self-conception as a poet, a perversion of the function of artist which Williams has elsewhere defined as the attempt to "embrace" one's fellow humanity and thereby ameliorate, at least temporarily, our existential condemnation to "solitary confinement inside our own skins" (III, 3).

Thus, at forty, Sebastian's life and work still depend, as does the viability of the foetus in the womb, on a symbiotic relationship with his mother for sustenance and nourishment. Freud explains such extended dependence as Sebastian's as the genesis of male homosexuality:

> A young man has been unusually long and intensely fixated upon his mother in the sense of the Oedipus complex. But at last, after the end of his puberty, the time comes for exchanging his mother for some other sexual object. . . . [however,] the young man does not abandon his mother, but identifies himself with her; he transforms himself into her, and now looks about for objects which can replace his ego for him, and on which he can bestow such love and care as he has experienced from his mother.[44]

115

Freud's theory clarifies the identification of the Venus Flytrap with both mother and son: just as Sebastian feeds his mother's unconscious incestuous desires, so he, in identifying with and imitating his mother's suffocating "love and care," assumes the Flytrap's role himself, and similarly attempts to seduce and devour all those within his reach: his mother, the young boys he sexually violates, and, finally, Catharine.[45]

Sebastian does attempt to escape the symbiotic relationship with his mother, first by his flight to a Buddhist monastery, which, however, represents psychologically only a retreat into a surrogate sanctuary or womb; for, according to Freud, the cloister is, like a neurosis, a place "in which were accustomed to take refuge all those whom life had undeceived or who felt themselves too weak for life."[46] His second attempt is represented by his literal divorce from his mother and his appropriation of Catharine as her surrogate. According to Catharine, during Sebastian's final trip without his mother, it was as if "something had broken, that string of pearls that old mothers hold their sons by like a . . . sort of--*umbilical* cord, *long--after* . . . " (p. 409) it should have been severed.

Predictably, however, Sebastian's belated attempt at independence results only in his final destruction. As his mother says, "Without me he died last summer" (p. 354). Jung explains the psychological consequences of such an abrupt divorce as Sebastian's from his "mother-imago" (the internalized influence of his mother, which is here also his "anima," projected image of the ideal woman), after having maintained for so long an abnormally strong attachment. Repressed, the ambivalent incestuous desires engendered in the son--simultaneously wished-for and guilt-ridden--are in danger of bursting forth with self-destructive violence:

> That is to say, the violence of the separation is proportionate to the strength of the bond uniting the son with the mother, and the stronger this broken bond was in the first place, the more dangerously does the "mother" approach him in the guise of the unconscious. This is indeed the <u>Mater saeva cupidinum</u>, "savage mother of desire," who in another form now threatens to devour the erstwhile fugitive.[47]

Thus, "suddenly last summer," Sebastian Venable emerges from the sanctuary of his mother's womb--like the newly-hatched turtles, vulnerable and (psychologically) defenseless--consciously desiring to escape from an all-consuming mother-love, but pursued by his unconscious desire to return to that womb. His own unconscious thus becomes "the Terrible Mother who devours and destroys, and thus symbolizes death itself."[48]

Sebastian's rebirth is therefore ironically destructive, giving rise neither to the self-knowledge of his own corruption nor to a conscious desire to atone for that corruption. Both his social and moral conscience remain dormant, his egocentricity and elitism intact. Of the starving children whom his own rapaciousness had corrupted, he says to Catharine: "Don't look at those little monsters. Beggars are a social disease in this country. If you look at them, you get sick of the country, it spoils the whole country for you" (p. 415). (Contrast Sebastian's egoistic responses of revulsion and repugnance with the social and spiritual concern awakened in *Cat*'s Big Daddy [III, 87-88] and *Iguana*'s Shannon [IV, 368-69] by similar confrontations with the starving poor of foreign countries.) People remain to Sebastian "items on a menu," *things* to be exploited, devoured, and afterwards discarded. His response to the threatening advances of the starving natives of Cabeza de Lobo is, finally, that of the petulant, panic-stricken child, a newly-born ego that desires to assert its independence--"I want to handle this thing" (p. 421)--but is foiled by its internalized infantile psyche, as evidenced by Sebastian's childish refusal to return to the safety of "that filthy" restaurant, merely because "That gang of kids shouted vile things about me to the waiters!" (p. 421). Too long psychologically incubated in the over-fastidious, neurotically solicitous environment of his mother's "womb," Sebastian's birth-cries lead only to his death-agony. Consciously desiring to escape from those who would devour him, he is at the same time pursued by an unconscious longing to attain that infantile sense of original unity which also represents the annihilation of self. Psychologically, then, Sebastian is devoured by his mother--womb become tomb. His cannibalization represents his being literally swallowed up by the contents of his own unconscious, consumed by embodiments of "the Terrible Mother, of the voracious maw, the jaws of death in which men are crunched and ground to pieces."[49]

IX. The Mythic Version: Attis and Cybele

That myth which is reenacted by Sebastian and Mrs. Venable in a debased and ironic version is the archetypal drama of the death and resurrection of the vegetation god who is sacrificed to his mother-goddess, and, through his sacrifice, is reborn.[50] The myth of Attis, the son-lover of Cybele, the great Mother-Goddess, most closely corresponds to the relationship between Sebastian and Mrs. Venable. By one account, Attis is said to have been driven mad by his mother's insane love for him and castrates himself;[51] but he is reconstituted and symbolically resurrected by his mother in the form of violets which spring from his blood.[52] According to Jung, the self-emasculation of Attis represents in the healthy process of individuation the psychological self-sacrifice of the libidinous urge to incest, a means of both expiating and transforming that otherwise destructive impulse.[53] The self-castration of Attis, then, psychologically symbolizes a ritual of purgation and atonement, a rite of renewal signalling the development of the personality toward selfhood. In the play's debased version, however, Sebastian is initially unmanned or emotionally castrated by his mother's psychological violation of the incest taboo, and his own ultimate "sacrifice" is neither voluntary nor regenerative. Upon Sebastian's death, not the violet, but Violet Venable springs up to attempt her son's resurrection, an act rendered unproductive by Catharine, whose truths about Sebastian effectively smash "our legend, the memory of--" him (p. 363).

Other parallels between Sebastian's story and the cult of Attis confirm their ironically analogous relationship. On the third day of the annual spring festival in celebration of Attis and Cybele, known as The Day of Blood, the sacrifice of Attis is reenacted by his priestly disciples, who, "stirred by the wild barbaric music of clashing cymbals, rumbling drums, droning horns, and screaming flutes," work themselves into an ecstatic frenzy culminating in their own self-castration and mutilation.[54] In ironic imitation, the "followers" of Sebastian devise analogous versions of drums, cymbals, and tubas from "tin cans strung together" (p. 417), "bits of metal . . . flattened out, . . . and clashed together" (p. 417), and "paper bags . . . with something on a string . . . pulled up and down" (p. 417) with which they play their own harsh, barbaric music in honor of their sacrificial victim whom they dismember. Furthermore, according to Frazer in his *The Golden Bough*, a more private ceremony in honor of Attis included both a sacramental meal and a baptism of blood: "In the

118

sacrament the novice became a partaker of the mysteries by eating out of a drum and drinking out of a cymbal, two instruments of music which figured prominently in the thrilling orchestra of Attis."[55] The cannibalization of Sebastian is made a demonic parody of that sacramental meal, accomplished with the aid of his own disciples' home-made instruments; using "those jagged tin cans they made music with," Sebastian's attackers "had torn bits of him away and stuffed them into those gobbling fierce little empty black mouths of theirs" (p. 422). Finally, whereas violets symbolize the rebirth of Attis, and the rose, the rebirth of his Greek counterpart Adonis, Sebastian's remains resemble only "a big white-paper-wrapped bunch of red roses [that] had been *torn, thrown, crushed!*" (p. 422).

In the play, then, the myth of Attis and Cybele is shattered and retold not as a ceremony of ritual sacrifice to ensure the renewed fertility of life, but as its demonic counterpart: a fable of the modern world's rapacity, exploitation, and lust. What remains is not the promise of life's spring-time renewal of fertility, but the wasteland's sterile "heap of broken images": an existential hell.

X. The Other Side--Ironic Symbols of Transcendence

Against this demonic, demythicized vision of life are set several images of a vestigial beauty, goodness, and humanity struggling to survive or evolve. Thus, interpolated between the harsh cries of "savage" creatures emanating from the primeval environment of the jungle-garden is the occasional clear, sweet sound of a song-bird: transcendent symbol of a spiritual yearning to rise above the corrupt corporeal world, representing a nostalgia for a return to Edenic innocence. As a symbol of such "wishful thinking,"[56] however, the bird's song serves simultaneously to elicit sympathy for the characters whose transcendent longings it evokes and to render those desires futile and ironic.

Such an ambivalence accompanies our response to Mrs. Venable's desire to attain a mythic immortality for Sebastian and herself; thus, as she tells Dr. Cukrowicz of Sebastian's work, "Her face suddenly has a different look, the look of a visionary, an exalted *religieuse*. At the same instant a bird sings clearly and purely in the garden and the old lady seems to be almost young for a moment" (p. 353). Again, "A bird sings sweetly in the garden" as the maliciously motivated but also personally tormented Mrs. Venable imagines the "blessing" of peacefulness said to accompany lobotomy: "After all that horror, after those nightmares: just to be able to lift up their eyes and see . . . a sky not as black with savage, devouring birds as the sky that we saw in the Encantadas" (pp. 366-67), thereby revealing her yearning for a restored innocence even as she pursues the damnable plan to mutilate Catharine. Correspondingly, the "subdued, toneless bird-cries in the garden turn to a single bird song" (p. 398) as Catharine reaches the climax of her story about the married stranger she meets at the Mardi Gras ball, evoking the romantic possibilities of their sexual encounter even as she narrates its sordid reality. Finally, as Catharine begins her "hideous" story of Sebastian's last summer, "the raucous sounds in the garden fade into a bird song which is clear and sweet" (p. 405), a parodic prelude to the demonic truth she tells.

The characterizations of Catharine Holly and Dr. Cukrowicz likewise testify to the play's thematic insistence on a universal yearning for love and goodness that still exists in the midst of this existential hell. Both characters, however, share the ironic simultaneity of mythic elevation and parodic debasement. Like Sebastian, Mrs. Venable, and the Holly mother and brother, Catharine and Dr. Cukrowicz share the dual nature of victim and victimizer; as such, they are rendered existentially complex versions of their allegorical, mythical, and fairy-tale prototypes. Ultimately, however, it is their humaneness or humanity--not their superhuman, legendary, or fairy-tale dimensions--which elevates them from the animalistic level of those around them who devour or are devoured.

XI. Catharine Holly: Ironic Saint

Catharine Holly is depicted as both innocent victim of Mrs. Venable and experienced accomplice of Sebastian, luring to him the young boys he victimizes: both saint and seductress. Her archetypal prototype is the maiden-in-distress waiting for rescue by her White Knight, as her fairy-tale analogue is Little Red Riding Hood, in danger of being devoured by numerous analogues of the Wolf--including the married stranger at the Mardi Gras ball, with his "hot, ravenous mouth" (p. 399). As the existential version of these mythic prototypes--the "fallen woman"--Catharine resembles Williams' own Blanche DuBois; although Catharine's similar dependence on "the kindness of strangers" leads at first to her psychological derangement, it ultimately proves her salvation.

Like Sebastian, Catharine is invested with the aura of sainthood, a symbolism at once mythic and ironic. Her surname, Holly, assumes the religious significance suggested by the holly plant's associations with the birth of Christ (its use in Christmas festivities and ceremonies) and by its symbolic designation as the holy tree from which the cross was made.[57] Holly is also associated with Christ's Crown of Thorns, "its prickly leaves signifying thorns and its scarlet berries the blood of Christ."[58] Symbolically, then, Holly refers both to Catharine's psychological martrydom and to her rebirth. Besides its Christian associations, however, holly, due to its evergreen nature, is also a pagan symbol of sexuality, specifically of the "male reproductive urge," and was used in such Dionysian orgies as the Roman Saturnalia.[59] Catharine Holly's own aggressive, "masculine" sexual tendencies are evidenced by her voluntary liaison with the married stranger at the Mardi Gras ball; by her attempted seduction of Dr. Cukrowicz; and by her admission that she knowingly acted as pimp for Sebastian, which is accompanied by a veiled allusion to her own early promiscuity: "I knew what I was doing. I came out in the French Quarter years before I came out in the Garden District" (p. 413). Her religious elevation to holiness is thus accompanied by her existential debasement. Accordingly, the Holly family is rendered a parodic version of the Holy Family: an unsanctified trinity of mother, son, and daughter, whose "father," as in *The Glass Menagerie*, is absent.

Catharine's Christian name elevates her to sainthood. As ironic analogue of a saint, Catharine is hospitalized in "St. Mary's," a private Catholic asylum run by nuns, secular equivalent of the traditional cloister. She is herself called "Sister" by her mother and brother (p. 375), but her designation as a nun is debunked as a case of mistaken identity: "I think it's me they're calling, they call me 'Sister,' Sister" (p. 375). Finally, in her attempt to save Sebastian from his savage fate, Catharine assumes the intentions of the saint, but again ironically fails to fulfill that sacrificial role. In the context of all these hagiographic associations, Catharine's "Bless you, Sister!" (p. 374) in response to the nun's sneezing assumes grotesquely parodic dimensions.

Although not explicitly identified with a specific saintly namesake as is Sebastian, Catharine is invested with traits strikingly similar to those of a particular prototype, St. Catherine of Bologna, a fifteenth-century virgin-martyr, according to Butler's

121

Lives of the Saints, whose correspondence with Catharine is sub-stantiated by several major parallels in the life and behavior of both.[60] When only an adolescent, St. Catherine lost her father and soon after entered a semi-monastic order (Butler, I, 536); simi-larly, Catharine Holly's father is a "lost" figure in the play, and she too lives a cloistered life in St. Mary's under the supervision of its attendant nuns. From an early age, St. Catherine was "sub-ject to visions, some of which indeed came from God, whilst others were of Satanic origin," and she suffered great spiritual conflict from not always being able to distinguish their source (Butler, I, 537). Significantly, the term which Dr. Cukrowicz uses to describe Catharine's own "Satanic" story of Sebastian is "vision" (pp. 417, 418); and Catharine herself, while under the trance induced by the truth drug, insists that her telling the events of Sebastian's fate cannot be willed, but come to her as involuntary or inspired images of truth: "Under the drug it has to be a vision, or nothing comes" (p. 416). The dramatic conflict of the play, in fact, rests on determining whether Catharine's "visions," like those of St. Catherine, are true or false; but, in the play, the "Satanic" story proves to be true, the sacred one (told by Mrs. Venable), fraudulent.

Like Catharine Holly, St. Catherine wrote an account of her trials in a diary in which she used the third person in reference to herself (Butler, I, 537). Catharine Holly tells us that after one of her own trials--the traumatic sexual encounter and subse-quent rejection by the married man at the Mardi Gras ball--"I began to write my journal in the third person. . . . the next morning, I started writing in my diary in the third person, singular, such as 'She's still living this morning, . . . *What's next for her*? *God knows*!'" (pp. 398-99), her latter expletive a skeptical, secular debasement of the saint's expression of Providential faith.

The most blasphemous vision inflicted upon St. Catherine by the Devil was an image of "the real presence of Jesus Christ in the Blessed Sacrament" (Butler, I, 537), in other words, a vision of mystical communion as the actual consuming of Christ's body and blood. Indeed, it is just such a demonic vision, the actual de-vouring of flesh and blood, that Catharine Holly witnesses in the cannibalizing of Sebastian Venable, the demonic Eucharistic Feast of an ironic Christ figure. As a final ironic parallel, St. Catherine is honored as the patron of artists (Butler, I, 539), an accolade Catharine Holly desecrates by smashing the legend of Sebastian's "artistic" life.

The visitation of Christ to St. Catherine is described in terms remarkably similar to those describing Catharine Holly's first impression of Dr. Cukrowicz, thus elevating him to the mythic stature of Savior. According to Butler, as a means of distinguishing between "divine visions and the artifices of Satan," St. Catherine had learned to recognize when it was our Lord who was really deigning to visit her, "by the holy light of humility" which she felt "at the approach of the Divine Guest" (Butler, I, 537). At such times, "Jesus would enter into her soul like a radiant sunshine, to establish there the profoundest peace." Catharine Holly's first impression of Dr. Cukrowicz is accompanied by just such an aura of radiance: perceived behind "the misty white gauze curtains" (p.374), he is described by Catharine as "too blond to hide behind window curtains, he catches the light, he shines through them" (pp. 374-75). Similarly, like the "Divine Guest" who enters the soul of St. Catherine in order to establish there "profoundest peace," Dr. Cukrowicz is charged with submitting Catharine to a lobotomy which, according to Mrs. Venable, "pacifies them, it quiets them down . . . . what a blessing to them, Doctor, to be just peaceful, to be just suddenly--peaceful" (p. 366), thus making demonic what had been sacred. Mrs. Venable also invests Dr. Cukrowicz with spiritual illumination, albeit sarcastically and in parody of its Christian significance. When Dr. Cukrowicz lights Mrs. Venable's cigarette with her lighter, he exclaims, "My Lord, what a torch!"; she then, "with a sudden, sweet smile," adds Portia's line from Shakespeare's *The Merchant of Venice* (V.1.91.): "So shines a good deed in a naughty world" (pp. 364-65).

Finally, just as St. Catherine expressed her spiritual love for Christ in physical, even erotic, ways, so Catharine Holly expresses her own desperate need for love and salvation to Dr. Cukrowicz in equally sexual terms. Compare Butler's description of St. Catherine's reception of the infant Christ, who is said to have appeared to her on Christmas night, with Williams' stage directions for the manner in which Catharine Holly embraces her own potential savior. Just as St. Catherine, "trembling with respect, but still more overcome with joy . . . took the liberty of caressing Him, of pressing Him against her heart and of bringing His face to her lips" (Butler, I, 538), so Catharine Holly, "dizzy" from her injection, "rises unsteadily" toward Dr. Cukrowicz, and "crushes her mouth to his violently . . . presses her lips to his fiercely, clutching his body against her" (p. 403).

In the play, however, the sublimated eroticism of St. Catherine is debased to Catharine's Holly's raw libidinous impulses, and the saint's devotion to the incarnated God is reduced, perhaps, to an Electra complex: Catharine's own search for a surrogate father. Deceived and degraded by even those who profess love for her, Catharine Holly is in danger of succumbing to the cynical beliefs held by Mrs. Venable and Sebastian of humankind's inability to transcend an inherently exploitative universe: "We all use each other and that's what we think of as love, and not being able to use each other is what's--*hate*" (p. 396). At the same time, however, the vestiges of the saint's altruism, honesty, and humility remain extant in her modern counterpart, and St. Catherine's major conflict--the struggle for her soul by the forces of good and evil--is enacted once again in the play's secularized *psychomachia*.[61] In its Freudian version, Catharine's conflict may be considered that of the ego's struggle for self-preservation, torn between being overwhelmed by the libidinous impulses of the id (personified by Sebastian and his analogues) and the desire for redemption by the super-ego, "the moral or judicial branch of personality," embodied by Dr. Cukrowicz.[62]

XII. The Psychiatrist as Existential Savior

In his relation to Catharine Holly, Dr. Cukrowicz is invested with the attributes of priestly confessor, moral judge, and, as her savior from lobotomy, a Christ-figure or "God." To Catharine's archetype of maiden-in-distress, he plays the role of the White Knight who rescues her, as well as that of the protective hunter-- "the responsible, strong, and rescuing father figure"--who frees her as "Little Red Riding Hood" from the belly of the wicked "wolves" (p. 399).[63] As the existential equivalent of these mythic figures, Dr. Cukrowicz is characterized as the rational, conscientious, "glacially brilliant" (p. 350) Apollonian seeker of truth: the modern psychiatrist who takes the place of priest in the profane, secular world. Thus, Dr. Cukrowicz displays throughout the play what Jung called the primary attribute of the modern psychiatrist, "an attitude of unprejudiced objectivity."[64] He remains objective even in the face of the bribe offered him by Mrs. Venable to "cut this hideous story out of her [Catharine's] brain!" (p. 423), in stark contrast to Sebastian's self-indulgent subjectivity, Mrs. Venable's malicious slander, and the Hollys' vested interest in the distortion of truth. Jung adds, however, that the kind of psychoanalysis Dr. Cukrowicz is engaged in with Catharine is possible only if the doctor is not repelled by his patient's revelations, no matter how shocking or corrupt; and "he can do this . . . only when he has already seen and accepted himself as he is," has recognized "the enemy within," or his own "shadow" (the negative side of the personality).[65]

That the ostensibly "innocent" (p. 368) Dr. Cukrowicz *has* a "shadow" side is amply documented in the play. He is not only the potential victim of Mrs. Venable's bribe but also the potential victimizer of Catharine, whose mental and emotional life or death is dependent on whether or not he decides "to bore a hole in my skull and turn a knife in my brain" (p. 389), as Catharine graphically describes her proposed lobotomy.[66] Within "Dr. Sugar" (p. 351), then, lies the "shadow" of Sebastian's own cannibalistic nature. As the "skilled surgeon" (p. 366) who mutilates and dismembers his patients, he also reflects the powers of a "savage" God. His headquarters, the state asylum, is significantly named "Lion's View," obvious corollary to the site of Sebastian's bestial murder, "Wolf's Head." Thus, Dr. Cukrowicz, on the one hand, represents the allegorical antithesis of Sebastian, or his *Doppelgänger*, that mythical archetype which symbolizes "a spiritual emanation of the self as it ought to be," who here, as elsewhere in literature, assumes the function of "the better of the two selves tracking down the crimes that the worser perpetrates."[67] At the same time, he also serves to validate Sebastian's vision of a universally savage world by his own medically sanctioned participation in its cannibalism. Beneath his mythical aura as Sebastian's antithesis, then, is to be found his psychological aspect as Sebastian's alter ego. Accordingly, Mrs. Venable comments: "You would have liked my son, he would have been charmed by you" (p. 359).

At the play's beginning, however, Dr. Cukrowicz is characterized as essentially innocent: a *naif* among the play's cynical figures, a "sweet" thrown to the wolves (as is implied by the English translation of his Polish name: "Sugar"). He believes at first that Mrs. Venable is truly concerned for Catharine's emotional well-being, and his conscience compels him to warn her about the risks of the operation he has been asked to perform on her, the effects of which he admits "haunt" him: "It may be that the person will always be limited afterwards, relieved of acute disturbances but--*limited*, Mrs. Venable" (p. 366). His obtuseness in understanding the malicious motives behind Mrs. Venable's offer of financial aid prompts her own cynical evaluation of his naiveté:

"You're such an innocent person that it doesn't occur to you, it obviously hasn't even occurred to you that anybody less innocent than you are could possibly interpret this offer of a subsidy as-- well, as sort of a *bribe*?" (p. 368).

At the end of the play, Dr. Cukrowicz's tacit decision that Catharine be spared the mutilation of lobotomy seems to suggest that the doctor has himself undertaken a psychological journey from innocence to experience. By his admission that "I think we ought at least to consider the possibility that the girl's story could be true" (p. 423), Dr. Cukrowicz enacts the role of ironic Savior, sparing Catharine from the "blessings" of his surgical skills rather than submitting her to the threatened lobotomy--that medical treatment which Williams himself called "a tragically mistaken procedure."[68] Yet, in this 1971 *Theatre* version of the play, revised from its original 1958 script, there is little to suggest that Dr. Cukrowicz has recognized the shadow within himself, the "savagery" of his own medical practices, even though he ultimately saves Catharine from them. His final utterance in this version of the play simply serves to underline the play's theme: that Catharine's story of cannibalism as well as Sebastian's vision of a "terrible" God is, indeed, "a hideous story but . . . a true story of our time and the world we live in" (p. 382).

What is missing--the steps by which the doctor's initial innocence becomes the dark recognition of the savagery he has himself perpetuated--may be found in the original 1958 script of the play (hereafter cited in reprint as Signet).[69] There, Dr. Cukrowicz is depicted initially not only as an essentially innocent man of conscience, but also as a humane, altruistic, idealistic, and truly religious figure who sincerely believes in the psychologically redemptive powers of lobotomy. As Sebastian's *Doppelgänger*, Dr. Cukrowicz is said to be looking for God, too, on his own "solitary safari" (Signet, p. 18), without benefit of scriptural guide or metaphysical map. Thus, to Mrs. Venable's story of Sebastian's equation of the predatory devouring of the newly-hatched sea turtles by the carnivorous birds with a similarly ruthless, savage God, Dr. Cukrowicz responds not with the neutral expression of comprehension--"I see" (p. 357)--as in the revised *Theatre* edition, but with the shocked incredulity of the Christian existentialist: "I can see how such a spectacle could be equated with a good deal of--*experience, existence*!--but not with *God*! Can *you*?" (Signet, p. 19). At the same time, in the play's original version a further link is made between Sebastian's and Dr.

Cukrowicz's "savage" side: the violent ward of the doctor's asylum is described as "The Drum"--a place "with very bright lights burning all day and all night" (Signet, p. 18)--a parallel to both the "blazing equatorial day" (p. 357) of the Galapagos Islands where Sebastian witnesses the mutilation of the sea turtles and the "blazing white hot" hell of Cabeza de Lobo where he suffers his own dismemberment.

Most important to the characterization of Dr. Cukrowicz in the 1958 script is the story he tells of the first lobotomy he performed on a young girl, with which reenactment Catharine is threatened. Recounted by Dr. Cukrowicz in Scene i of the original play, the story is told as a fairy tale with a happy ending, devoid of any recognition on the part of the doctor that his genuinely altruistic intentions may have yielded destructive consequences, despite his subsequent admission to being haunted by the risks involved in undergoing lobotomy and his expressed fear that "the person will always be limited afterwards" (Signet, p. 30; *Theatre*, p. 366), the latter remark retained in both versions of the play. The major significance of Dr. Cukrowicz's story of his first lobotomy performed on the "young girl" (Signet, p. 18) is that it is made analogous to Catharine's projected operation in several important ways, thereby evoking a sense of menace beneath the doctor's rendition of it as an unqualified success. In both cases (Catharine's and the anonymous girl's), their apparent insanity is identified by their "babbling." Before "the girl's" lobotomy, Dr. Cukrowicz tells us that, "her speech, everything that she'd babbled, was a torrent of obscenities" (Signet, p. 19). Similarly, Mrs. Venable, in both the play's versions, refers to Catharine's "hideous" story about Sebastian as babbling: "She *babbles*! They couldn't shut her up in Cabeza de Lobo or at the clinic in Paris-- she babbled, babbled!" (Signet, p. 27; *Theatre*, p. 364). In the first case, the girl's obscene babbling is stilled by the lobotomy, just as lobotomy is intended to stop Catharine's babbling, or at least destroy her credibility: "After the operation, who would *believe* her, Doctor?" (Signet, p. 30; *Theatre*, p. 367). After "the girl's" operation, on "a nice afternoon, as fair as this one," she is said to have looked up and whispered, "Oh, how blue the sky is!" (Signet, p. 19). On the surface, the girl's response indicates a state of mind restored to the "blessed" innocence and "peacefulness" which Mrs. Venable characterizes as the outcome of Catharine's proposed lobotomy also. At the same time, the juxtaposition of the girl's reference to a "blue . . . sky" with Dr. Cukrowicz's observation that the weather that day was indeed "nice" and "fair" suggests that the girl's perception was strictly in accord with surface reality and, though sane, perhaps also emotionally "limited"--testimony to that psychological loss which haunts Dr. Cukrowicz as lobotomy's major drawback.

In that original 1958 script are drawn other parallels to suggest that beneath surface realities lie dark truths and, paradoxically, that both altruistic and selfish motives may yield similarly destructive consequences. Even those actions and attitudes which on the surface sharply distinguish Dr. Cukrowicz from his "shadow" antitheses--Sebastian and Mrs. Venable--have at a deeper level parallels with them. For instance, Dr. Cukrowicz tells us that after the girl's operation, he felt "proud and relieved," as if "I'd delivered a child that might stop breathing" (Signet, pp. 18-19), on the surface a clear indication of the doctor's compassion and solicitude, evoking the images of salvation and rebirth. In similar terms, however, Mrs. Venable describes Sebastian's delivery of his annual "Poem of Summer," a product which took nine months of preparation, "the length of a pregnancy" (Signet, p. 14; *Theatre*, p. 354), which was also "hard to deliver," and Mrs. Venable proudly adds, "*Without* me, *impossible*" (Signet, p. 14; *Theatre*, p. 354). The parallel suggests that such solicitude may have destructive as well as constructive consequences.

Furthermore, the concern and compassion Dr. Cukrowicz shows toward his patient in the story--"I stayed with the girl . . . holding onto her hand" (Signet, p. 18)--is both contrasted to Sebastian's inability to love and compared to Mrs. Venable's suffocating mother-love. Unlike Dr. Cukrowicz's behavior toward his patient, Sebastian rejects Catharine when she most needs him, after she'd "made the mistake of responding too much to his kindness, of taking hold of his hand before he'd take hold of mine" (Signet, p. 74; *Theatre*, p. 406), a rejection that ultimately leads to his destruction: "I tried to hold onto his hand but he struck me away and ran, ran, ran in the wrong direction" (Signet, p. 39; *Theatre*, p. 374). Catharine concludes, "If he'd kept hold of my hand I could have saved him!" (Signet, p. 40; *Theatre*, p. 375). On the other hand, Mrs. Venable ostensibly shows the same concern for Sebastian as does Dr. Cukrowicz for his patient; when Sebastian suffered one of his frequent anxiety attacks, Mrs. Venable would "reach across a table and touch his hand . . . [just] touch his hands with my hand until his hands stopped shaking" (Signet, p. 76; *Theatre*, p. 408). Their parallel attitudes are reinforced by analogous tactile imagery and the similar linguistic structures of their expressions. Moreover, just as Dr. Cukrowicz "stayed with the girl, holding onto her hand," so Mrs. Venable proudly claims to have similarly helped Sebastian to recover from his delirium and withdrawal from the world; thus, even though called home to her dying husband, Violet Venable "stayed with my son. I got him through that crisis too" (Signet, p. 21; *Theatre*, p. 358).

From the juxtaposition of these parallels afforded by the inclusion of Dr. Cukrowicz's story and his more fully developed characterization in the 1958 script, a more complex dimension to the play's theme emerges: that the truth is essentially paradoxical and its surface appearances, deceptive. Thus, the love intended to save may ultimately destroy; the embrace may devour; and what seems to be insane and obscene babbling may be but "a true story of our time and the world we live in" (Signet, p. 47; *Theatre*, p. 382). In the play's original version, then, Catharine's Byronic remark that truth lies "at the bottom of a bottomless well" (Signet, p. 68; *Theatre*, p. 401) is given added significance.[70] Finally, it is just this--the paradoxical nature of truth and the unconscious primitive impulses that lie beneath even the most consciously civilized behavior--that Dr. Cukrowicz learns as the play's literal quest-figure in the original 1958 script. As an active seeker of truth through whose questions the play's subterranean secrets are drawn to the surface, Dr. Cukrowicz undergoes a moral development in the play's original version, and his final utterance suggests his own redemption as well as Catharine's. By contrast, in the revised 1971 edition, Dr. Cukrowicz is relegated to little more than a sounding board for Catharine's story, his quest reduced to a dispassionate, objective interrogation, and the final recognition of his own "shadow" left in doubt.

In that original script, Dr. Cukrowicz's final statement--"I think we ought at least to consider the possibility that the girl's story could be true"--reverberates far beyond its immediate application to Catharine's "hideous" tale of Sebastian's cannibalization. In the doctor's anonymous allusion to "*the girl's story*" [emphasis mine] rather than his specific reference to "Miss Catharine," as she is formerly called by Dr. Cukrowicz, his final utterance recalls the story of his first lobotomy performed on a similarly un-named "girl" whose torrent of "obscene" babblings he had stilled. The evocation of that memory is reinforced by Dr. Cukrowicz's reminiscent delivery of the line which, according to Williams' stage directions, is to be spoken "after awhile, reflectively, into space" (Signet, p. 93; *Theatre*, p. 423). In the original version, then, Dr. Cukrowicz's admission that "the girl's story could be true" refers not only to Catharine but to that other "girl" as well, and raises to consciousness his recognition of the possibility that the obscene babblings of his first patient might have been as darkly true as Catharine's. Accordingly, what had appeared to be his first patient's redemptive apprehension of a "blue sky" may have actually represented not a clarified state of mind but a forever "limited" perception of a world inherently black, which, perhaps, only the lobotomized mind still perceives as fair or "blue." Thus, what Dr. Cukrowicz had thought to be his finest social and moral achievement may have been, in reality, a tragically "savage" act. It is implied, then, in the original version that only by recognizing his own shadow, his own complicity in the world's savagery, is Dr. Cukrowicz able to arrest the cycle of victimization, thereby truly creating some light in an otherwise dark and destructive world.

In the play's 1971 revised version, Dr. Cukrowicz fulfills the same symbolic role and thematic function as Catharine's savior, but his own moral development is not made as clear. All that remains of the structure which had traced his moral development from his triumphant story of his first lobotomy patient to his final refusal to perform the same operation on Catharine are two passages of dialogue: the first in Scene i when he expresses to Mrs. Venable his concern for the "risk" involved in lobotomy, and the second at the beginning of Scene iv when he is delayed in his meeting with Catharine because of an urgent phone call from Lion's View about "a patient." In the original 1958 version, it is strongly implied that the phone call is about some problem that has developed with the girl on whom Dr. Cukrowicz performed his first lobotomy; for in both versions, Dr. Cukrowicz prefaces his comment by asking Mrs. Venable to recall their former conversation about such a patient: "Don't you remember our talk? I had to answer a phone call about a patient that--" (Signet, p. 54; *Theatre*, p. 389); the explanation is left incomplete. In the *Theatre* revision, however, because the story about Dr. Cukrowicz's first patient is deleted, the line remains without specific referent, and can only allude to Dr. Cukrowicz's general expression of concern for the risks faced by all patients of lobotomy.

Without the first story, however, it is too much to assume that an audience, or even a reader, would recall these two scant passages expressing and implying, respectively, Dr. Curkowicz's concern for the dangers of lobotomy; and, on the basis of such meager evidence, conclude that his final decision to forgo Catharine's lobotomy also signifies the dark realization of his own complicity in the world's savagery. Rather, his decision to spare Catharine from lobotomy is, in the play's 1971 revised version, based entirely on his belief in the truth or sanity of her story; in short, he refuses to submit a *sane* patient to the danger of lobotomy, a rational *medical* decision but hardly suggestive of moral insight into his own subterranean "shadow." We can only assume that he will continue to perform the brutal operation of lobotomy on those patients he judges appropriately *insane*, despite his understanding of the operation's risks. To be sure, the doctor's final musing, "reflectively, into space" (p. 423), suggests his recognition of the world's savagery--as recounted in Catharine's story and as demonstrated by Mrs. Venable and the Hollys--but gives no clue that he has understood his own participation in it. In the final version, then, Dr. Cukrowicz remains Catharine's existential savior, but his own moral journey--from the idealistic surgeon who proudly tells his story of lobotomy's redemptive powers to the quietly reflective man who saves Catharine from what he must now realize are his "savage" skills--can no longer be clearly traced.

XIII. Coda

In "Foreword" to *Sweet Bird of Youth* (1959), the play produced directly after *Suddenly Last Summer* which employs a similar sacrificial myth, Williams tells of an "unmailed letter" in which he had written: "We are all civilized people, which means that we are all savages at heart but observing a few amenities of civilized behavior" (IV, 3). It is just this "heart of darkness" beneath humanity's civilized veneer that Williams explores in *Suddenly Last Summer*.

By making Dr. Cukrowicz exempt from the realization of his own participation in the world's savagery, however, Williams has undermined the universality of his own theme. In the play's original version, as in Conrad's tale of the "impenetrable darkness" at the heart of the human psyche, Williams had presented the simultaneous revelations by two individuals of "the horror" of their own inherent capacity for savagery. As polar aspects of the human psyche, both Sebastian and Dr. Cukrowicz (like Kurtz and Marlow) make the descent into their own subterranean regions--the one self-propelled, the other as vicarious witness--and both discover there primitive impulses which link man with nature. Unlike Kurtz, however, Sebastian never attains that self-knowledge which raises Conrad's figure to tragic stature; instead, he projects his internal discovery outward and finds in predatory nature metaphysical justification for the indulgence of his own savage appetites, which ultimately consume him. Like Marlow, on the other hand, the original Dr. Cukrowicz understands but refuses to perpetuate the savage impulses he discovers lie beneath his healing efforts: his "restraint" is Catharine's redemption. Just as Marlow, by refusing to shatter the illusion of love held by Kurtz's "Intended" thereby invests value into that quality and preserves it, so the original Dr. Cukrowicz, by his own act of mercy and moral restraint, ensures and affirms the survival of those virtues even as he realizes their rare and vulnerable existence.

In the original version of the play, then, Dr. Cukrowicz embodies a theme intrinsic to Williams' own humanistic code: that in the absence of any sign of the existence of an all-loving, all-merciful God, mere mortals must be "God" to each other. From the play's shattered myths and debased transcendent symbols evolves in the original 1958 script a tentative hope in the survival of compassion, understanding, and humane-ness in an otherwise infernal world. In the play's 1971 revised version, Dr. Cukrowicz is also cast in the role of "God," the arbiter of Catharine's fate, but his formerly moral restraint is relegated to the realm of medical ethics, and his apparently continued ignorance about his own savagery makes the play's world an even darker place.

CHAPTER SEVEN

SWEET BIRD OF YOUTH

Palm gardens by the sea and olive groves
on the Mediterranean islands all have that
lament drifting through them. 'Lost, lost'. . . .
They're all places of exile from whatever we loved.

I. The Dream of a Comeback: Two Memory-Stories

In *Sweet Bird of Youth* (1959), two major memory-stories inform the play's structural pattern. Accordingly, two main characters complicate the structure by their respective and antithetical memories of past events: the one memory so idyllic that the play's male protagonist is obsessed with its re-creation; the other so humiliating that the female protagonist is obsessed with escape from and obliteration of it. Thus, even as Chance Wayne, anachronistic Adonis and ironic romance knight, attempts the quixotic quest to recapture his adolescent experience of first love with "my girl" (Heavenly Finley), his traveling companion, Alexandra del Lago (alias the Princess Kosmonopolis), an aging film star whom Chance serves as lackey and stud, seeks only escape and oblivion from her memory of a failed film "comeback" (IV, 34). Ostensibly, then, the two begin at cross-purposes, and, in the pursuit of their respective goals, each reverses or exchanges initial positions. From the peak of romantic optimism, Chance descends to the abyss of despair and disillusionment while the Princess, who begins at what she believes to be the nadir of her career, ultimately achieves a qualified return to fame.

Ironically, however, each aspires to or flees from a non-existent dream and nightmare, respectively. Chance has unknowingly rendered impossible the reenactment of his dream even before his quest begins. Reaching for that material success--in this case, stardom--which is a perversion of the mythic American Dream of spiritual aspiration, Chance has degenerated from "the finest, nicest, sweetest boy in St. Cloud" (p. 63) to a beach-boy, lothario, and stud, whose youthful experience of ideal love with Heavenly has deteriorated into multiple loveless reenactments with aging, wealthy women. As a result of his promiscuity, Chance has unwittingly defiled Heavenly--her very name symbolic of that unattainable goal to which he aspires: a return to youth and an ascent to stardom.[1] Having infected Heavenly with venereal disease, he desecrates her both in image and substance. Her consequent hysterectomy--"a whore's operation" (p. 59)--casts down the inviolate ideal she represents to the level of a mutilated animal: "spayed like a dawg" (p. 103), "gutted and hung on a butcher's hook, like a chicken" (p.120). Rather than the mythic reunion of heaven and earth to which Chance aspires, then, it is the story of Heavenly's mutilation which is reenacted by Chance. At the play's end, he surrenders himself to the castration which renders his dreams, like hers, desecrated and dismembered.

Conversely, the Princess learns that the failure from which she flees is equally illusory: her own screen comeback had been successful all along. In one sense, then, what she had believed to be an unsuccessful comeback to film stardom is reenacted in a successful version at the end of the play. However, the news of her public acclaim is so tempered by her personal realization of the transience of youth, beauty, and stardom itself, that the Princess, like Chance, is forced to relinquish the impossible dream of "coming back" in favor of its existential alternative--"to go on" (p. 122). Like Chance, the Princess, too, faces castration: "Age does the same thing to a woman" (p. 120). The play ends, then, as the Princess leaves to confront her audience again while Chance stays behind to surrender to an act of violent destruction, their lives having intersected at a moment of apparently antithetical desires, in the pursuit of which each ultimately realizes the same fate: the "castration" of illusions and the hope of ever coming back to a youth forever lost to them both.

In essence, then, despite their apparent cross-purposes, both Chance and the Princess begin by seeking the same impossible goal: a comeback or return to youth, an ideal elevated in the course of the play above personal meaning to a primordial nostalgia for that mythical Golden Age of paradisiacal beauty and innocence. In this existential present, however, both also encounter the same implacable antagonist: "Time," whose scythe not only clips the wings from the sweet bird of youth pursued by Chance and the Princess, but also "castrates" them of all heroic virtues, mythic aspirations, and transcendent ideals. All of the other characters in the play undergo a form of castration as well.[2] Heavenly's father, Boss Finley, a corrupt, secular Godhead, is castrated of his illusion of omnipotence by his mistress, Miss Lucy, who accuses him of sexual impotence. Miss Lucy herself undergoes a symbolic castration when

134

Boss Finley, in retaliation for her insult, slams the lid of his gift-box on her fingers. An innocent black is literally emasculated by Boss Finley's henchmen as a racist warning to violators of a mythical white Southern chastity; and a heckler who challenges Boss Finley's hypocritical pose as populist messiah suffers the fate of having his voice (and perhaps his life) cut off. In its sordid reiteration of acts of castration, symbolic and literal, the play portrays a world bereft of transcendent values, whose inhabitants are grotesquely diminished from the mythical prototypes evoked by their names, images, and aspirations: a world whose setting is designated by Williams simply as "Modern" and ironically as "Easter Sunday" (p. 9). In its rapacious dedication to achieving the materialistic goals of power and success, this modern world is described by the Princess as "the beanstalk country, the ogre's country at the top of the beanstalk, the country of the flesh-hungry, blood-thirsty ogre" (p. 98); and depicted by the martyred heckler as a spiritual wasteland where is heard only "the silence of God, the absolute speechlessness of Him . . . a long, long and awful thing that the whole world is lost because of" (p. 105). If a "comeback" expresses the nostalgic yearning for mythical and spiritual values by the characters in this play, "castration" represents its inevitable existential outcome.

II. Chance Wayne: Ironic Adonis

In this play, the romantic and mythical prototypes of the characters are so radically undermined by the comparison that the tension between ideal image and existential reality is stretched to the point of caricature. Simultaneously romantic and ironic, each characterization evokes both a mythical prototype and the "castrated" modern version to which the ideal has been debased, thereby magnifying the disparity between idyllic past and demythicized present. As the hero *manqué* of the play, Chance Wayne is cast in the role of an aging romance knight engaged in a quest to rescue Heavenly, the damsel-in-distress, from her corrupt politician father and to raise her and himself to the level of "stars" in a movie to be called, appropriately, "Youth": a goal doomed to failure by the physically and morally corrupt means used by Chance to attain it. Specifically, Chance is endowed with the mythical attributes of Adonis,[3] the Eastern fertility god who historically becomes the Greek archetype of beautiful but transient youth. Beloved by Aphrodite, he is killed by a jealous Ares in the likeness of a wild boar.

Williams first evokes the association of Chance with Adonis (as well as that of the Princess with his mythical consort, Aphrodite) by his emphasis on the symbolic or "non-realistic" (p. 9) ambience of the play's setting. Its suggestion of an Eastern, Mediterranean, or "vaguely Moorish" (p. 13) atmosphere extends the play's immediate location, "somewhere along the Gulf Coast" (p. 13), to the mythic regions of the Asiatic-Greco gods. More specifically, both Adonis and Aphrodite are identified with Cyprus -- reputedly their birthplace and sanctuary[4]--and "Cyprus" is the first of several exotic places characterized by the Princess as "places of exile from whatever we loved."[5] All are "Palm gardens by the sea and olive groves on Mediterranean islands" through which wafts the lament, "Lost, lost, never to be found again" (p. 103). Indeed, that setting designated by Williams as the play's "most important and constant" is a similar "grove of royal palm trees" (p. 9) outside the Royal Palms Hotel where Chance and the Princess stay, suggesting that their present location is also a "place of exile," their having irrevocably "lost" the ideal attributes of youth and beauty embodied by their mythical prototypes. Also, "Lamentations" are a major part of the ceremonial rites of mourning for Adonis;[6] significantly, Williams designates as the play's thematic music "a wind among these very tall palm trees" which, when it blends with music, "will be identified . . . as 'The Lament'" (p. 9).

The most important point of identification between Adonis and Chance Wayne, however, rests in their shared fate: castration.[7] Although Adonis is said to have been gored by a wild boar (an analogue, perhaps, of emasculation), his mythic counterpart, Attis, literally unmanned himself; and, according to Sir James Frazer, Attis is so closely identified with Adonis that the two figures are often confused or conflated.[8] Furthermore, a major part of the ritual mourning for Attis on the Day of Blood during his annual spring festival is the self-castration of his worshippers and disciples, a fertility rite in imitation of their emasculated god's sacrifice.[9] Just so, Chance submits to a similar castration in the springtime of Easter Sunday, evoking not only the emasculation of Attis/Adonis but also Christ's crucifixion (an analogous mutilation or dismemberment).

Both Attis/Adonis and Christ, however, are resurrected deities, and their "lamentations" are followed by a Festival of Joy and Easter celebration, respectively. Unlike these divinities,

Chance's self-sacrifice signals no anticipation of either renewed fertility or spiritual salvation. Although he has cast himself in the role of savior, vowing to rescue the defiled Heavenly and to "give her life back to her" (p. 107), his redemptive efforts fail. (Note the similarities between Chance and Val Xavier as ironic saviors.) Thus, although the references to palm trees, olive groves, and lamentations evoke not only the Adonic myth but also Christ's triumphant entry into Jerusalem on Palm Sunday (as well as his subsequent retreat to the Mount of Olives, his betrayal in the Garden of Gethsemane, and his destined crucifixion), Chance's own "homecoming," his betrayal of Heavenly, and his final dismemberment serve only to further reinforce the vast distance between him and his mythic prototypes. Finally, then, although Chance's surname, Wayne (wane), suggests his association with such "waxing and waning" gods as Attis and Adonis (so-called because of their seasonal representation of winter's sterility followed by spring's renewed fertility[10]), Chance remains, unlike these personifications of rebirth and resurrection, "on the wane" from the beginning. As his first name implies, Chance, the youthful beneficiary of "Sheer Luck!" (p. 50)--ultimately falls victim to indifferent natural forces--Hardy's "Crass Casualty" and "dicing Time"--in an inherently absurd and god-forsaken universe.

More authentic, perhaps, is Chance's affinity with the adolescent hero of the fairy tale "Jack and the Beanstalk," a comparison initially suggested by the Princess' frequent allusions to their both being lost in "the beanstalk country . . . the country of the flesh-hungry, blood-thirsty ogre" (p. 98), her metaphor for the ruthless, rapacious nature of the modern materialistic world in which both Chance and the Princess strive to succeed. Like Jack, both Chance and the Princess are "climbers." As Chance says, "In a life like mine, you just can't stop. . . . you've got to keep going right on up from one thing to the other" (p. 48). The Princess' "beanstalk" (identified by Bruno Bettelheim as a phallic symbol)[11] may be considered the sexual dominance she wields and pays for, turning her into the very ogre or "monster" (p. 43) who, in the tale as in the play, threatens to devour aspiring young boys like Chance. Chance's "beanstalk" refers more literally to his sexual powers or phallic potency. Like Jack, Chance believes in the magic power of his "seed" or phallus as the means to achieve wealth and fame: "Slept in the social register of New York! Millionaires' widows and wives and debutante daughters" (p. 47). The other parallels, however, between the fairy tale and Chance's story are inverted, and ultimately ironic. Thus, just as Jack each time

returns home a hero after successfully wresting the treasure from
the ogre at the top of the beanstalk, so Chance also perodically
returns to his home-town and Heavenly after his social and sexual
conquests. Ironically, however, Chance's is a tale of missed oppor-
tunites (or "chances") and of successive failures, until the only
"treasure" he brings back to Heavenly is the venereal disease with
which he corrupts her.

Chance, like Jack, may be said to be engaged in an "oedipal
conflict with the ogre,"[12] represented in the play by Heavenly's
father, Boss Finley. In the fairy tale, however, Jack wins the
oedipal struggle by cutting down the beanstalk, which psychologically reflects his relinquishing childish fantasies of magical
phallic powers.[13] According to Bettleheim, by cutting down the
beanstalk Jack initiates the development of psychic maturity: freed
from his youthful belief in "the magic power of the phallus as the
means for gaining him all the good things in life . . . Jack is
ready to give up phallic and oedipal fantasies and instead try to
live in reality."[14]

In the play, however, Chance *loses* the oedipal battle with
Boss Finley to win Heavenly, and his submission to castration
(i.e., cutting down the "beanstalk") does not clearly signal the
development of either his psychological or moral maturity. Chance
laments the waning of his sexual appeal and powers, but he gives
little indication that he has outgrown his youthful belief in their
importance. To Chance, who believes that "Love-making" is "maybe
the only one [vocation] I was truly meant for" (p.47), life without
the youthful powers of the phallus is truly not worth living.
Shortly after the Princess tells Chance that his sole distinction
was "your youth . . . It's all you had, and you've had it" (p.119),
Chance himself admits his life has become meaningless: "I couldn't
go past my youth, but I've gone past it" (p. 122). His submission
to castration as an attempt to make his death meaningful ("Something's got to mean something, don't it?" [p. 121])--an act which
has been interpreted as a gesture of sacrificial atonement for
Heavenly's defilement[15]--is thus vitiated by his admission that
Time and its ravages have castrated him already. In psychological
terms, then, Chance remains "stuck in the phallic phase" of development,[16] unwilling to give up his belief in the supremacy of youth
and unable to go on living without his youthful fantasies. Not
Chance but the Princess bravely faces her own "castration" of
youthful dreams and prepares to "go on" (p. 124), to resume the
struggle with the ogre, symbol of the corruption inherent in

living, and with Time, ravager of youth and beauty: "I've climbed back alone up the beanstalk to the ogre's country where I live, now, alone" (p.119).

III. The Princess Kosmonopolis: A Fallen Aphrodite

The characterization of the Princess Kosmonopolis (or, Alexandra del Lago) encompasses both her existential role as a survivor--a hard-as-nails realist--and her romantic one as a disillusioned idealist. The disparity between her mythicized image and her actual nature, however, is often so great as to render her a grotesque version of the mythological, legendary, and fairy-tale prototypes she evokes: "like a princess from Mars or a big magnified insect" (p. 23). At the same time, whereas Chance makes an inexorable descent to pathos and the parody of his mythic analogues, the Princess truly experiences a psychological rebirth in the re-awakening of humane and compassionate feeling, which elevates her final demythicized character to a certain heroic stature.

Her first name, Alexandra, evokes the mythical regions of Eastern Asia, Greece, and the Mediterranean germane to the play's symbolic geography, as her grandiose manner recalls Alexander the Great, the flamboyant, domineering figure who conquered and united those regions, naming each of its major cities Alexandria, after himself.[17] However, her alias, "the Princess Kosmonopolis," translated loosely as "the state of the cosmos or universe,"[18] testifies to the degenerative state of the modern age as reflected by her corrupted, ruinous condition. It has been pointed out that the name Alexandra is a variant of Cassandra,[19] the mythical prophetess whose function the Princess fulfills by her forewarning Chance of his destiny as another "Franz Albertzart," gigolo to "a woman of seventy" who will lead him around by an invisible chain like "a blind, dying lap dog" (pp. 113-14). In the original version of the play, the Princess was named Ariadne del Lago, (alias the Princess Pazmezoglu),[20] evoking the mythical princess who safely guided Theseus out of the labyrinth of the Minotaur. In this revised version of the play, Alexandra retains Ariadne's function as Chance's guide, but her attempt to persuade him to "go on" remains futile. As her surname del Lago (Spanish or Italian, "of the lake") suggests, the Princess is also identified with the Arthurian Lady of the Lake and assumes her dual nature: to her Sir Lancelot (Chance), she represents both a nurturing anima-figure and the *femme fatale* whose seduction is deadly.

As companion to Chance in his role of an aging Adonis and ironic fertility god, the Princess represents as well a vulgarized version of the mythical Aphrodite, Goddess of Love and mother-consort to Adonis. Significantly, Aphrodite is also known as Astarte (or Ashtart), Phoenician goddess of fertility and sexual love,[21] whose star was deemed "the most beautiful of the heavenly bodies, Venus,"[22] an image diminished in its personification by the Princess to that of a fading film star. As a diminished Aphrodite, the Princess has reduced the meaning of love to a mere "dependable distraction" (p. 44), an anodyne like the drugs and liquor she uses to forget her fears, loneliness, and lost youth. No longer the irresistible, "beautiful golden goddess,"[23] this version of Aphrodite reflects only the darker anima aspects of "monster"--the "treacherous and malicious" figure who exerts "a deadly and destructive power over men"[24]--and of the Terrible Mother, "devouring maw of the underworld"[25] or *vagina dentata*, whose equivalent in the play is "the flesh-hungry, blood-thirsty ogre at the top of the beanstalk." Her sexual exploitation of Chance is thus depicted as yet another form of castration; to her warning of his actual castration, Chance replies: "That can't be done to me twice. You did that to me this morning, here on this bed" (p. 120). Unlike the ritual sacrifice (often in the form of castration) undergone by Attis/Adonis to their mother-consorts Astarte/ Aphrodite in order to achieve rebirth,[26] Chance's sexual submission to the Princess signals no such growth in him. Instead, Chance's perception of the Princess as castrator serves only to reinforce his own characterization as a *puer aeternus*, or eternal adolescent; for, according to Erich Newmann, "a male immature in his development, who experiences himself only as male and phallic, perceives the feminine as a castrator, a murderer of the phallus."[27] (Compare the similar perception of an aggressive woman as a psychological archetype of the Terrible Mother held by Tom Wingfield toward Amanda, Brick toward Maggie, Sebastian toward Violet Venable, and Shannon toward Maxine.) Thus, Chance rejects the maternal love aroused in the Princess, deflating her momentary endowment with the attributes of her Great Mother prototypes, Aphrodite and Astarte: "Come here, kiss me, I love you. Come here. . . . [Then to Chance with arms outstretched] What a child you are. . . . Come here. . . . [He ducks under her arms, and escapes]" (p. 54). In the diminished figure of the Princess, then, the mythical goddesses of love, sacrifice, and rebirth have become, like her own youth, "dead, as old Egypt" (p. 123).

The Princess is also characterized as a grotesque version of the fairy-tale princess "Sleeping Beauty" (p. 19). At the beginning of the play, her struggle out of drugged sleep and nightmare is but a parody of the symbolic rebirth signified by the fairy-tale princess' reawakening.[28] Ironically, however, it is the Princess' role as "Sleeping Beauty" which allows Chance to fulfill his only authentic act as savior. Upon awakening, the Princess calls for her oxygen mask, "as if with her dying breath" (p. 21). Chance fits the oxygen inhalator over her nose and mouth, in parody of the fairy-tale prince's kiss, symbolically saving her life. What is merely a farcical version of the miracle of rebirth at the beginning of the play, however, gains substance later on. As a result of Chance's act, the Princess experiences a true reawakening of tenderness and compassion, her monstrous egoism transformed to altruistic concern: "Chance, the most wonderful thing has happended to me. . . . I felt something in my heart for you. . . . I felt something for someone besides myself. . . . I almost died this morning, suffocated in a panic [but] . . . You gave my oxygen to me" (pp. 96-97). Chance's incidental act of "kindness" (p. 97) and the consequent awakening of compassion in the Princess represent all that's left of the mythical Aphrodite's inspirational love or Sleeping Beauty's miraculous rebirth, but its significance is momentous in this spiritual wasteland.

IV. Heavenly and Boss Finley: Inverted Christian Archetypes

The two other major characters in the play, Heavenly and her father, the political demagogue Boss Finley, represent defiled and corrupt versions of Christian ideals and archetypes, serving to reinforce the loss of transcendent spiritual values in the modern world. However, because their function is naively allegorical and their characterizations stereotypical, they emerge as cardboard angel and villain, respectively. Together they evoke both the poignancy and perversions engendered by spiritual desolation, but largely by way of their own dramatic lifelessness.

In name and image, Heavenly evokes the entire complex of associations inherent in the play's mythic yearnings: popular, pagan, and Christian. She suggests both Venus and Virgin, stars and stardom, the earthly paradise and those transcendent regions where mythically exist eternal youth, beauty, and angelic innocence. As remembered by Chance, she evokes the numinous image of the youthful Venus rising from the sea-foam--Goddess of Love and Beauty, symbol of spring and fruitfulness: "She had on a silky wet tank suit and fans of water and mist made rainbows about her" (p. 51).[29] Symbol also of that Siren "success," Heavenly represents that ideal which Chance would always "just about reach" (p. 51) but which would finally "disappear," like Heavenly herself, "throwing up misty rainbows" (p. 51). Heavenly's image, then, is illusory. Initially corrupted by Chance himself, Heavenly is also sexually exploited by her father, who forces her to have relations with a "fifty-year-old money bag that you wanted something out of . . . and then another, another" (p. 68), and she is finally "castrated" of her symbolic significance altogether: "George Scudder's knife . . . cut the youth out of my body" (p. 71). Although she retains a mythical beauty, her appearance masks a "dry, cold, empty" spirit (p. 71): "The embalmers must have done a good job on me" (p.67). The point is made: "heaven" exists no more, the possibility of a return to youthful innocence and love is dead, and the nascent Venus is destined to become the ironic Aphrodite embodied by the Princess: "an old childless woman" (p. 71).

Significantly, then, there is "no answer" when Chance repeatedly tries to make contact with Heavenly by phone; and there is no epiphany, no reunion between "heaven" and earth. There is instead, in Act II, Scene ii, only a brief, distant, silent confrontation between Heavenly and Chance just before she is to appear at her father's rally in the beguiling guise of a virgin, symbol of white Southern chastity, an act misinterpreted by Chance as Heavenly's alignment with the racist, hypocritical stance of her father: "Chance has seen that Heavenly is going to go on the platform with her father. . . . He stands there stunned" (p. 99). The "Gulf of misunderstanding" which previously described the lack of relationship between Chance and the Princess now opens up between him and Heavenly. Their meeting is more nearly divorce. Significantly, this scene in which Chance feels defeated and betrayed takes place while he stands "on the steps leading to the Palm Garden" (p. 99), one of those "places of exile from whatever we loved" (p. 103), here become Chance's demythicized Garden of Gethsemane as well as a "garden of Adonis," symbol of the transience of youth and beauty, where grow only ephemeral plants that quickly wither and die.[30]

Heavenly's donning "the stainless white of a virgin" (p. 72), however, is not blatant hypocrisy but a martyr's act of self-sacrifice. She agrees to the masquerade in an attempt to save Chance, whose life her father had threatened after her initial refusal to participate in his politically expedient rally: "How do you want him to leave, in that white Cadillac . . . or in the scow that totes the garbage?" (p. 72). Although Heavenly's gesture is futile, by thus sacrificing her integrity for the possibility of Chance's salvation, she partially redeems her mythic stature, emerging finally as an image of martyred innocence, fallen angel, and secular saint.

Boss Finley, evil antithesis to Heavenly's goodness, represents the anti-Christ of this spiritual wasteland, the sacred archetype of communion become cannibal—the "flesh-hungry, bloodthirsty ogre" at the top of the beanstalk (p. 98)—and an embodiment of the corruption of power. Political tyrant, Boss Finley perpetrates acts of racism, sadism, and murder in the guise of God's apostle: "When I was fifteen I came down barefooted out of the red clay hills . . . Because the Voice of God called me" (p. 106). Like Satan, his name is legion, and his characterization is thus appropriately derivative of other literary figures similarly corrupted by illusions of omnipotence. As political demagogue, Boss Finley resembles no other literary figure so closely as Willie Stark, Robert Penn Warren's ruthless political "Boss" in *All the King's Men*.[31] (Warren's character is modeled on Huey P. Long, former Governor of Louisiana, a state which is, like "St. Cloud," on the Gulf Coast.) Like Boss Finley, Willie professes to be just a "country boy" struck by "the powerful force of God's own lightning" to camouflage his corrupt acts.[32] Boss Finley's larger-than-life TV image also recalls both *1984*'s apotheosis of fascism, "Big Brother," and *The Great Gatsby*'s billboard-size close-up of T. J. Eckelberg's spectacled eyes, symbolizing the gigantic loss of moral vision in a world become a "valley of ashes," graced only by the faded image of a blind, indifferent God. In his delegation of Chance's murder to his son, Tom Jr., accompanied by his insistence that he remain ignorant of its gory details ("I don't want to know how, just go about it" [p. 59]), Boss Finley resembles Bolingbroke, Shakespeare's exemplar of moral confusion in *Richard II*, who similarly wants Richard dead, but attempts to evade responsibility for the delegated deed: "Though I did wish him dead, I hate the murtherer, love him murthered" (V. vi. 39-40). Finally, as an inverted image of Christ, Boss Finley grotesquely parodies His crucifixion and resurrection: "Last Friday, Good Friday, . . . a hideous straw-stuffed effigy of myself, Tom Finley, was hung and set fire to. . . . Today is Easter Sunday and I am in St. Cloud" (p. 108). Only evil is resurrected in this play. By his perversion of archetypes of divine justice and sacred salvation, Boss

Finley predictably makes "St. Cloud" infernal (p. 110), a hell of heaven.

Although Boss Finley is cast in the role of evil incarnate, he is, at one point, intended to arouse our sympathy for what he once was or might have been. In Act II, Scene i, as he gazes at Heavenly, he is inspired by her beauty and her resemblance to his deceased wife to feel an emotion approaching awe, which momentarily elevates his moral stature: "In her father, a sudden dignity is revived. . . . he becomes almost stately. He approaches her . . . like an aged courtier [who] comes deferentially up to a crown princess or infanta" (pp. 66-67). This lapse in his corrupt image is only temporary, however, resembling the similar abeyance of evil in Milton's Satan as he gazes at Eve just before causing her fall:

> . . . her heavenly form
> Angelic, but more soft and feminine,
> Her graceful innocence, her every air
> Of gesture or least action overawed
> His malice. . . .
> That space the Evil One abstracted stood
> From his own evil. (Paradise Lost IX. 457-64)

Boss Finley, then, is depicted not only as castrator but, like the other characters in the play, as "castrated" also--a diminished and defiled version of Christian deity and romantic gallantry. As a sexual parallel to his castrated mythic image, he is accused by his mistress, Miss Lucy, of "being too old to cut the mustard" (p. 65). Like Chance and the Princess, Boss Finley is a victim of Time; his youthful sexual powers gone, he is an impotent version of once-sacred omnipotence.

V. Chance and Heavenly: a Modern Abelard and Heloise

The tragic romance of Abelard and Heloise, the immortalized twelfth-century lovers, is also evoked by the story and characterizations of Chance and Heavenly, their twentieth-century counterparts.[33] In broad outline, the story of Abelard and Heloise tells of the illicit romance between the dashing, handsome scholar-teacher and his beautiful young pupil whom he seduces when she is only a virginal adolescent, causing to blossom in both of them such an ecstasy of passionate love that they regard it as transcending sin and lust. Their sexual pleasures are brought to an abrupt end, however, when Abelard is castrated by Heloise's uncle and surrogate-father, the Canon Fulbert of Notre Dame. The two are thus forever separated from the fulfillment of their grand passion, Heloise entering a convent, Abelard a monastery, where they remain until death.[34] The major parallel between the two love stories, of course, lies in the similar fate of Chance and Abelard: castration. Not only is the history's major catastrophe paralleled in the play, but particular attributes of the principal characters and significant details of their story are made analogous also.

The historical Heloise is said to have been "orphaned at an early age";[35] Heavenly has similarly lost her mother. Consequently, both are left to the charge of male guardians: Heloise to her uncle, Fulbert; Heavenly to her father, Boss Finley. As Bernard DuKore points out in his essay on affinities between the two love stories, an obvious parallel between the characters is "the initial-letter resemblances between Fulbert and Finley, and Heloise and Heavenly."[36] Less obvious, perhaps, is the similarity between the etymologies of the two girls' names. According to Abelard, Heloise's name, like Heavenly's, has divine echoes: "God has specially marked you out for heaven by calling you Heloise, derived from his own name of Elohim."[37] Significant also is the fact that Heavenly's mother is Roman Catholic (p.71), the faith of the medieval lovers. Like Heloise, Heavenly at fifteen (p. 50) gives herself to the grand love of her life when she is still a virginal adolescent; and like Heloise after she is deprived of her lover, Heavenly announces her intention to enter a convent, "If they'll let me, accept me" (p. 71). In the play's original version, Heavenly further demonstrates a nun-like piety by offering a prayer for spiritual purity to the Virgin: "Oh, Lady, wrap me in your starry blue robe. Make my heart your perpetual novena. . . . "[38] The historical Heloise kept alive to her death the flame of her passion for Abelard, even while clothed in a nun's habit; as an inverted parallel, Heavenly hypocritically dons "the stainless white of a virgin" but does so only to demonstrate the magnitude of her love for Chance.

Abelard and Chance also share more than a similar tragic fate. According to Heloise, Abelard was, like Chance, the handsome, charming heart-throb of "countless women."[39] As Bernard DuKore points out, Abelard candidly acknowledges his sexual conquests "in a manner suggestive of Williams' hero," boasting that at the time he met Heloise, he "enjoyed such renown and was so outstanding for my charm of youth that I feared no repulse by any woman whom I should deign to favor with my love."[40] Indeed, Abelard's irresistible attractiveness to women seems to have engendered what in the play Chance calls "Sex-envy" (p. 90). Recalling Abelard's romantic appeal, Heloise writes:

> "Your poems and love songs. . . set women's hearts yearning for you, and those verses, mostly celebrating our love, soon spread my name through many lands and sharpened the jealousy of countless women. . . . What queen, what princess did not envy both my joys and my bed?"[41]

Ultimately, both Abelard and Chance suffer the revenge of sex-envy: castration.

Significantly, even the cast of characters assigned to perform the grisly deed are similar. As the incident is recounted by Marjorie Worthington in *The Immortal Lovers*, it was Heloise's uncle-guardian "Fulbert, some of his kinsmen, and a Spanish doctor" who entered Abelard's room, overpowered him as he slept, and castrated him.[42] Correspondingly, in the play, it is Heavenly's guardian (in this case, her father) who orders the mutilation, her brother and his friends who are to carry it out, and, at least in the play's original version, the corrupt doctor, George Scudder, who is to assist in the "operation" and attend to its aftermath.[43]

Ultimately, however, Heavenly and Chance are depicted as debased versions of Heloise and Abelard, the love story of their prototypes diminished by time, history, and circumstance. Unlike Heloise, who remained physically faithful to her first and only lover, Heavenly is sullied by her forced relationships with other men, the political cronies of her father. Whereas Heloise, before Abelard's castration, married and bore him a son, Heavenly is denied marriage "for love" (p. 69) and is rendered forever sterile and childless after a hysterectomy. Finally, although both women make supreme sacrifices for their lovers, Heavenly's is made corrupt by its mendacity and ignominious purpose. While Heloise demonstrates her everlasting fidelity to Abelard after his mutilation by entering a convent in the prime of her youth, Heavenly is denied her similar desire to enter a convent and must yield instead to her father's corrupt political ambitions: "This state is a Protestant region and a daughter in a convent would politically ruin me" (p. 71). She is led to believe that in order to save Chance's life she must appear at her father's political rally wearing "the stainless white of a virgin" as an exemplum of White Southern Womanhood's innate purity, the ideal itself a racist fiction. Heavenly's "collapse" (p. 109) at that rally is but a dynamic symbol of the corresponding collapse of the ideals of purity, fidelity, and transcendent love in the corrupt secular world.

Similarly, Chance Wayne ultimately represents Abelard's antithesis, primarily by virtue of their contrasting responses to a mutual fate. Abelard responds to his castration by humbly submitting to divine will. After the deed is done, Abelard accepts his most "cruel and shameful" punishment as just retribution for his sexual excesses: "By how just a judgment of God was I stricken in that portion of my body wherein I had sinned."[44] He fervently embraces the monastic life, grateful for that dismemberment (a literal *coup de grace*) which led to his religious conversion and a lifetime of devotion to God. The play suggests that Chance's castration may be similarly considered just retribution for his despoiling of Heavenly. However, in the secular world of *Sweet Bird of Youth*, Chance Wayne regards his impending castration not as submission to God's will but to Time's scythe, which inevitably cuts down all those material and sensual means by which modern man attempts to counter the spiritual emptiness of his world. Both renounce the physical life, but to Chance, Time is an executioner, not a redeemer.

VI. Demythicization: "The enemy, time, in us all"

In *Sweet Bird of Youth*, the demythicization of each character is dramatically presented in terms of his or her castration, literal or symbolic. Youth, beauty, and ideal love are here the objective correlatives of that "original state of unconscious wholeness and perfection" which, according to Jungian psychology, is experienced by the infantile ego, and whose mythical analogues include Paradise, the Golden Age, and childhood itself; thus, in a very real psychological sense, "Heaven lies about us in our infancy."[45] The inevitable loss or "castration" of these qualities by the scythe of Time reduces both the individual and his mythicized world to diminished, defiled, and demythicized versions of once-perfect archetypes and ideals. In *Sweet Bird*, then, castration is the symbolic act which divests the characters of their inflated infantile egos, deflates their mythicized images, and exiles them from the "heaven" of youthful illusions.

The difference between the responses of Chance and the

Princess to the divestment of their illusions results in a tragi-comic ending. The Princess, despite having fully recognized the castrating effect of Time on her youthful beauty and talent, opts to confront the fallen world of existential reality and "to go on" (p. 124). By contrast, Chance chooses to stay with full knowledge of the tragic fate that awaits him. The apparent nobility or courage of Chance's decision to submit to the violence of literal castration, however, is undermined by its multiplicity of motives.

On the one hand, it may be construed that the guilt of having irreparably defiled Heavenly, of causing her sterilization, and of destroying his dream of reclaiming her moves Chance to submit to the similar violation of castration. His decision then may be interpreted as a gesture of sacrificial atonement which renders him, like her, "a dead, dried-up vine" (p. 71): in its intent a morally redemptive act. Williams himself has elsewhere defined atonement as "the surrender of self to violent treatment by others with the idea of thereby clearing one's self of his guilt,"[46] a way of gaining integrity, or at-onement. Thus, as interpreted by Peter L. Hays, "Chance's self-sacrifice takes the form of that of the 'novices' of Adonis, but for the same reasons as Christ's: to atone."[47] Viewed in this light, Chance's decision to stay elevates him at the end of the play to moral if not mythic stature; his voluntary submission to castration equals the resurrection of his own moral integrity. According to Hays, by refusing to flee with the Princess, Chance is showing greater strength and determination than ever before. Although Chance does not achieve the springtime renewal of an Adonis, he is credited by Hays with achieving "a very personal and psychological resurrection, at-onement only with himself (and perhaps with the audience, too), as he ironically gains in manliness at the moment he faces the loss of his manhood."[48]

Chance himself lends some credence to this interpretation. There is little question that Chance is obsessed with his return to and reclamation of Heavenly throughout the play (although whether his quest is for her substance or her image is a question to be treated subsequently). Furthermore, upon learning that Heavenly is to appear at the rally with her exploitative father, Chance claims that if she were to be so hopelessly lost to him, he would prefer suicide to life: "If I believed it . . . I'd dive off municipal pier and . . . keep on swimming till sharks and barracuda took me for live bait" (p. 90). Finally, after he realizes that Heavenly is truly lost to him, he implies that his decision to stay is an attempt to invest in his death that meaning lacking in his life:

"Something's got to mean something, don't it. . . . I mean like your life means nothing, except that you never could make it, always almost, never quite? Well, something's still got to mean something" (p. 121). Atonement for Heavenly's defilement would, indeed, "mean something."

Williams never makes clear, however, that atonement is, in fact, Chance's motive in submitting to death and dismemberment. Not once does Chance expressly assume responsibility for his part in the defilement of Heavenly, seemingly a prerequisite to atonement for that act. Instead, upon learning of his infecting her with venereal disease, he gives only tacit admission to his own responsibility: "I left town before I found out I--[was infected myself]" (p. 102), at least thereby clearing up the ambiguity about his guilt or innocence caused earlier in the play by Aunt Nonnie's claim that "Heavenly says it wasn't Chance that--she says it wasn't Chance" (p. 62). Furthermore, Chance lamely excuses his failure to inform Heavenly of the disease by a second attempt to evade, or rather transfer to her, his responsibility: "I thought if something was wrong she'd write me or call me--" (p. 103). Finally, although Chance makes vague references to the need for instilling meaning into his dying, he does not mention Heavenly at all after voicing his decision to stay (pp. 121ff).

What *is* made explicit in the final act of the play is Chance's inability to survive the inevitable consequences of Time: its "castrating" effect on youth, beauty, and romantic dreams. It is as symbol of those qualities that Heavenly had value for Chance, not as substance; and it is the loss of those qualities in himself more than in her that Chance laments. Consequently, Time is cast as the chief antagonist to Chance's quest, not Boss Finley. Heavenly and her father are thus relegated to dramatic superfluity in the final act of the play, seen in retrospect as melodramatic ploys to the platitudinous metaphysic which usurps their dramatic function.

In the final act of the play, then, Chance reveals that his decision to stay is based on the simple fact that he would rather die than live without "youth." His physical castration is but the dramatic enactment of a loss already incurred. Thus, to the Princess' warning that staying would result in castration, Chance replies: "That can't be done to me twice. You did that to me this morning, here on this bed" (p. 120), where he played the role of paid, aging stud, forecast as his destiny. His decision to stay, then, is based on his belief that "Whatever happens to me's already happened" (p. 121)--the loss of his youthful dreams and powers. Chance confirms that it is the loss of his youth that determines his decision to submit to castration after the Princess tells him candidly that his youth was all he had, "and you've had it" (p. 119), a sentiment that Chance subsequently echoes: "I couldn't go past my youth, but I've gone past it" (p. 122). He thus partici- pates in his own demythicization, not by admitting his inherent flaws, but by depicting himself as the anti-heroic victim of Time: "Time--who could beat it, who could defeat it ever? Maybe some saints and heroes, but not Chance Wayne" (p. 123). His final appeal to the audience extends his individual dramatic situation to platitudinous universality: "I don't ask for your pity, but just for your understanding--not even that--no. Just for your recogni- tion of me in you, and the enemy, time, in us all" (p. 124).[49]

Chance Wayne, the modern degenerate of Abelard, Adonis, Christ, Arthurian romance-knight, and fairy-tale hero Jack, is perhaps the most diminished of Williams' mythic analogues--deflated by time, history, and, ultimately, by his own shallow self-concern. His is not the tragic protagonist's recognition of his moral weaknesses or flaws of character, but the pathetic appeal of an "innocent" victim of the inevitable process of aging. The play ends, then, "Not with a bang but a whimper"--the whine of one of Williams' most "hollow men."

CHAPTER EIGHT

THE NIGHT OF THE IGUANA

> Who wouldn't like to suffer and atone for
> the sins of himself and the world if it
> could be done in a hammock with ropes
> instead of nails, on a hill that's so much
> lovelier than Golgotha, the Place of the
> Skull.

I. A "Secular Scripture"[1]

The Night of the Iguana (1961) signals an important shift of
emphasis in the dramatic structure of those plays controlled by the
"demonic" memory of their protagonists. For the first time in
those plays structured by a demonic memory-story--the protagonist's
recollection of a past transgression which he is doomed to repeat
in the play's dramatic present--the seemingly inevitable tragic
consequences of reenactment are transcended. The stories of a
corrupt past are told; they are compulsively reenacted; however, at
the moment of his deepest despair, the Reverend T. Lawrence Shannon
is, as if miraculously, released from his bondage to the past and
its crucifying conflicts, due solely to his "providential" (IV,
280) encounter with Hannah Jelkes, a secular "saint" (p. 266),
whose intervention proves to be the existential equivalent of an
act of divine grace. Furthermore, although Shannon experiences a
fall from an ironically elevated self-image, he neither withdraws
into insanity because of it nor suffers violent retribution for his
past crimes or inherent corruption. Instead, he survives and is
reformed, if not transformed, by the ministrations of Hannah, who
also represents a new departure in Williams' characterization; for
she is elevated to heroic stature and remains undefiled--a model of
limitless compassion, selfless devotion, and stoical courage in the
face of the world's suffering and her own loneliness and despair.
Thus, although Shannon represents the archetypal figure of the
guilt-haunted wanderer in flight from his own and the world's
corruption at the play's beginning, he emerges the existential
savior at its end. *The Night of the Iguana*, then, moves from a
Freudian case study of sexual neurosis and spiritual malaise
through a psychological "dark night of the soul," in which are
embedded an ironic "Passion Play performance" (p. 345) and a parody

of a saint's martyrdom, to conclude as the existential analogue of a medieval miracle play, complete with the protagonist's resurrection, a redemptive "act of grace" (p. 373), and a tableau of the Pieta.[2]

Largely as a result of the protagonist's liberation from a psychological hell, a demonic past, and the closed circle of reenactment, much of the play's movement appears to correspond to what Northrop Frye calls the "ascent theme" of romance: a movement from the demonic night world, where the imprisoned self experiences increasing "isolation and immobility" and where "much of what goes on . . . is cruelty and horror," to a higher world, the chief conceptions of which are "escape . . . discovery of one's real identity, growing freedom, and the breaking of enchantment" (or, in this case, enchainment), in preparation for the ascent to an idyllic world of romance or the attainment of divine epiphany at the end of the spiritual quest.[3]

The play's resemblance to the transcendent events of Christian myth, traditional romance, and the spiritual quest is, however, ultimately qualified; for the "miracle" of Shannon's psychic rebirth is tempered by the intractable nature of the reality into which he is reborn. Released from his bondage to the past, the play's protagonist discovers himself "stuck" (p. 365) in an inherently unredemptive present--marked by an absent or "oblivious" (p. 305) transcendent deity, by the existential isolation and metaphysical loneliness of its suffering inhabitants, and by an irreconcilable dichotomy between flesh and spirit. The cycle of romance, then, ends not in Shannon's ascent to a higher world, but in his acceptance of a thoroughly fallen one. His mythic rebirth results not in the fairy-tale metamorphosis of the frog revealed as prince, but in its ironic inversion: a self-proclaimed "gentleman born and bred" (p. 334) who comes to accept his subterranean animal nature and who, in so doing, makes the more complex transformation from childish "self-indulgence" (p. 345) to the maturity of compromise and concern for another. Accordingly, his dark night concludes not in "the upward journey of a creature returning to its creator," but with the protagonist's instruction in a "secular scripture," which, according to Frye, "tells us that we are the creators"[4] who, the play adds, must needs "play God" (p. 370) to each other.[5] In the protagonist's recognition that each must be "God" to the other, however, lies the redemptive message of the play and its ironic ascent theme.

Freed from his past obsessions and accepting of his fallen nature, Shannon is able to join with another in a union which, although thoroughly corrupt in its arrangement, nevertheless represents an act of self-transcendence. Thus, at the end of his "dark night of the soul," Shannon descends a naturalistic version of St. John's mystic ladder of divine union to embrace "the earth's obscene, corrupting love" (p. 371) in a darkly comic "marriage" to Maxine, thereby ameliorating to some degree the *angst* of "solitary confinement inside our own skins" (III, 3) which the play posits as the inescapable fact of human existence.[6] The protagonist remains in a naturalistic version of the night world, but his bondage has become a bond; he has learned "how to live beyond despair and still live," which, in Williams' own words, is the play's theme.[7] Despite Shannon's miraculous liberation from his past identity, then, not escape, but endurance is the theme of the play; not transcendent salvation, but the sharing of human suffering; not ascension to a higher world, but the acceptance and amelioration of this one.

II. Setting as Symbol

The play is set in a world that is thoroughly naturalistic, a primeval "rain forest" which is described in the stage directions as "among the world's wildest and loveliest" places (p. 253). Its jungle is a "home" (p. 373) to both the reptilian iguana and the "wild orchid" (p. 279); and the sea beyond its lovely "still-water morning beach" (p. 253) is infested with "sharks and barracudas" (p. 347), thus symbolizing both a "cradle of life" (p. 278) and a watery bier. The product of "oblivious" (p. 305) natural forces, its "steamy, hot, wet" tropical climate is subject to the natural cycle of "fast decay" (p. 369) and lush regeneration, as the name of the hotel, "Costa Verde" (Green Coast), implies. The dilapidated hotel is at once a sanctuary from the horrors and savagery of an ostensibly civilized world, engaged in this "summer of 1940" (p. 253) in yet another barbaric war, and a gathering place for its victims and victimizers: the "rapaciously lusty" (p. 255) Maxine Faulk, the hotel's proprietor, who opportunistically caters to a group of Nazis on holiday with as little moral discrimination as nature itself; the aggressive "Medeas" (p. 306)--Judith Fellowes and Charlotte Goodall--who invade the hotel in pursuit of Shannon, the play's transgressor in flight from the world's corruption and his own; and, finally, one who is testimony to the victory of the human will over naturalism altogether, the humane "saint" (p. 266),

Hannah Jelkes, accompanied by her "ninety-seven-year young" grand-father, Nonno.

Beneath the play's naturalistic detail, however, is the arche-typal geography of the pilgrim's spiritual quest: having wandered through the "underworlds" of "God's world" (p. 338), Shannon makes the climb up the mountain or "jungle-covered hilltop" (p. 253)--traditional locus of epiphany--seeking "something outside and be-yond himself" (p. 326). In this case, however, the Christian epiphany is rendered ironic: on the mountaintop Shannon confronts only the naturalistic deity of "Lightning and Thunder" (p. 305), whose comparison to "a giant white bird attacking the hilltop of the Costa Verde" (p. 325) recalls Sebastian Venable's image of a demonic God reflected in the flesh-eating birds in *Suddenly Last Summer*.[8] Unlike Sebastian, Shannon ultimately finds salvation rather than damnation here; but only by descending from his ele-vated position in acceptance of the world's fallen nature, as well as his own, is he led in the play's final scene beside the lovely "still-water beach" in a thoroughly secular version of the Twenty-Third Psalm.

The play's immediate stage set is no less ambiguous than its contextual world in its juxtaposition of demonic and redemptive imagery. As a microcosm of the existential universe, the structure of the Costa Verde hotel simultaneously reflects the inherent isolation of its inhabitants and offers the possibility of their communion, or, at least, communication. Along the back wall of the hotel are the doors to "a line of small cubicle bedrooms" (p. 253), each cubicle a concrete symbol of existential isolation: the separate, self-contained world of individual consciousness which Williams has elsewhere described as "the cell in solitary where each is confined for the duration of his life" (III, 3). Directly in front of those "cells," however, serving as the stage, is the hotel's wide verandah--the communal gathering-place for the play's lonely inhabitants--which offers the opportunity for "broken gates between people so they can reach each other, even if it's just for one night only" (p. 352). In the center of the verandah is a canvas hammock which becomes a dynamic symbol in the course of the play, changing significance as it reflects the protagonist's psychological development; representing, in turn, a womb-like sanc-tuary in which Shannon periodically regresses to "infantilism" (p. 343); a crucifying cross to which he is bound and from which he is resurrected; and, finally, an analyst's couch from which he rises, able to endure the *angst* of existential isolation. Beneath the

154

verandah for half the play is a captive iguana, symbol of all the play's representatives of suffering humankind trapped in a god-forsaken world which offers no hope of divine assistance or transcendent salvation. The iguana is identified especially with Shannon--the "minister of God" (p. 304)--who is tied to an animal or sexual nature which he can neither accept nor deny, and only in the release of which can he finally accept the fallen world as "home" (p. 373).

The archetypal model for the play's set is a naturalistic version of the three-tiered stage of the morality play: its "oblivious" deity emanating from the stormy heavens above, the captive iguana in its "hell" below, and the protagonist literally suspended in the hammock between, engaged in a struggle for psychic salvation. Accordingly, the play's two central female characters--Maxine Faulk and Hannah Jelkes--resemble the polarized morality figures of Vice and Virtue, or, as Nancy Tischler suggests, psychologized extensions of Shannon's own nature: "his flesh and spirit, bad and good angels, id and superego."[9] They resemble as well "the doubled heroine" of romance: the dark, sensual, often demonic seductress and her light, virginal spiritual counterpart.[10] Although the protagonist is indeed "saved" by the end of the play, in this modern *psychomachia* and ironic romance, it is Vice who wins-- not Shannon's soul, but his body. Ironically, the sensual victory of Vice (Maxine) is brought about by the spiritual aid and tacit approval of Virtue (Hannah), who, by miraculously liberating Shannon from his sexual anxieties and spiritual conflicts during one night's conversation, assumes the role of the play's *deus ex machina*. Thus, the conclusion of the traditional morality play is fulfilled by its ironic inversion: the protagonist saves his psyche (if not his soul) by accepting his shadow side, surrendering to Vice his body, and giving up altogether his spiritual pretensions, while Virtue, having contributed to his existential salvation, remains uncorrupted but alone. The "spinster's loss, widow's gain" (p. 364) with which the play ends creates an ambivalent mood; for, according to Frye, the device of the doubled heroine, which often concludes as it does here with "one girl . . . heading for the choice of one of her suitors and marriage to him, the other for virginity or devotion to a cause," produces simultaneously the antithetical moods of "allegro" and "penseroso"--"the two major cadences of romance."[11] In the fallen world, the play suggests, this duality is not to be resolved: spirit and flesh are not to be united; the divided self remains divided; and salvation depends on accepting and enduring the particular limitations of one's inherently incomplete nature.

III. The Stories and their Reenactment

The stories told by and about the Reverend T. Lawrence Shannon throughout all three acts of the play comprise his "psychological history" (p. 329): a history of recurrent "crack-ups" engendered by his sexual compulsions and spiritual conflicts. "At the end of [his] rope" (p. 271) when the play begins, Shannon, the stories reveal, is tied by a long umbilical cord to a childhood past dominated by a sexually-punitive "Mama and God" (p. 329) to whom he remains in thrall. The telling of the stories alternates with their reenactment in the play's recent past and dramatic present, forming a self-enclosed circle of repeated transgressions, subsequent guilt, and emotional collapse.

As the play opens, Shannon is in the midst of attempting to escape from his most recent reenactment of an event from his past which he recounts in full to Hannah Jelkes in Act II: his sexual seduction of an "innocent, underage" girl (p. 274). In flight from his transgression and on the verge of another crackup, the middle-aged "defrocked" (p. 275) minister, become the guide for Blake Tours, arrives with his bus-load of Baptist schoolteachers at the Costa Verde hotel, seeking rest and refuge in the hammock on the hotel's verandah--also a recurrent event, according to the hotel's proprietor, Maxine Faulk: "He cracks up like this so regular that you can set a calendar by it. Every eighteen months he does it, and twice . . . here" (p. 341).

Shannon's disclosure of his involvement with Miss Charlotte Goodall, a young girl "a month less'n seventeen" (p. 261), comes out in bits and pieces throughout the play's three acts, as Shannon attempts to justify his promiscuity as the need for "human contact" (p. 268); to defend himself against the charge of "statutory rape" (p. 267) made by Judith Fellowes, the "butch vocal teacher" (p. 261) outraged at Shannon's treatment of her "Charlie" (p. 298); and to extricate himself altogether from the affair in his callous rejection of Charlotte herself. Most significant to Shannon's characterization in all these exchanges is his repeated refusal to assume any responsiblity for his libidinous acts. Thus, to Maxine's gibe that Shannon "took the young chick and the old hens are squawking about it," (p. 261), Shannon tersely counters, "The kid asked for it" (p. 261). His definition of "statutory rape" casts *him* in the role of the injured party and passive victim: "That's when a man is seduced by a girl under twenty" (p. 267). To Miss Fellowes' charge that Shannon took Charlotte to "filthy" (p. 335), "ghastly" (p. 335) places off the scheduled tour, Shannon emphatically denies the role of initiator: "I showed her what she told me she wanted to see. . . . All that I did was offer my services to her when *she* told *me* she'd like to see things not listed in the brochure . . ." (p. 336). Even in his exchange with Charlotte herself, Shannon shifts the responsibility for his sexual indulgence to her, reminding her that "When I brought you home that night I told you good night in the hall, just kissed you on the cheek like the little girl that you are, but the instant I opened my door, you rushed into my room and I couldn't get you out of it . . ." (p. 297).

In Shannon's defense, it must be said that Charlotte's depiction in the play is hardly that of a shy virgin or shrinking violet. In Williams' stage directions, she is described as pursuing Shannon with the passionate tenacity of a "teen-age Medea" (p. 294), Jungian archetype of the seductive young witch or negative anima:[12] a description echoed in Shannon's own characterization of Charlotte and Miss Fellowes as "the teen-age Medea and the older Medea" (p. 306), respectively. Like Medea, among whose siren's charms was a "sweet magical song,"[13] Charlotte is depicted as a "musical prodigy" (p. 261) who attempts to ensnare Shannon by singing "I Love You Truly" (p. 262) at one of the tour's nightly recitals. According to Shannon, "Miss Bird-Girl opens her mouth and out flies, 'Larry, Larry, I love you, I love you truly!' That night, when I went to my room, I found that I had a roommate" (p. 262). The roommate is, according to Shannon, his "spook" (p. 262), the spectre of existential loneliness that drives him to such "human contact" as he has with Charlotte Goodall, however brief and loveless.[14] Like Medea, Charlotte offers "help" (p. 298) to her "Jason" and desperately begs him to "marry me" (p. 297). Like Jason, the seducer of young girls, Shannon reneges on a commitment to marital fidelity, confessing to Charlotte his inability to love and pointing out their mutual emotional instability: "The helpless can't help the helpless" (p. 298).

Whatever Charlotte's resemblance to the aggressive Medea, however, Shannon's self-portrayal as passive victim martyred to the voracious sexual appetite of an adolescent girl borders on the pathological, as does his treatment of Charlotte after their love-making. As recalled by Charlotte, "I remember that after making love to me, you hit me, Larry, you struck me in the face, and you twisted my arm to make me kneel on the floor and pray with you for forgiveness" (p. 298)--behavior which Shannon admits is recurrent and compulsive: "I do that always when . . . I don't have a dime left in my nervous emotional bank account" (p. 298). Sexual indulgence followed by shame, guilt, punishment, and the desire for absolution from a transcendent authority is the pattern of Shannon's neurosis. His integrity shattered, Shannon "cracks up," unable to reconcile his elevated image as "gentleman" (p. 275) and "a minister of God" (p. 304) with his biological drives and sexual outbursts, or his calling as shepherd with his compulsive behavior as wolf.

In Act II, Shannon tells Hannah Jelkes the story of which this incident is a reenactment: it is an almost identical tale of sexual indulgence with "a very young Sunday-school teacher" (p. 302), which took place only a year after Shannon had assumed his duties as "an ordained minister of the Church" (p. 275) and is partial cause for his subsequent dismissal, occasioned by his committing "Fornication and heresy . . . in the same week" (p. 302). That act of fornication was, apparently, Shannon's first, for he describes himself previous to that incident as one whose sexual impulses had been severely repressed: "the goddamnedest prig . . . even you could imagine" (p. 303). In this first incident, as in its reen-actment, Shannon claims the role of passive victim, himself seduced by the girl who had "asked to see me privately in my study" where "she declared herself to me--wildly" (p. 302). As with Charlotte Goodall, sex and religion, pleasure and punishment are intertwined. As Shannon recounts the incident (characteristically phrasing its climax in the syntax of the passive voice), "I said, let's kneel down together and pray and we did, we knelt down, but all of a sudden the kneeling position turned to a reclining position on the rug of my study and . . . When we got up? I struck her . . . and called her a damned little tramp" (p. 303). This incident leads to the girl's attempting suicide and Shannon's confrontation with the "accusing faces" (p. 303) of his congregation.

The second part of this story, also told to Hannah in Act II, serves to link Shannon's sexual aberrations with his spiritual conflicts. On that Sunday after his sexual transgression, Shannon, rather than humbling himself in contrition before his "smug, dis-approving" (p. 303) congregation, delivers an outraged polemic against their concept of God, charging that "All your Western theologies, the whole mythology of them, are based on the concept of God as a *senile delinquent* . . . a bad-tempered childish old, old, sick, peevish man" engaged in "blaming the world and brutally punishing all he created for his own faults in construction" (p. 303). Shannon's description of the God conceived by Western theology resembles a folklore version of the Old Testament God of Wrath--the often arbitrary moral authority of the Calvinists--whom Northrop Frye in his study of William Blake describes portrayed in Genesis as "a fussy, scolding, bad-tempered . . . deity who orders his disobedient children out of his garden after making clothes for them, who drowns the world in a fit of anger and repeoples it in a fit of remorse."[15] Indeed, a literary analogue of Shannon's Old Testament God is Blake's Old Nobodaddy--"Father of Jealousy" and sadistic tyrant--whom Frye describes as a primitive version of "the God of official Christianity" invented by state religion, who is also tyrannical and negligent at once: "This God is good and we are evil; yet, though he created us, he is somehow or other not responsible for our being evil, though he would consider it blasphemous either to assert that he is or to deny his omnipotence."[16] That Shannon becomes a guide for "*Blake*" Tours, dedicated to exposing the "underworlds . . . of God's world" (p. 338), is not, perhaps, without allusive import.

Expelled from the church, Shannon, as tour guide, begins his "demonic" quest, "collecting evidence" of his "personal idea of God, not as a senile delinquent" (p. 304), but as an "oblivious majesty" (p. 305)--an amoral force of nature, indifferent alike to the beauty of its creations and the suffering of its creatures: an immanence indiscriminately reflected in the "majestic apocalypse" (p. 305) of a blazing sunset, in convulsions of "Lightning and Thunder" (p. 305), in the mutilation of "stray dogs vivisected" (p. 305), and in the shocking plight of human beings reduced by hunger to foraging in a mound of excrement for "bits of undigested . . . food particles" (p. 369). That Shannon still yearns for belief in a transcendent father figure who is neither punitive nor oblivious, however, is apparent from his continued performance of rituals that have no meaning in a universe dominated by the naturalistic forces he calls "God" (p. 326). Thus, his prayers for forgiveness go unanswered; his repeated intention to "go back to the Church" (p. 323) remains unfulfilled; the letters he writes to his Old Bishop seeking reinstatement and making "a complete confession and complete capitulation" (p. 268) are never mailed; and the hands he extends under the rainfall "as if he were reaching for something outside and beyond himself" (p. 326) receive no baptismal blessing.

The conflict between faith and disbelief that still rages within Shannon is also dramatized by his struggle with his clerical collar. In Act II, just before he tells Hannah the story of his dismissal from the church, Shannon dons several pieces of his clerical garb in an attempt to convince his party of ladies that he is still a "*frocked*! --minister of the Church" (p. 300). However, as Hannah attempts to help him fasten his collar, the button pops off, and, in frustration and rage, Shannon "rips the collar off, crumples it and hurls it off the verandah" (p. 301), ironically "defrocking" himself.

IV. A Freudian Analysis

In Act III, both Shannon's sexual neurosis and related spiritual conflicts are traced to their mutual source by Maxine, who retells Shannon's own Freudian analysis of how his "problems first started" (p. 329), a history originally related by Shannon to Fred, Maxine's recently deceased husband. According to Maxine, Shannon had told Fred that his Mama used to put him to bed before he was ready to sleep, so he "practiced the little boy's vice" (p. 329). After spanking Shannon for masturbating, his mother told him that his sexual self-indulgence "made God mad as much as it did Mama" and that she had to punish him for it, "so God wouldn't punish you . . . harder." Because Shannon loved both God and Mama, he repressed his sexual drives, but "harbored a secret resentment" against them both: "And so you got back at God by preaching atheistical sermons and you got back at Mama by starting to lay young girls" (p. 329).

Freudian psychology validates Shannon's simplified analysis of his conflicts. According to Freud, such a "repetition compulsion" as that from which Shannon apparently suffers, which gives its victims "the impression of a pursuing fate, a daemonic trait in their destiny," is revealed through psychoanalysis to have its source in "infantile influences."[17] When the specific infantile influences may be traced to parental restraint of sexual pleasure, such repression of the child's "auto-eroticism" by "education and mental forces like shame, disgust, and morality" is internalized by the individual psyche as the superego or conscience.[18] Furthermore, for those in whom "the libido has never forsaken its infantile fixations," there is an outbreak of illness through "inhibition of development."[19] According to Freud, it is "the dread of castration" that persists as "fear of conscience" in "the conception . . . of an inexorable higher being who metes out punishment."[20] When the individual revolts against the internalized "censorial institution" in the desire to liberate himself from its influence, "his conscience then encounters him in a regressive form as a hostile influence from without."[21]

Although Shannon repeatedly denies "ever having preached an atheistical sermon" (p. 271), it is clear that his repudiation of the punitive God of Western theology is also an act of rebellion against the childhood authority who threatened him with "harder" punishment (i.e., castration) for his sexual pleasure, his inherent sexuality being that "fault" in his own "construction" for which his internalized parent continues "brutally punishing" (p. 304) him. In simplified Freudian terms, Shannon's rejection of that God as a "senile delinquent" can be explained as a symbolic enactment of the Oedipal ritual of "killing" his father in an attempt to free himself from sexual anxiety and guilt, but he is prevented from developing relationships with "normal grown-up women" (p. 264) by his identification of them with his Mama who "tied up" his sexual freedom: "All women, whether they face it or not, want to see a man in a tied-up situation" (p. 345). Glenn Embrey suggests that Shannon's subsequent conception of God as a force "oblivious" to humankind is an attempt to liberate himself from his fear of punishment for his sexual indulgences: "Sex becomes safe if he can deny his mother's idea of God, so he tries to collect evidence for this denial."[22]

However, Shannon's attempts to replace a punitive "Mama and God" with a naturalistic deity oblivious to his sexual sins proves unsuccessful. Instead, he remains in bondage to his parental moral authorities, internalized as his own superego. Thus, Shannon's refusal to assume responsibility for his sexual seduction of innocent young girls reveals the extent to which he still fears incurring the wrath of his childhood Mama/God. Indeed, in his physical punishment of his sexual partners, he assumes the role of his punitive parental figures; and his compulsion to pray after indulging in sex demonstrates his continued need for their forgiveness and absolution. That Shannon cannot bear a world abandoned by a judgmental God is indicated by his terror of the "spook"--the spectre of existential isolation and metaphysical loneliness. Thus, his rebellions against God are always followed by his letters of "confession and capitulation" and a resolve to "go back to the Church" (p. 323). Finally, in a futile attempt to gain forgiveness from an internalized Mama and absolution from an oblivious God,

Shannon periodically "cracks up," thereby retreating into neurosis, regressing to a state of infantile helplessness where he can no longer be held responsible for his acts of disobedience and rebellion. As Glenn Embrey suggests, Shannon, "in effect . . . wants to become a good boy again."[23]

V. A "Voluptuous Crucifixion"

Shannon's story of his childhood sexual trauma is both reenacted and infused with symbolic significance in Act III. Threatening to commit suicide, Shannon, caught and tied up in the hammock by Maxine as he was once restrained by his Mama in the crib, hysterically identifies his condition as "Regression to infantilism, ha, ha . . . The infantile protest . . . the infantile expression of rage at Mama and rage at God and rage at the goddam crib, and rage at everything" (p. 343). In the womb-like hammock on Maxine's verandah, then, Shannon reenacts his childhood role of the innocent victim martyred for his sexual sins and thereby gains some measure of absolution through an act of expiatory "self-abuse" or self-punishment. According to Freud, such a "flight" from "unsatisfying reality . . . [which] takes place over the path of regression, the return to earlier phases of the sexual life . . . is never without an individual gain in pleasure for the patient."[24] As Maxine suggests, Shannon's "suffering" is largely self-imposed and masochistic: "He's acting, acting. He likes it!" (p. 341).

As a psychic projection of Shannon's internalized Mama, the "rapaciously lusty" (p. 255) Maxine represents the negative aspect of the feminine archetype, the "Terrible Mother," perceived as "the womb of the earth become the devouring maw of the universe"[25] or, as Shannon calls her, "a sort of bright widow spider" (p. 317) who threatens to trap, ensnare, and "tie up" his sexuality. The masculinity of Maxine's first name reflects her dominating, aggressive nature, while her last, Faulk, is a pun on her sexual function.[26] According to Erich Neumann in *The Great Mother*, psychic depression causes the irruption of the archetype of the Terrible Mother, whose attraction is so great that the ego, "unable to withstand it, 'sinks' and is 'swallowed up.'"[27] Neumann adds that "a male immature in his development, who experiences himself only as male and phallic, perceives the feminine as a castrator, a murderer of the phallus"; and that "the individual who is no longer in the original and natural situation of childlike containment experiences the attitude of the Feminine as restricting and hostile."[28] Thus, to

162

The Night of the Iguana

Shannon, in the depths of a psychic depression, at an arrested stage in his psychosexual development, and yet struggling to escape from the womb of childhood traditions and taboos in which he remains captive, Maxine represents the Terrible Mother, who, in her negative function of "holding fast, fixating, and ensnaring," of "not releasing what aspires toward independence and freedom," is perceived as "dangerous and deadly."[29]

Shannon's "tied-up situation" (p. 345)--sexual, spiritual, and psychological--evokes his analogy to the phallic iguana which mirrors his condition beneath the verandah where it, too, is "caught," "tied up," and "at the end of his rope" (pp. 366-67). Like the iguana, "hitched" to a post and "trying to scramble away" (p. 356), Shannon's own animal or sexual nature strives to be free of the restraints imposed on it by his internalized Mama and God. The iguana's torment is reflected in Shannon's self-laceration as he attempts to remove the gold cross from around his neck with an "animal outcry" (p. 340) of rage and frustration. Like the iguana caught as a feast for Maxine, Shannon, too, is threatened by Maxine's "rapaciously lusty" appetite. Both the iguana and Shannon briefly escape from Maxine's grasp, but just as the iguana is captured again, so is Shannon retrieved and roped into the hammock, where, surrounded by the sadistic Germans, he is tormented "like an animal in a trap" (p. 343).

Whereas Shannon's sexual conflicts are reflected in the captive iguana, his psychological or spiritual conflicts evoke his analogy to an ironic Christ-figure or martyred saint. It is Hannah who identifies Shannon as a self-willed martyr and his masochistic crackups in the comfort of Maxine's hammock as a self-indulgent and "voluptuous" crucifixion:

> Who wouldn't like to suffer and atone for the sins of himself and the world if it could be done in a hammock with ropes instead of nails, on a hill that's so much lovelier than Golgotha, the Place of the Skull, Mr. Shannon? There's something almost voluptuous in the way that you twist and groan in that hammock--no nails, no blood, no death. Isn't that a comparatively comfortable, almost voluptuous kind of crucifixion to suffer for the guilt of the world, Mr. Shannon? (p. 344).

Significantly, Shannon's response to Hannah is a paraphrase of Christ's final words to his Father, "My God, my God, why hast thou forsaken me?" (Matt. 27.46), as he asks, "Why have you turned against me all of a sudden, when I need you the most?" (p. 344).

Not only Christ's crucifixion is imitated by Shannon, but his life and resurrection as well. Indeed, Shannon has enacted the role of an ironic Christ throughout the play.[30] Like Christ, Shannon denounces the concepts of established religion, excoriates its practitioners as philistines, and is expelled from the "temple" to continue a nomadic ministry in the world.[31] With messianic zeal, Shannon gives his "disciples" a "priceless chance to feel and be touched" (p. 338). Unlike Christ, however, Shannon leads his parties of ladies to the "underworlds . . . of God's world," collecting evidence not of a loving and merciful Father, but of a cruel and oblivious deity. As the demonic son of that "oblivious majesty," Shannon also refuses to assume responsibility for the suffering he inflicts on others, whether they be his sexual partners or the ladies he shepherds into "filthy," "ghastly" (p. 335) places where they consume bad food and pick up dysentery. Significantly, he is betrayed to the tour's authorities by Judith Fellowes: her first name suggests her role as a Judas[32] and combined with her last name reinforces her role as an ironic or traitorous disciple of Shannon's ministry. In response to the charges made against him, Shannon characteristically depicts himself as an innocent victim crucified by the world's cruelty and lack of compassion. To Jake Latta, who wrests the bus key from him and takes over his tour, Shannon plays the role of passive victim: "O.K., O.K., you've got the bus key. By force. I feel exonerated now of all responsibility" (p. 334).

In his subsequent scene in the hammock, the Rev. T. Lawrence Shannon not only enacts the "voluptuous" crucifixion of an ironic Christ but also parodies the martyrdom of his patron saint, St. Laurence.[33] According to legend, St. Laurence suffered the grisly martyrdom of being bound upon a gridiron with glowing coals under it and was slowly roasted to death.[34] However, according to St. Augustine, "the martyr felt not the torments of the persecutor . . . so passionate was his desire of possessing Christ."[35] Instead, St. Laurence, after he had been "roasted" for a long time, is said to have quipped to his executioner, "It is cooked enough, you may eat."[36] In the play, Shannon enacts a debased version of this auto-da-fé when a lighted cigarette falls into the hammock to which he is bound. Unlike the saint's blissful disregard of his torture, however, Shannon panics at the first sensation of physical discomfort. "Twisting and lunging about in the hammock," Shannon cries out in anti-heroic contrast to the saint, "It's under me, under me, burning. Untie me, for God's sake, will you--it's burning me through my pants! . . . Untie me, untieeeee meeeeee!" (p. 348).

Other parallels between the saint and his secular counterpart are equally disparaging of Shannon's failure to live up to the fortitude and piety of his namesake. As a deacon of the Church, St. Laurence was charged with the distribution of alms among the poor, whereas Shannon is accused of extorting money from Charlotte, of profiting from his sale of anti-dysentery pills to the tourist party, and of cheating them out of the advertised tour altogether, after they'd saved "all year" (p. 345) to take it. Finally, St. Laurence's grim witticism about being ready to "eat," which demonstrates the saint's sacrificial willingness to offer himself in Christian communion, both reflects Shannon's perception of himself as sacrificial victim to Maxine's "rapaciously lusty" sexual appetite and directly contrasts with his unwillingness to give himself up to it.

The demythicization of Shannon's inflated self-image as a messianic Christ-figure and martyred saint is accomplished by the compassionate but candid evaluation of Shannon by Hannah, and is dramatized by his existential "resurrection" from the hammock-- "Out! Free! Unassisted!" (p. 351)--a dynamic symbol of his psychological rebirth from "infantile regression" and release from his psychological bondage to his childhood past. Hannah exposes Shannon's imitation of the crucified Christ as masochistic and "self-indulgent" (p. 345); his suicidal plans as a fantasy by which he hopes to achieve another means of "painless atonement" (p. 347); his self-styled role of messianic tour guide, engaged in a demonic quest "through hell" (p. 345) to expose the brutal "truth about God" (p. 304), as a personal vendetta undertaken "for your own pleasure" (p. 345); and his cynical impersonation of a priest administering a last supper of "hemlock" (p. 346) to Nonno as "childishly cruel" (p. 346), the behavior of "a small, cruel boy" (p. 346). At the same time, Hannah's harsh criticism of Shannon is tempered by her recognition of his fundamental "decency and bit of goodness" (p. 347), her sympathetic understanding of his struggles to attain it, her admission that she "respects" him, and her gentle ministrations to help him through the night. By her therapeutic insights and sympathetic understanding, Hannah helps Shannon take the first steps from childish self-indulgence to compassionate maturity.

In Jungian terms, Shannon's symbolic enactment of the crucifixion signals a crisis in the process of individuation, his
initial sense of betrayal and abondonment representing "the limbo
of despair following the death of an old life orientation and
preceding the birth of a new one."[37] According to Jungian scholar
Edward Edinger, as a psychological experience "crucifixion is a
paralyzing suspension between opposites [for the ego]. It is
accepted reluctantly out of the inner necessity of individuation
(the wholeness-making process) which requires a full awareness of
the paradoxical nature of the psyche."[38] To experience crucifixion, then, is to consciously acknowledge and accept all the
opposing facets of one's whole nature--the sensual and the spiritual, the ego and the shadow (or negative aspects), the divine and
the demonic. If the ordeal of crucifixion is accepted, it leads to
"the birth of a more comprehensive personality," symbolized by the
resurrection.[39] According to Edinger, "It is the willing endurance
of the opposites within oneself, the acceptance of one's shadow,
rather than indulging in the cheap way out by projecting it onto
others, which brings transformation."[40] With Hannah as his psychotherapist, then, Shannon begins the difficult task of self-
acceptance, of acknowledging both the light and "the dark side[s]"
(p. 353) of his nature and of enduring the crucifying conflicts
they engender. Paradoxically, by so doing, Shannon divests himself
of his imitation of Christ and, in effect, picks up his own cross
or burden of individuality; according to Jung, "It is no easy
matter to live a life that is modelled on Christ's, but it is
unspeakably harder to live one's own life as truly as Christ lived
his."[41]

Ingrid Rogers suggests that the "bitter" (p. 350) poppy-seed
tea Hannah gives to Shannon to help him through the night parallels
the "bitter cup" of destiny given to Christ during his agony in the
Garden of Gethsemane.[42] In the scripture, Christ first attempts to
evade his destined death and prays, "O my Father, if it be possible, let this cup pass from me" (Matt. 26.39). Ultimately,
however, Christ embraces his fate: "Nevertheless, not as I will,
but as thou *wilt*." In broad parody of Christ's agony, Shannon,
while still confined in the hammock, initially resists his symbolic
death as self-indulgent child; he "gags and chokes" (p. 350) and
finally spits out the bitter tea. However, after his resurrection
from the hammock, he is able to accept life's "bitter cup" with the
help of Hannah, whose guidance and example make it "much more--
palatable" (p. 360).

VI. Hannah and Nonno: Spiritual Guides

A New England spinster who has devoted her entire life to the care and companionship of her grandfather--the "ninety-seven-years young" (p. 280) minor poet, Jonathan Coffin--Hannah Jelkes is described by Williams as looking like "a Gothic cathedral image of a medieval saint, but animated" (p. 266). Accordingly, she embodies the saintly attributes of selflessness, compassion, tolerance, asceticism, and a stoical fortitude in the face of adversity. Her saintliness, however, is thoroughly humanized; for it is not by prayer, faith, or any supernatural aid that she and her grandfather have endured, but by their own resourcefulness. Although her speech is sprinkled with scriptural allusions, their context makes clear that any redemption from the play's fallen world must be achieved by human, not divine, will. Thus, although Hannah describes their finding sanctuary at the Costa Verde hotel as "providential" (p. 280), it is her own strength and determination that propels them to the top of Maxine's mountain, and her own wiliness that allows them to stay when Maxine declares there is, in effect, no room at the inn. Similarly, Hannah simultaneously invokes and disclaims the role of miracle worker when she describes their only alternative to staying as heading "out to sea--and I doubt that we could make it divide before us " (p. 282). Her gentle advice to Shannon that he minister unto his congregation, not by exposing them to the brutal truths about a naturalistic universe but by "Lead[ing] them beside still waters because you know how badly they need the still waters" (p. 305), places the responsibility of the Good Shepherd firmly in human hands. In short, Hannah represents the human embodiment of that spiritual strength and goodness which Shannon had failed to find in a transcendent being.

In her redemptive role as Shannon's spiritual mentor who effects his psychological rebirth, Hannah evokes the Jungian archetype of the Good Mother: the "life-giving, 'kindly' aspect" of the unconscious whose functions are those of "bearing and releasing," growth and development.[43] Hannah's "totally feminine and yet androgynous-looking" features--"almost timeless" (p. 266)--combined with her wise counsel suggest the feminine archetype of Sophia (or, Philosophia), psychic symbol of spiritual transformation and the highest feminine wisdom: "a spiritual whole in which all heaviness and materiality are transcended" in "a wisdom of loving participation."[44] According to Mircea Eliade, androgyny is also "an archaic and universal formula for the expression of wholeness."

167

More than a state of sexual completeness, androgyny symbolizes "the perfection of a primordial, non-conditioned state," or "a general formula signifying *autonomy, strength, wholeness.*"[45] As an embodiment of archetypal wholeness, Hannah evokes other analogues of feminine spiritual wisdom: her chastity combined with her maternal warmth evokes the image of the Virgin Mother, Mary; her ministrations to Shannon cast her in the role of a Beatrice whose inspiration led Dante from his own inferno of despair to spiritual enlightenment; and her loving attentions to her grandfather suggest her analogy to a redeemed Cordelia fulfilling Lear's dream of their imagined life together. Significantly, Hannah's name in Hebrew means "grace" or "He [God] has favored me."[46]

Correspondingly, Nonno's first name, "Jonathan," means "Jehovah has given" or "the Lord's gift,"[47] and his initials, J. C., suggest his role as a spiritual guide or Christ-figure. "Nonno" itself is Italian for "grandfather." As Mary Constance Drake suggests, Nonno is "a kind of Tiresias [archetype of the blind seer] or Jungian 'wise old man' combined with the mad or 'inebriate' poet . . . [who] accepts and endures life with ancient wisdom."[48] According to Jung, the archetype of the wise old man, like the figure of Sophia, represents the spiritual factor in the psyche, which "always appears when the hero is in a hopeless and desperate situation from which only profound reflection or a lucky idea . . . can extricate him."[49] In addition, "the figure of the superior and helpful old man tempts one to connect him somehow or other with God . . . the Ancient of Days."[50] Like Tiresias, in whom the two sexes meet, Nonno--the "gentle man" (p. 319)--is also a symbol of androgyny or wholeness.

Thus, Nonno represents a positive human version of the narrowly-conceived deity whom Shannon rejects. Like the Old Testament God whom Shannon denounces, Nonno is also a "childish," "sick," "senile," "old, old man" (p. 303); unlike Shannon's concept of that Puritan God, however, Nonno remains a gallant, cheerful "gentleman," an irrepressible life-force even as he bears the knowledge of imminent and inevitable death in his very name (Coffin).[51] As a human incarnation of "God," Nonno offers Shannon a viable alternative to a punitive father figure and thus transforms his outrage to compassion, his acts of rebellion to those of charity. Just as Hannah teaches Shannon how to live, so Nonno teaches him how to die. Nonno's refusal to "go gentle into that good night" is suggested by his name's Italian pronunciation [non no], an explicit protest against death until the meaning he

168

has invested in life--his last poem--is finished.

The poem (pp. 371-72) which Nonno completes just before his death at the end of the play simultaneously evokes a Wordsworthian nostalgia for a paradisal world peopled by "beings of a golden kind" (l. 14) and recapitulates the fall from that ideal state, as imaged in "the plummeting to earth" of a branch of ripened fruit doomed to inevitable decay and "intercourse" with "earth's obscene, corrupting love" (l. 16). The poem evokes the degeneration of the mythic Golden Age as well as humankind's exile from a Biblical Eden and its consequent separation from God. Like Hannah, who endures the *angst* of existence in a fallen world "Without a cry, without a prayer/ With no betrayal of despair," Nonno, in the face of imminent death, asks for a similar "Courage" to dwell "in the frightened heart of me" (l. 24).

Together, Hannah and Nonno represent the spiritual parents of Shannon, whose own name, with the exception of the initial letter, is a combination of theirs,[52] and means in Irish "Grandson of little Seanach (old or wise)."[53] The orthographic interrelationship of their three names points up the lesson Hannah teaches Shannon: the mutual interdependence of each on the other as a means to ameliorate the existential and metaphysical isolation of suffering humankind in a naturalistic universe.

Significantly, Hannah and Nonno have a transforming effect on Shannon from their very first meeting. At his first sight of Hannah, Shannon, sobbing with rage and frustration, is instantly "pacified" (p. 266); and he immediately offers to help bring her grandfather up the hill, in direct contrast to his repeated refusal to aid his party of ladies in any way. Almost instinctively, Shannon defends Hannah and Nonno against Maxine's evaluation of them as "a pair of loonies" (p. 278) and mediates with Maxine to permit them to stay at the Costa Verde "for just one night" (p. 285). Uncharacteristically, he offers Hannah his own cubicle when he discovers she has been given one with a leaky roof, and he sustains the old man's illusion of his earning money from poetry-reading by tucking five dollars into his pocket. In Williams' own words, Nonno "touches something in him [Shannon] which is outside of his concern with himself" (p. 315). Indeed, the kindness, patience, tolerance, and "infinite gentleness" (p. 285) with which Shannon responds to Nonno represents such a transformation of Shannon's egocentric nature that Hannah at one point has cause to observe, "He [Nonno] thinks you're me, Mr. Shannon" (p. 313).

As his psychic alter-ego, Hannah does in fact share some of Shannon's qualities and experiences. Like Shannon, Hannah arrives at the Costa Verde at the end of her rope, financially bankrupt and emotionally "overdrawn" (p. 313) with concern and worry for her grandfather. Beneath her forced cheerfulness and stoical composure is the desperation of one who, like Shannon, has "got to bluff and keep bluffing even when hollering 'Help' is all you're up to" (p. 269). As the "quick sketch artist" (p. 284) who has had to live by her wits--ingratiating herself with strangers to whom she sells flattering portraits--Hannah is identified by Shannon as a "hustler . . . a fantastic cool hustler," to which characterization Hannah responds, "Yes, like *you*, Mr. Shannon" (p. 306). Hannah's "ethereal" (p. 266) appearance thus masks a tough realism, of which, like her financial situation, she is neither "proud" nor "ashamed" (p. 292) but accepts as a necessity for survival.

Like Shannon, Hannah is a world traveler who has journeyed not only to the underworlds of God's world but also to the subterranean depths of her self--the "dark," "unlighted," "shadowy" side of her nature (p. 353). She is qualified to help Shannon through his own dark night of the soul because she, too, has battled the "spook"-- the spectre of existential loneliness--which she calls her "blue devil" (p. 352). Finally, like Shannon, Hannah is representative of an existential human nature sentenced to "solitary confinement inside our own skins" (III, 3). Thus, Hannah's chastity--"a sort of fastidiousness, a reluctance, toward intimate physical contact" (p. 348)--is directly antithetical to Shannon's compulsive sexuality, making it "impractical" for them to "travel together" (p. 364). Like John Buchanan and Alma Winemiller in *Summer and Smoke* and *Eccentricities of a Nightingale*, Shannon and Hannah are embodiments of an inherent dichotomy between flesh and spirit. In that respect, they represent what Angus Fletcher calls "divided androgynes," the separated halves of an original union between body and soul which, "like the two sexually halved creatures in Aristophanes' myth of Eros," are continually seeking a reunion that, according to the theme of this play, is not to be consummated in this imperfect world.[54] Unlike Shannon, however, Hannah accepts the particular limitations of her ascetic nature: to Shannon's "touch," she responds simply, "It isn't for me" (p. 364). She has thereby achieved a measure of psychic integrity, transforming even her inadequacies into virtues by sublimating the need for "human contact" into the altruistic expressions of compassion, kindness, and understanding toward another. Just such a sharing of herself is what releases Shannon from his own "solitary confinement," making it possible for him to accept his inherently incomplete nature and to achieve, if only momentarily, the semblance of a reunion with his divided self.

The pivotal scene between Hannah and Shannon in Act III marks a distinct shift in the play's focus, mood, and direction. From noisy, violent activity, a mood of desperation, and a tragic direction, the play is suddenly transformed to a quiet, contemplative dialogue that "arrests time" in its Wordsworthian focus on the "philosophic mind," which finds "Strength in what remains behind." Significantly, the play's psychological focus also shifts from its Freudian emphasis on the sexual conflicts which derive from Shannon's personal unconscious to a broader concern with what Jung calls "the spiritual problem of modern man": the need for a shared religious mythos through which humankind's psychic yearning for wholeness is fulfilled.[55] In the symbolic roles of teacher, priest, and Jungian psychotherapist, Hannah seeks to restore just such religious values as "faith, hope, love and understanding" to Shannon as student, patient, and spiritual quester.[56] Thus, she identifies Shannon's problem as "the oldest one in the world--the need to believe in something or in someone--almost anyone--almost anything . . . something" (p. 352), and offers as her own belief a redemptive humanism: "Broken gates between people so they can reach each other, even if it's just for one night only" (p. 352). She tells him that she battles her own "blue devil" of existential *angst* through involvement in her "work" (p. 355), in others, and, finally, by enduring, "just by . . . enduring" (p. 353). By looking "out of myself, not in" (p. 355), Hannah discovers in Shanghai a semblance of God in the faces of "the old and penniless dying" (p. 355), whose eyes, "as clear as the stars in the Southern Cross" (p. 356), reflect a redemption from suffering in the prospect of death itself--a beatific vision of blessed peace.

Besides endurance, Hannah counsels tolerance and acceptance. In response to Shannon's question about the nature of her love life, Hannah relates two stories which comprise her only "love experiences" (p. 363): the first at age sixteen when in a Nantucket movie theatre "a young man sat down beside me and pushed his knee against mine" (p. 361), and the last in Singapore when a lonely Australian ladies' underwear salesman achieved sexual "satisfaction" (p. 362) with a piece of her clothing. To Shannon's incredulity that she would call these "dirty little episodes" love-experiences, Hannah replies, "Nothing human disgusts me,

171

Mr. Shannon, unless it's unkind, violent" (pp. 363-64). To the Singapore story, Hannah adds that its moral is "Oriental": "Accept whatever situation you cannot improve" (p. 363).

Not only the "moral" of these particular stories but Hannah's entire philosophy approaches the teachings of Eastern or Oriental religions. Referred to by Shannon as "Miss Thin-Standing-Up-Female-Buddha" (p. 347), Hannah, dressed in a Japanese Kabuki robe, practices the Zen art of deep breathing when she begins to panic, and she ceremoniously makes poppy-seed tea, a mild sedative, to help Shannon through the night. According to Alan Watts, "the quietening, clarifying, and slightly bitter taste" of tea is used by Buddhist monks as "a stimulant for meditation" and by secular Japanese as "a frank escape from the turmoil of the world," while the Zen technique of deep breathing affords another way of "letting go."[57] The substance of Hannah's teachings evokes the Sanskrit words from the Upanishad which end Eliot's *The Waste Land*: "Give, sympathize, control," keys to ameliorate the existential isolation of "each in his prison" (1. 414). Finally, Hannah's compassion not only for human suffering but also for the "pain and panic" (p. 370) of the tied-up iguana suggests an Eastern understanding of the interrelatedness of all forms of life. Her saintly virtues are Buddhist virtues as well: tolerance, compassion, serenity, self-lessness, asceticism, and an all-encompassing love.[58] She resembles, then, not only the Western archetype of feminine spiritual wisdom, Sophia, but also her Eastern counterparts: the Chinese deity Kwan-Yin, the goddess who "'hears the cry of the world' and sacrifices her Buddhahood for the sake of the suffering world," and the Hindu goddess Tara, symbol of spiritual transformation, who "leads out beyond the darkness of bondage, [as] the primordial force of self-mastery and redemption."[59] In her philosophy of acceptance, endurance, charity, and self-reliance, Hannah echoes the central idea of the Buddha: "'Work out your own salvation with diligence.' How? It is immaterial."[60] By her Oriental teachings, then, Hannah releases Shannon from conflicts engendered by the taboos and traditions of Western culture and guides him to a self-acceptance that is also self-transcendence. The hands that Shannon had stretched out under the "oblivious" rainfall as if he were "reaching for something outside and beyond himself" (p. 326) are finally grasped by Hannah, as the two of them, on the verandah outside their separate cubicles of self-confinement, temporarily assuage their mutual loneliness and fears in a secular ritual of communion: the redemptive humanism of "a little understanding exchanged between them, a wanting to help each other through nights

The Night of the Iguana

like this" (p. 352).

The play's Oriental allusions are not confined to Hannah, however. Significantly, Hannah's Oriental moral--"Accept whatever situation you cannot improve"--had been expressed previously in less elegant terms by Maxine, who offers Shannon the philosophy of "the Chinaman in the kitchen": "'No sweat' . . . All the Chinese philosophy in three words, 'Mei yoo guanchi'--which is Chinese for 'No sweat'" (p. 330). In fact, Shannon's own paraphrase of Hannah's Oriental "moral" seems closer in essence to Maxine's vulgarized version: "'When it's inevitable, lean back and enjoy it'--is that it?" (p. 363). Furthermore, both Hannah and Maxine counsel a philosophic attitude of compromise to Shannon. After Shannon is rejected by Hannah as her traveling companion and complains of "winding up with . . . the inconsolable widow [Maxine]" (p. 365), Hannah tells him, "We all wind up with something or someone, and if it's someone instead of just something, we're lucky, perhaps . . . unusually lucky" (p. 365). Earlier, Maxine had expressed to Shannon a similar view of the compensatory value of compromise: "We've both reached a point where we've got to settle for something that works for us in our lives--even if it isn't on the highest kind of level" (p. 329). Finally, the flagrantly sensual Maxine assumes an Oriental aura at the end of the play when she reappears to begin her relationship with Shannon: "It is apparent that the night's progress has mellowed her spirit: her face wears a faint smile which is suggestive of those cool, impersonal, all-comprehending smiles on the carved heads of Egyptian or Oriental deities" (p. 373). Maxine's look of serene satisfaction not only reflects, perhaps, the afterglow of the sexually sated (recalling the look of "narcotized tranquillity" associated with "the faces of Eastern idols" [I, 62] that Stella Kowalski wears after a night of lovemaking with Stanley in *Streetcar*), but it also suggests her affinity to Hannah as a guide to Shannon's survival, if not his salvation. That Maxine assumes Hannah's Oriental ambience, then, is not so incongruous as it appears, for Maxine has, throughout the play, attempted to help Shannon in her own "simple, sensuous" manner as much as has Hannah in her role of "guardian angel" (p. 327); but, as Hannah suggests to Shannon, "[you've] just been so much involved with a struggle in yourself that you haven't noticed when people have wanted to help you, the little they can" (p. 324).

Primarily because of the positive value invested in the Oriental attributes given Hannah, Glenn Embrey suggests that "the

173

play creates a definite contrast between East and West, in which the Eastern attitudes of stoicism and fatalism are offered as a positive alternative to the Western preoccupations with guilt and suffering."[61] Other Oriental allusions in the play, however, do not constitute a clear dichotomy between Eastern attitudes as positive and Western attitudes as negative; nor do they, at first sight, seem to form a coherent symbolic pattern. Thus, Shannon repeatedly threatens to "take the long swim to China" (p. 323), his metaphor for suicide in which the "Orient" represents escape and oblivion. Herr Fahrenkopf (Head-Driver or Leader), one of the Nazis who ostensibly represent "the cruelty and violence of the Western world" in direct contrast to the kindness and compassion of the "Oriental" Hannah,[62] is inexplicably depicted performing muscle-flexing exercises in poses much like "the preliminary stances of Japanese Suma wrestlers" (p. 295). Finally, although Nonno's "calm resignation before death" may be considered "Oriental,"[63] his last words echo those of the crucified Christ: "It is *finished*!" (p. 371).

The Oriental allusions throughout the play, then, do not so much constitute a clear dichotomy between East and West as they suggest a universality to human nature and the human condition that encompasses "Africa, Asia, Australia" (p. 338), includes German Nazis and Mexican beachboys, and can be found in the play's American citizens from New England, Texas, and Virginia. The wisdom of "China" may be found in the Gothic saintliness of a New England spinster who practices an Emersonian philosophy of self-reliance and self-transcendence as well as in the "affable" (p. 255) vulgarity of an equally self-reliant sensualist like Maxine. Conversely, the impulse to violence may be found in a Mexican kid "poking out [the] eyes [of iguanas] and burning their tails with matches" (p. 368) as well as in Nazi barbarism and the stylized martial art of Japanese wrestling. Incidents of sexual perversion engendered by "loneliness" (p. 363) take place in a Nantucket movie theatre as well as on a sampan in Singapore. Finally, the re-demptive vision of death reflected in "the old and penniless dying" of Shanghai (p. 355) is seen also in the eyes of the old and dying Nantucket poet, Nonno. Thus, Williams presents as universal both the light and "shadowy" sides (p. 354) of the human psyche and offers through Hannah a timeless corrective of love.[64]

174

VII. "A little act of grace"[65]

At the end of their "one night . . . communication" (p. 352),
Hannah asks Shannon to cut loose the iguana, one of "God's
creatures" (p. 373), symbolic of suffering humankind imprisoned in
a world marked by "faults in [its] construction" (p. 304) and
dominated by forces oblivious to its "pain and panic" (p. 370).
Shannon's freeing of the iguana signifies the liberation of his own
sympathies in his recognition of mutual fellow-suffering: "See?
The iguana? At the end of its rope? Trying to go on past the end
of its goddam rope? Like *you*! Like *me*! Like Grampa with his last
poem!" (pp. 367-68). It is also symbolic of his realization that
in a world abandoned by an all-loving, all-merciful deity, each
must be "God" to the other.[66] Thus, Shannon cuts loose the iguana
"because God won't do it and we are going to play God here" (p.
370). Just as Coleridge's Ancient Mariner found his own curse
lifted when he blessed the watersnakes in sympathetic recognition
of the interrelatedness of all life--"And from my neck so free/ The
Albatross fell off" (ll. 289-90)--so Shannon, by freeing the iguana
in a similar "act of grace" (p. 373), is released from his own
strangulating loneliness and despair.[67]

Shannon's release of the iguana signals also the release of
his own instinctual or animal nature. His subsequent acceptance of
the "simple, sensuous" (p. 308) Maxine whom he had previously
rejected represents as well the acceptance of his own sexual na-
ture--the "dark," "unlighted," "shadowy side" (p. 353) of his
psyche--for which he had formerly refused to accept responsibility.
Released from his infantile sexual fixations, Shannon is thus
able to "lay off the young ones and cultivate an interest in normal
grown-up women" (p. 264), to use his sexuality to engender "a
little understanding" rather than for "ravaging" (p. 369) innocence. Correspondingly, Maxine's "mellowed" appearance suggests
that she is no longer projected by Shannon as the devouring Terrible Mother, but is perceived simply as another lonely human being
who "needs somebody" (p. 374) to get through the existential night.
Her newly-acquired "Oriental" aura (p. 373) suggests that Maxine
will serve a purpose similar to Hannah's as Shannon's help-mate,
their relationship being one of mutual benefit and understanding,
"even if it isn't on the highest level" (p. 329).

Having internalized Hannah's altruistic philosophy of looking
"out of myself, not in" (p. 355), Shannon is liberated from his
"hell" of self-confinement, able to minister unto another.[68] The

sympathetic understanding exchanged between Hannah and Shannon, then, is reenacted in a vulgarized version between Shannon and Maxine. Shannon assumes the role of Fred, Maxine's deceased husband, who is characterized as having been so "patient and tolerant" (p. 270) of Maxine's promiscuity that his understanding made him "bigger than life-size" (p. 270); in effect, Shannon's similarly enlarged sympathies now make him eligible to "fill his [Fred's] shoes" (p. 268).

VIII. "The Way Down is the Way Up"

At the end of the play, Shannon is released from the recurrent reenactment of his sexual and spiritual conflicts, having learned that God's viable existence is to be found in human relationships and that salvation derives from ministering to each other (an existential philosophy that recalls Blake's "All deities reside in the human breast"). Thus, he gives to Hannah his "gold cross that I never want on me again" (p. 367), symbol of his final disavowal of his inflated role as messianic anti-Christ and his self-righteous posturing as "an ordained minister of the Church." In Jungian terms, Shannon may be said to have given up his imitation of Christ's life in order to assume the burdens and responsibilities of his own. Having accepted his own fallen nature, Shannon offers himself to Maxine's "rapaciously lusty" appetite in place of the iguana that "Mrs. Faulk wants to eat" (p. 368): an act of voluntary self-sacrifice which is also self-transcendence. Significantly, in the play's original Broadway production, Shannon reappears from the nether-regions beneath the verandah after having released the iguana, with its rope around his own neck[69]: a gesture which suggests a comic parody of marriage, with Shannon in the role of the proverbially reluctant suitor who is finally "caught" and "hitched" to the scheming female who pursues him.

The relationship between Shannon and Maxine is based finally on a business partnership--the mutual exploitation of their sexuality--proposed by Maxine: "I've got five more years, maybe ten, to make this place attractive to the male clientele. . . . And you can take care of the women that are with them" (p. 374). Businesslike also is Shannon's calculating attitude toward being "stuck here" (p. 365) with Maxine: "So I stay here, I reckon, and live off la patrona for the rest of my life. Well, she's old enough to predecease me. She could check out of here first" (p. 369). At the prospect of Maxine's proposal, however, Shannon "chuckles happily"

(p. 374) in ribald approval. Thus, at the end of Shannon's "dark night of the soul," he descends a naturalistic version of St. John's mystic ladder of love, upon which "to go down is to go up."[70] The literal descent of Shannon and Maxine down the hill to the "still water beach," with Maxine "half leading half supporting" (p. 374) Shannon, fulfills Hannah's image of the true minister who leads his congregation "beside still waters because you know how badly they need the still waters" (p. 305); the evocation of her biblical counsel thus lends a redemptive humanism to their whorish coupling as slut and stud. Similarly, St. John's paradoxical tenet for spiritual ascension--the way down is the way up--is turned by Maxine into a double entendre which is at once a sex joke and a marriage vow of emotional commitment: to Shannon's fear that "I can make it down the hill but not back up," Maxine responds with lusty confidence, "I'll get you back up the hill" (p. 374). By their vulgarization of Hannah's spiritual philosophy of acceptance, endurance, compromise, and compassion, Shannon and Maxine find mutual salvation in their embrace of "the earth's obscene, corrupting love" (p. 371): an existentially viable "intercourse" (p. 371) which is also a comic act of accommodation to a world "no longer gold" (p. 371). The significance of their relationship is best expressed, perhaps, in the Prologue to *Camino Real* by Williams' Don Quixote, who observes that in a world where "so many are lonely . . . it would be inexcusably selfish to be lonely alone" (II, 436).

For Shannon and Maxine, then, the play ends as a comedy, albeit a dark comedy; for their relationship has within it those elements of "the pragmatic," "the expedient," "the fleshly," "the cynical," and, ultimately, "success within the existent order" (rather than triumph over the existent order) which Robert Heilman has defined as characteristic of "black humour": "the acceptance (even the overacceptance) of the unacceptable."[71] Black comedy also implies collaboration with the world, "cooperation and collusion," and "submission as the groundwork for subsistence [and] survival"; thus, "we do what we have to do to get on, to get in, to make out, to go up . . . to keep from going under."[72]

No less ambiguous is the tragicomic mood evoked by the play's final depiction of Hannah and Nonno. Nonno's liberation from his "dying-out efforts to finish one last poem" (p. 370) coincides with Shannon's release of the iguana and extends that act's symbolic meaning, creating a mood of celebration. Although the completion of Nonno's poem also marks the completion of his life, Nonno's "It is finished!" (p. 371) is at once a cry of triumph and of Christ-like faith in death as redemption from a life which is implicitly compared to a crucifixion. Although death may be the only redemption from suffering in a fallen world, Nonno's last words are not nihilistic. Having finished what Hannah calls "your loveliest poem" (p. 373), Nonno drifts into his final sleep with the words, addressed to her, "Yes, thanks and praise . . . " (p. 373). Here, as throughout the play, the existence of "God" is left an "Incomplete sentence" (p. 305), to be fulfilled through acts of human goodness and love.

At Nonno's death, Hannah also experiences an ambivalent release, for she is left simultaneously unburdened and alone. Throughout the play, Hannah exemplifies the stoical attributes of the "orange branch" personified in her grandfather's poem, which "observe[s] the sky begin to blanch/ Without a cry, without a prayer/ With no betrayal of despair" (p. 371). In the play's final moments, however, she reveals the extent to which her nomadic life with her grandfather has exhausted her "emotional reserve" (p. 313); for her last words comprise just such a "prayer," a "cry," and a "betrayal of despair": "Oh, God, can't we stop now? Finally? Please let us. It's so quiet here, now" (p. 375). In an ironic reversal of Cordelia's death scene when Lear holds a mirror before her face and believes the illusion that "The feather stirs; she lives!" (l. 265), Hannah extends a hand before Nonno's mouth to see if he is breathing: "He isn't" (p. 375). For a moment, Hannah exemplifies the solitary figure of existential tragedy; alone, loveless, and bereft of all illusions, "she looks right and left for someone to call to. There's no one" (p. 375). The play ends, however, with the spiritually redemptive tableau of the Pieta: as Hannah "bends to press her head to the crown of Nonno's" (p. 375), she is elevated to the figure of the *Mater dolorosa*, archetype of maternal compassion for suffering humankind, and Nonno, to the secular analogue of her divine Son.

IX. Beyond Reenactment: Beyond Credibility?

More fully than in any other of his plays, Williams in *The Night of the Iguana* sets forth a philosophy of life rooted in self-transcendence which offers a way of coping with the modern sense of spiritual isolation and metaphysical loneliness occasioned by what J. Hillis Miller calls "the disappearance of God." Like Sartre's Orestes in *The Flies*, who defiantly asserts in the face of life's inherent meaninglessness that "Human life begins on the far side of despair," the characters in *Iguana*, in Williams' own words, "reach the point of utter despair and still go past it with courage."[73] Because of the play's emphasis on survival and endurance, it represents what its early critics called a "new departure"[74] from Williams' previous work, both in structure and sensibility: a "profound change"[75] from the violent and fatalistic conclusions of such plays as *A Streetcar Named Desire*, *Orpheus Descending*, and *Suddenly Last Summer*, wherein the protagonists, unable to escape, accept, or transcend the fallen world and its inherent corruption, are doomed to repeat their past transgressions and are ultimately destroyed by them.

In *The Night of the Iguana*, the structure of fatalistic reenactment is transcended; the protagonist's "repetition compulsion, broken. The pivotal scene which marks the release of the play's protagonist from the closed circle of recurrence is the exchange in Act III between Shannon and Hannah--their "one night . . . communication" outside their separate cubicles on the verandah of the Costa Verde hotel. At the beginning of that scene, Shannon undergoes the divestment of his elevated self-image as an apocalyptic messiah or demonic anti-Christ, reenacting in a psychological version the crucifixion of his inflated ego and his resurrection or psychic rebirth as anti-heroic, existential man who must learn how to live in a demythicized world without despair or self-deception. The remainder of that scene is devoted to just such instruction, delivered by Hannah Jelkes as she expounds a philosophy of life which counsels the acceptance of one's limitations, a stoical endurance in the face of inevitable suffering, and the exchange of "a little understanding" to assuage the inescapable afflictions of existential *angst* and metaphysical silence. At the end of this scene, and ostensibly as a result of Hannah's guidance, Shannon, unlike most of the protagonists previously examined, is liberated from his past concerns, conflicts, and compulsions--psychological, theological, and sexual--and accepts both his inherent limitations and metaphysical isolation. The transcendence of the fatalistic structure of reenactment thus results in the play's essentially affirmative ending.

At the same time, the protagonist's sudden release from the determinants of his past identity raises the question of his conversion's credibility, especially since there seems to be little continuity established between the concerns addressed by Hannah and the literal overnight transformation of Shannon from a guilt-ridden

179

sexual neurotic--his characterization developed throughout more than half the play--to the cavalier libertine freed of all sexual anxiety depicted at its end. As Glenn Embrey complains, "an hour's exposure to human compassion, a cup of poppy tea, and a bit of Oriental wisdom hardly seem sufficient to eradicate habits and attitudes hardened over the past ten years."[76] Particularly difficult to see is how anything the chaste, ascetic Hannah says or exemplifies leads to Shannon's new-found freedom from *sexual* guilt or cures him of his pedophilic compulsions, his release from both being logical prerequisites for his final acceptance of Maxine. Thus, Embrey finds it "incredible" that Shannon should "chuckle happily" at the prospect of his promiscuous partnership with Maxine, "this from a man who previously has been obsessively guilty about, disgusted by, and terrified of sex."[77] Embrey concludes that "the optimistic conclusion simply ignores the psychological portrait [of Shannon] Williams works out so carefully during the course of the play."[78] Similarly, Jacob H. Adler finds Shannon's easy capitulation to Maxine's salacious scheme "inconsistent with all that has gone before, unless it can be taken as . . . drunkenness," although Adler accepts the idea that Shannon's "return from masochism to normal acceptance of life" may be plausibly accounted for by "Hannah's kindness and the insight she helped him to attain" during their night's conversation.[79] Ironically, however, in his "Note of Explanation" to *Cat on a Hot Tin Roof*, Williams himself declared implausible such a sudden change of character as is evinced by Shannon. In explaining his objection to Elia Kazan's "happy ending" of the play's Broadway version in which Brick undergoes a psychic transformation after his talk with Big Daddy, Williams protested Brick's "apparent mutation" on the grounds that, "I don't believe that a conversation, however revelatory, ever effects so immediate a change in the heart or even the conduct of a person in Brick's state of spiritual disrepair" (III, 168). Yet, in *Iguana*, just such a conversation is made to effect instantaneous change in the heart and conduct of an equally soul-sick protagonist.

Shannon's transformation, however, owes less to the determinants of realistic motivation than to the dictates of the play's mythic substructure--its archetypal sequence of death and rebirth--which is given viability and direction by the characterization and function of Hannah Jelkes, the humanized *dea ex machina* on whom both Shannon's survival and the play's essentially affirmative message depend. In her transcendent roles as "saint" (p. 266), "guardian angel," (p. 327), and a human analogue of divine grace,

Hannah imparts the "providential" (p. 280) framework of a Christian (and Buddhistic) universe to the play's inherently godless world, and thereby seemingly "banishes the power of naturalism" to determine character.[80] Solely due to Hannah's intervention, then, Shannon is redeemed from the constrictions and consequences of his past identity. The "miracle" of Shannon's psychic rebirth at the conclusion of his "dark night of the soul" gives epiphanic significance to his one night's conversation with Hannah and transformative value to the redemptive message their communion represents: the play's affirmation that a semblance of both God and grace may still be realized in an existential universe through human acts of charity and compassion, thus providing a way "to live beyond despair and still live." Designed primarily for the conveyance of that message, *Iguana* is concluded in a manner much like the Broadway version of *Cat on a Hot Tin Roof*, in which Maggie plays a similar role of a *dea ex machina* who effects the miracle of reviving the spiritually dead and psychologically divided Brick by her single-minded conviction that "life has got to be allowed to continue even after the *dream* of life is--all--over" (III, 57).

Like the other plays examined in this study, *The Night of the Iguana* is developed on two levels, referred to in this play as "the realistic level" and "the fantastic level" (p. 317); when Shannon asks Hannah "which is the real one, really," Hannah replies, "I would say both, Mr. Shannon" (p. 317). What begins, then, as a "realistic" study of Shannon's character, conflicts, and compulsions ends with the "fantastic" miracle of his psychic rebirth. Whether that is cause for complaint or inspiration depends, perhaps, on the literary or epistemological bias of the play's viewer--the degree to which he is able or willing to engage in a Coleridgean "suspension of disbelief." Whereas John Simon in his 1962 review of the play complained that because of its lack of strict causality, "things happen by the author's will to make a point rather than by a necessity clearly communicated to the audience,"[81] Northrop Frye offers an observation that seems to justify *Iguana*'s fulfillment of its mythic formula of rebirth: "The feeling that death is inevitable comes to us from ordinary experience; the feeling that new life is inevitable comes to us from myth and fable. The latter is therefore both more true and more important."[82]

CHAPTER NINE

AFTER *IGUANA*: WILLIAMS' COMIC MODE

"Accept whatever situation you cannot improve."

The Night of the Iguana

I. The Structural Pattern: The Comic Alternative to Romantic Tragedy

The pattern based on a protagonist's mythicized memory-story and its ironic reenactment that structures Williams' major plays from 1945 to 1961 continues to inform his drama after *The Night of the Iguana* (1961), with one significant difference: the pattern is predominantly comic, not tragic, in mode. Five full-length plays representative of Williams' work in the sixties and seventies employ the comic mode of the pattern: *The Milk Train Doesn't Stop Here Anymore* (1962-64), *The Two-Character Play* (1967-75; also titled *Out Cry*), *Kingdom of Earth* (1968-75; also titled *The Seven Descents of Myrtle*), *Small Craft Warnings* (1972), and *A Lovely Sunday for Creve Coeur* (1979). Significant aspects of the pattern also appear in three plays contemporaneous in origin with the works previously examined: *Summer and Smoke* (1948), its revised version *The Eccentricities of a Nightingale* (not published until 1964), and *Camino Real* (1953). Though each traces a protagonist's "fall" from romantic illusions, all of these plays (both early and late) conclude in the essentially comic spirit which also marks the outcomes of *The Rose Tattoo*, the Broadway version of *Cat on a Hot Tin Roof*, and *The Night of the Iguana*. All end with their protagonists' liberation from a remembered past (idyllic or demonic) and with their acceptance of existential givens. In effect, all express the theme of *Iguana* itself: "Accept whatever situation you cannot improve."

According to Robert Heilman in *The Ways of the World: Comedy and Society*, just such an attitude of acceptance constitutes the hallmark of comic style: the "acceptance of the world."[1] Heilman defines acceptance as "a perception of the world as a livable middle ground that is not celestial but is not infernal either"; it is an "accommodation to actuality."[2] To accept is "to see what is possible, probable, or inevitable and yet, though these may not be wholly desirable or admirable, to make do."[3] Thus, the protagonists of these plays are neither emotionally transfixed by memories of the past nor violently destroyed by conflicting desires; instead, they survive, by making the necessary adjustments to a life "in which much falls short of expectation."[4] Their comic strength lies in "being unillusioned without becoming disillusioned."[5]

Unlike Williams' romantic tragedies, the emphasis in these plays is not on what has been lost in a mythicized past, but on what can be made of the mundane present. To that end, several of these plays conclude not with a memory's reenactment but with its comic reversal. Thus, Williams has so altered the fundamental pattern in these plays that what is perceived as an irrevocable loss in the plays of his predominantly tragic mode is instead accepted in the comic spirit of compromise, albeit often a "dark" comedy, marked by the acceptance (or over-acceptance) of the minimal, the expedient, the corrupt, or the "second-best."[6] The comic spirit of survival that remains a secondary motif or foil in the plays of Williams' predominantly tragic mode is fully developed in these plays as a viable alternative to romantic despair and existential *angst*.

These additional plays, then, both early and late, represent further comic variations of the fundamental pattern which also structures *The Rose Tattoo* and *The Night of the Iguana*. Through their structural modifications, they effect the transformation of romantic tragedy to existential comedy, demonstrating through themes of acceptance, accommodation, and endurance that "if the descent is . . . sometimes performed in sorrow, it can also take place in joy."[7] Whereas the Edenic myth of a paradise lost or the infernal myth of the imprisoned self damned to the endless repetition of a demonic past informs Williams' romantic tragedies, it is Camus's existential "Mythe de Sisyphe" which provides the vision for its comic alternative: a vision best expressed by Williams in the words of *Camino Real*'s Byron: "*Make voyages!--Attempt them!--* there's nothing else . . . " (II, 508).

II. Early Plays in the Comic Mode: *Summer and Smoke*, *The Eccentricities of a Nightingale*, and *Camino Real*

Though *Summer and Smoke* and *The Eccentricities of a Nightingale* differ distinctly from *Camino Real* in dramatic style, all are informed by the structural pattern of recollection and reenactment which traces the loss of romantic illusions. In these three plays, however, the pattern is altered in ways which shift its focus from a protagonist's transfixion by the mythic past to his or her tactics for survival in a diminished, demythicized present.

In *Summer and Smoke*, the structural pattern based on a protagonist's mythicized memory-story followed by its ironic reenactment is condensed to a single *mundane* reference and its subsequent recurrence, rather than providing the architectonics of the entire drama. As a further modification of the pattern, memory is here made to serve as the vehicle by which the play's protagonist is *released* from her romantic illusions, rather than representing that obsession to which she remains in thrall. Thus, Alma Winemiller's incidental reference in Scene i to Mrs. Ewell, "the merry widow of Glorious Hill" (II, 148) who waits at the train station to seduce the traveling salesmen, points the way to Alma's own sexual liberation, for she assumes Mrs. Ewell's role of "fallen woman" at the end of the play. Because Alma's story is too slight to carry anticipatory or predictive value at the time it is made, however, its significance when reenacted is understood only in terms of dramatic recall: "that device which is the reverse of foreshadowing."[8] The *primary* structural pattern of the play is based on the intersecting of its two protagonists' lives in symmetrical reversal, allegorically representing the irreconcilability of spirit and flesh personified respectively by Alma, the minister's daughter, and John Buchanan, the doctor's son. Hence, the chaste and idealistic Alma--"Alma is Spanish for soul" (p. 130)--ironically exchanges her romantic view of life for John's naturalistic one just as he embraces her former spirituality. The play ends, then, in a bittersweet mood of comic compromise: Alma gives up her romantic dreams of achieving with John the marriage of body and soul and settles for a temporary sexual liaison with a traveling salesman she picks up at the train station: a compensatory act which permits her to "keep on going" (p. 254) and provides some physical consolation for the loss of her spiritual ideals.

In *The Eccentricities of a Nightingale*, the revised version of *Summer and Smoke*, the promiscuous Mrs. Ewell is replaced as Alma's role model by her cavalier Aunt Albertine; the formerly brief reference to Alma's prototype is developed into a full-blown anecdote; and the structural pattern of recollection and reenactment is strengthened. In this "substantially different" version of the play,[9] characterization centers more directly on Alma's internal conflict: between her spiritual yearnings for an enduring love of "*transcendental*! *tenderness*" (II, 15) and her sexual desires which struggle for release from a restrictive environment and repressive conventions. The role of John Buchanan is thus reduced to that of a passive, secondary figure, even as he is symbolically elevated in Alma's eyes to the mythicized stature of a would-be savior. In this play, the memory-story of the scandalous Aunt Albertine who escaped the repressive life of the rectory by running away with a traveling toy inventor, Otto Schwarzkopf (her "shadow" side), is reenacted twice by Alma: first, in a one-night sexual encounter with John Buchanan; then, when he fails to fulfill the role of redeemer, with a young traveling salesman. Although the escapade of Aunt Albertine ends in fiery catastrophe, she dies still grasping a button she'd torn from the sleeve of her lover, leaving Alma with the lesson, "don't . . . die empty-handed!" (p. 87). As the reincarnation of Aunt Albertine, Alma exchanges both her romantic dreams and puritanical propriety for sexual liberation, with no regrets.

In his 1976 reworked version of *Eccentricities*,[10] Williams reinforces the prophetic quality of the Aunt Albertine story by adding Alma's revelation that "Alma isn't really my name. I was christened Albertine."[11] Also clarified in this version is a formerly puzzling story of a snake that swallowed its blanket and died, here made psychologically analogous to the situation of John Buchanan, whose own animal instincts are similarly smothered by the over-protective love of his mother.[12] In each successive revision of these two plays, then, Williams strengthens the relationship between a recollection and its reenactment. Unlike the memories of Amanda and Laura Wingfield, Blanche DuBois, and Brick Pollitt, however, Alma's recollections offer a strategy for survival which is fulfilled by their existential reenactment.

Whereas memory is rendered mundane in *Summer and Smoke* and *Eccentricities*, *Camino Real* evokes the mythic past in its most phantasmagoric form, suggesting in style and content a grandiose theatrical adaptation of the "mythical method" used by Eliot in *The Waste Land*.[13] As such, this play comprises a stylized abstract of Williams' own mythical method. Combining elements of the medieval dream vision and the Renaissance masque or pageant with an ironic treatment of the romance quest, the play's structure both evokes the nostalgic "remembrance of things past" and encourages the continued search for meaning in an inherently absurd present. Its

historical, literary, and legendary figures--Don Quixote, Jacques
Casanova, Proust's Baron de Charlus, Marguerite Gautier (Camille),
Lord Byron--represent debased modern versions or "reincarnations"
of once viable heroic and romantic ideals, displaced from their
mythic contexts to the confines of existential reality. Exempla of
the romantic sensibility doomed to defeat in the modern demythicized world, they are "mostly archetypes of certain basic attitudes
and qualities with those mutations that would occur if they had
continued along the road to this hypothetical terminal point in it"
(II, 419): that point which marks "the end of the *Camino Real*
[the Royal Road] and the beginning of the *Camino Real* [the Real
Road]" (p. 435). In the acceptance of this fallen state, however,
resides the play's comic ascent theme. Thus, Kilroy--the play's
protagonist-quester and All-American anti-hero--undergoes a vulgarized, but successful, version of the ritual death and rebirth of
a mythic fertility god.[14] Stripped of his romantic illusions, he
is led to embrace the existentialist philosophy uttered by the
play's Byron become a Sisyphean absurd hero: "*Make voyages!--
Attempt them*!--there's nothing else . . . " (p. 508). Having
conquered despair, Kilroy assumes the role of Don Quixote's new
companion, and they strike out together for the "Terra Incognita"
(p. 431) ahead. While *their* resumption of an unillusioned quest
for meaning in a dark, uncertain reality represents the existential
resurrection of the quixotic spirit, the aging Casanova and faded
Camille who are left behind in the confines of Camino Real imbue
its former ideal of romantic love with a deeper humanism. Through
mutual compassion, kindness, and understanding, they effect the
"miracle" of love's survival in the spiritually barren "wasteland"
(p. 432) of the modern world: "*The violets in the mountains have
broken the rocks*!" (p. 591). By so doing, they restore to the
Camino Real a modicum of its former idealism and moral value. The
existential reenactment of the romantic past in this play thus
leads to the comic themes of regeneration, rebirth, and renewal.

III. After *Iguana*: The Comic Reversal of the Tragic Pattern

In "Foreword" to his *Memoirs* (1975), Williams claimed to be
"quite through with the kind of play that established my early and
popular reputation," adding that "Since *The Night of the Iguana*,
the circumstances of my life have demanded of me a continually less
traditional style of dramatic writing."[15] Although Williams' drama
after *Iguana* undergoes several stylistic changes (primarily in his
use of "absurdist" techniques), its thematic concerns and struc-

tural pattern remain fundamentally the same, with one significant difference: a comic *peripeteia*, or reversal, follows his protagonists' fall from mythicized memory to existential reality, thus rendering his plays of the sixties and seventies predominantly comic rather than tragic in mode. In 1960, Williams announced just such a modification of his dramatic mode: "I'm through with what have been called my 'black' plays. . . . For years I was too preoccupied with the destructive impulses. From now on I want to be concerned with the kinder aspects of life."[16] Thus, Williams' plays after *The Night of the Iguana* (1961) all conclude in the comic mode of *Iguana* itself: with their protagonists' ready acceptance of or accommodation to a demythicized reality rather than their despair of or destruction by it. Moreover, though several of these plays are absurdist in style, all remain traditional or Aristotelian in structure: consisting of a definite beginning, middle, and end which depends on an *anagnorisis*, or moment of *self-*recognition, for their climax and denouement. Thus, the structural pattern that controls the form and content of Williams' drama up to *Iguana* continues to inform his subsequent plays, including *The Milk Train Doesn't Stop Here Anymore*, *The Two-Character Play*, *Kingdom of Earth*, *Small Craft Warnings*, and *A Lovely Sunday for Creve Coeur*.

Despite Williams' claim to the contrary, then, the plays following *Iguana* do not so much mark either a structural or thematic change from the kind of drama that established his "early and popular reputation" as they represent an increasing emphasis on the comic strain that has informed his work from its beginning, and which is fully developed as a viable alternative to tragic despair as early as *Summer and Smoke* (1948). If a genuinely new note may be discerned in Williams' drama, it resides precisely in the greater degree to which this comic attitude is stressed. In several of these plays of the sixties and seventies, the shift in emphasis from tragic to comic mode is so complete that the sense of mythic loss or romantic disillusionment that had earlier been evoked even in Williams' plays of a predominantly comic mode is instead denied altogether or presented as a parody of that former tragic vision.

The Night of the Iguana may itself be considered the turning point of Williams' shift from tragic to comic mode only insofar as it represents the purgation of the "destructive impulses" dominant in the plays which precede it; and as it emphasizes the comic attitudes of acceptance, accommodation, and endurance which, although present in Williams' drama long before *Iguana*, are dominant thereafter. *Iguana*'s "Oriental" philosophy of acceptance--"Accept whatever situation you cannot improve" (IV, 363)--becomes the major theme of Williams' drama in the sixties and seventies. *Iguana* also anticipates by its protagonist's release from the reenactment of a demonic memory the comic reversal of tragic experience in these plays. As happens in both the Broadway *Cat* and *Iguana* itself, this reversal of a tragic fate toward which the protagonist seems to be heading is often so abrupt or unexpected that it evokes the sense of the miraculous as well as that of the manipulative. According to Northrop Frye, the comic ending is often effected by just such a "twist in the plot," involving a "metamorphosis of character" brought about by "unlikely conversions, miraculous transformations, and providential assistance."[17]

Among the "less traditional" stylistic techniques with which Williams experimented in his full-length and one-act plays of the sixties and seventies are several which derive from or have been most closely associated with the Theatre of the Absurd. These include the use of ellipsis, incomplete sentences, and "cross-talk," or chiasmus, in dialogue (*In The Bar of a Tokyo Hotel*, 1969; *I Can't Imagine Tomorrow*, 1970; *The Two-Character Play*, 1975); the device of the play-within-a-play to blur the lines between art and life, illusion and reality (*The Two-Character Play*); a more extensive use of interior monologue and the confessional aside (*Small Craft Warnings*, 1972); and a more self-conscious use of black humor--which Williams claims to have "invented"[18]--both verbal ("the jokes of the condemned"[19] in *The Two-Character Play*) and visual (the "slapstick tragedy" of *The Gnädiges Fräulein*, 1966). Williams' use of these absurdist techniques, however, does not so much signal a radical departure from either the form or content of his earlier work as it represents an organic outgrowth of existentialist themes and concerns fundamental to his dramatic vision: such themes as the difficulty of human communication; the conflict between subjective impressions and objective reality; and the inherent absurdity of a universe marked by metaphysical silence and the existential condition of the fragmented or divided self condemned to "solitary confinement inside our own skins" (III, 3).

Several other significant themes which are expressed discursively in *Iguana* are conveyed by stylistic or structural means in the plays which follow it. Williams' syntactic use of ellipsis and incomplete sentences, for instance, is semantically anticipated by Shannon's resorting to an "Incomplete sentence" (IV, 305) whenever he attempts to define the inexpressible mysteries of an absurd universe. In addition, the technique of cross-talk dialogue--in which one character completes another's thought--linguistically conveys *Iguana*'s theme of the need for "broken gates between people" so they can reach each other in the communal exchange of "a little understanding" (IV, 352). Finally, Maxine's observation that "No one's bigger than life-size" (IV, 270) is incarnated by the antiheroic protagonists of Williams' plays of the sixties and seventies. Rather than representing inflated egos doomed to psychic fragmentation or neurotic withdrawal, the protagonists of these plays readily accept their existential limitations and, in the process, may be said to achieve a measure of psychic integration or, in Jungian terminology, "individuation." Unlike the romantics of Williams' tragic mode, the protagonists of these plays are survivors: they embody the comic spirit of diminished expectations and realistic adaptations, surviving what's possible and accepting what's not. The comic outcomes of several of these plays suggest existential analogues or mundane versions of mythic resurrections, miracles, and epiphanies, often brought about, as in *Iguana*, by a "providential" (IV, 280) encounter with the "kindness" of a stranger, thus evoking echoes of Williams' former themes and characters.

(1) The Milk Train Doesn't Stop Here Anymore

In the play immediately following *Iguana*, *The Milk Train Doesn't Stop Here Anymore* (1962; revised in 1964 to the version discussed here), the wealthy, widowed, and imperious Flora GoForth initially resists accepting her impending demise. Her tenacious hold on both her riches and her life evokes her analogy to "a golden griffin . . . a mythological monster, half lion and half eagle" (V, 7), which builds its nest of gold and keeps vigilant guard against plunderers.[20] Ultimately, however, she is led peacefully and serenely to accept her human mortality by a symbolic Angel of Death, Christopher Flanders (whose last name evokes Flanders Field). An itinerant poet-priest, an ironic St. Christopher,[21] and the ascetic "reincarnation" of Mrs. GoForth's fourth and last husband--"the one I married for love" (p. 10)--Chris has assumed the mission of easing into death the wealthy, aged, infirm, and hopeless: divesting them of both their fears of death and, it is implied, their wealth, with the gentleness of a lover. As an ironic version of St. Christopher, protector of travelers, who earned his sainthood by assuming the burdens of the world when he unknowingly carried the Christ-child safely across a river,[22] Chris tells an inverted tale of his helping an old man *divest* himself of a painful, disease-ridden life by leading him into the ocean to drown, a role he subsequently reenacts by helping the fearful Flora (appropriately nicknamed "Sissy") find the courage to "go forth" similarly unburdened to her "heavenly sleep" (p. 14). As an ascetic version of Mrs. GoForth's last husband, Chris refuses to reenact the sexual role of her marriage partner, thereby purging Flora of her voracious desire for life and preparing her for the embrace of death.

Just as in *Iguana*, wherein the plot's tragic direction is suddenly reversed owing to Shannon's "providential" (IV, 280) encounter with an existential analogue of divine grace, so in *Milk Train*, also a "sophisticated fairy tale" (p. 3), the essentially "comic" ending derives from the timely appearance of a stranger who "came here to bring me God" (p. 113). Whereas Hannah guides Shannon to accept the realities of life, however, Chris leads Flora GoForth to the attitude expressed by *Iguana*'s Nonno, of accepting "Without a cry, without a prayer,/ With no betrayal of despair" (IV, 372) the fact of inevitable death. The "Oriental" philosophy of the acceptance of life and death alike is here dramatically reinforced by the device of a pair of "stage assistants," intended to function, according to Williams, "in a way that's between the Kabuki Theatre of Japan and the chorus of Greek theatre" (p. 3): to ritualize, universalize, and, by their somewhat vaudevillian routine, theatricalize as spectacle the existential experience of death. Because Flora's physical demise is accompanied by a sense of spiritual awakening, the play concludes in the comic mood of rebirth and resurrection rather than in a tragic mood of loss; it ends, appropriately, with the bugle sounds of "Reveille," not "Taps" (p. 119).

(2) The Two-Character Play

Unlike the discursive, quasi-philosophical style used in *Iguana* and *Milk Train* to present the existential problems of "loneliness, the impenetrable mystery of the universe, [and] death,"[23] *The Two-Character Play* (1967-75) employs absurdist imagery to objectify the pyschological reality of the existential human predicament. Here, the existential world appears as a locked, abandoned, empty theater from which there is "no exit," and the divided psyche as two actors (brother and sister) condemned to "solitary confinement" inside their own subjective experience,

i. e., a "two-character play." The play is structured primarily, then, by the Pirandelloesque device of the play-within-a-play, a technique anticipated in Williams' own dramaturgy as early as *Battle of Angels*, *The Glass Menagerie*, and *Camino Real*, each of which employs the device of a frame story to merge past with present, dream with reality, remembered experience with its reenactment. Within this essentially static psychodrama, the linear pattern precipitated by a protagonist's memory-story plays a crucial role. Rather than ending with the tragic consequences of reenactment, however, the play concludes, as does *Iguana*, with its protagonists' liberation from a demonic past and their acceptance of their own flawed natures.

Thus, in *The Two-Character Play*, Felice and Clare, the brother and sister acting team, who have been previously condemned to repeat endlessly the events of their tormented past in dramatized reenactments of the "Two-Character Play," are suddenly released from the demonic memory which had controlled their lives--the murder of their mother by their father and his subsequent suicide-- when Clare, playing the surrogate role of their mother as murderer, *refuses* to pull the trigger which would end the life of her brother Felice, thereby reversing the tragic conclusion toward which they seemed destined. Instead, it is suggested that they choose to yield to their incestuous urges rather than play out the conflicts and frustrations which had driven their parents to madness and death.

In mythic terms, the incestuous union of brother and sister symbolizes a return to a primordial unity;[24] in Biblical typology, the erotic brother-sister union imaged in the Song of Solomon (from which derives the play's epigraph, "A garden enclosed is my sister, my spouse" [4.16]) represents an invocation to the holy marriage between God and man;[25] and, as a Jungian archetype of wholeness, brother-sister incest signifies by its conjunction of opposites-- "the highest and the lowest, the brightest and the darkest, the best and the most detestable"--a prelude to psychic integration or "individuation."[26] Thus, Felice and Clare--who resemble no other mythical counterparts so much as that cursed pair of the House of Atreus, Orestes and Electra--divest themselves of the tragic repetition of the past by accepting, in the spirit of love and forgiveness, their own inherently flawed natures. As divided androgynes of a single personality which ultimately accepts its own shadow-side,[27] their concrete symbol is a large two-headed sunflower, a "monster of nature" which nevertheless holds within it

192

the possibility of becoming a "marvel of nature" (V, 330) were its existence to be admitted and accepted. By just such a "tender admission" (p. 370) and acceptance, Felice and Clare attain a measure of self-integrity denied to Williams' tragically bifurcated figures. The play ends, then, in the "dark" comic gesture of Felice and Clare's embrace: a gesture which simultaneously releases them from their obsessive reenactment of the tragic past, and offers the sole mitigation from the unalterable circumstances of alienation, confinement, and death to which the existential condition condemns them.

(3) Kingdom of Earth

Williams' next major full-length play, *Kingdom of Earth* (1968-75), reenacts as "funny melodrama"[28] the Biblical stories of two rival brothers as well as the fall of Lot's wife and Noah's salvation from The Flood. In this secular rendition of "the survival of the fittest," the boorish, animalistic Chicken triumphs over his effete, sickly half-brother, Lot--usurping his birthright, his bride (Myrtle), and, finally, his life. Chicken ultimately assumes the role of an ironic savior by hauling onto the rooftop of his farmhouse the maternalistic, pragmatic Myrtle in order that they may survive together the Mississippi floodtide and, as ironic counterparts of the chosen Noah and his wife, fulfill God's commandment to inherit, "be fruitful . . . and replenish" (Genesis 9.1) a thoroughly debased "kingdom of earth." The play's three characters--the vulgar, phallic Chicken; the disillusioned but resilient Myrtle (who prides herself on having always "kept my haid above water" [V, 142]); and Lot, the "weak sister" and aspirant to "the kingdom of heaven"--are clearly comic versions of *Streetcar*'s Stanley, Stella, and Blanche, respectively.[29] As in *Streetcar*, those who survive in "the kingdom of earth" are the strong, the sexual, and the pragmatic. Here, however, the play's theme affirms the value of naturalistic existence--no matter how corrupt--rather than lamenting the loss of romantic ideals. Unlike Blanche, Lot is an essentially unsympathetic character: selfish, sexless, and fully as depraved in his own way as Chicken. His vision of the kingdom of heaven is embodied in the decadent opulence of his mother's parlor: heaven's pearly gates and streets of gold become the gaudy baroque furnishings of velvet drapes, gold chairs, and a crystal chandelier.[30] Dressed in his mother's "gauzy white dress" and a "picture hat . . . trimmed with faded flowers" (p. 211), the transvestite Lot parodies Blanche DuBois, and his death scene in the

193

rose-colored parlor grotesquely devaluates her romantic tragedy.

Set against Lot's decadent romanticism is Chicken's apostrophe to sexual vitality as earth's sole transformative value, which echoes Stanley Kowalski's similar tribute to "things that can happen between a man and a woman in the dark" (I, 321). To Chicken, as to Stanley, "There's nothing in the world, in the whole kingdom of earth, that can compare with one thing, and that one thing is what's able to happen between a man and a woman"; he adds, in the vernacular of Big Daddy, "The rest is crap" (p. 211). Finally, Myrtle, like Stella, descends to corruption in order to survive: a descent which is at the same time a literal ascent (and a symbolic assent) to life.

In this comic re-vision of *Streetcar*'s predominantly tragic mode, then, Williams has so shifted the emphasis of his dual vision as to bring to the fore the existential comedy inherent in Stanley Kowalski's Dionysian spirit and Stella's instinctual realization that "Life has got to go on" (I, 406), while debasing the "belle reve" of Blanche DuBois and exorcising through parody her romantic tragedy.

(4) Small Craft Warnings

Small Craft Warnings (1972), Williams' first commercial success after *The Night of the Iguana* (1961), also effects the comic reversal of romantic despair. The play dramatizes the stormy reshuffling of relationships in the course of one evening among the patrons of "Monk's Bar," whose bartender-proprietor acts as father-confessor to the down-and-out members of his adopted "family": Leona, the generous earth-mother; the frail, promiscuous Violet; coarse, priapic Bill; alcoholic Doc; and two homosexual transients --young, enthusiastic Bobby and the older, jaded Quentin. In the course of the play, each member of this representative human community is "spotlighted" and set apart from the others to tell his story or offer his reflections on life in individual monologues or confessional asides, a device which serves to objectify their isolated existential condition as vulnerable "small craft, each with his crew of one, himself that crew and captain."[31]

Within that structure, Leona Dawson's idealized memory of her "angelic" homosexual brother--one of Williams' fragile, moth-like creatures who was "too beautiful to live and so he died" (V, 248)--

194

is revived or "reincarnated" by the young homosexual Bobby: "Oh, my God, you've got the skin and hair of my brother and even almost the eyes!" (p. 263). Leona thus offers Bobby her maternal warmth and companionship in an effort to realize her dream of living with her brother, whose "death-day" she is commemorating. Leona's attempt to recapture an idyllic memory of the past sets the stage for the romantic disillusionment of an Amanda Wingfield, the tragic destruction of a Lady Torrance, or the "spiritual disrepair" of a Brick Pollitt. However, unlike the protagonists of Williams' romantic tragedies, who are emotionally transfixed and ultimately destroyed by their mythicized memories, Leona is able to turn the "One beautiful thing!" (p. 248) in her past into a source of enrichment for the present: "I cry! I cry! . . . No, I don't, I *don't* cry! . . . I'm proud that I've had something beautiful to remember. . . . Without one beautiful thing in the course of a lifetime, it's all a death-time" (pp. 247-48). Because memory here serves to sustain rather than destroy the protagonist, Leona is also able to absorb Bobby's gentle rejection of her offer of companionship with philosophical equanimity, optimistically consoling herself with the belief that she'll soon find someone else "that needs a big sister with him, to camp with and laugh and cry with" (p. 285). Thus, Leona, like the Princess, Stella, and Hannah, opts for "going on" as the only alternative to romantic despair.

In her capacity to view the existential search for meaning in life as a continuous adventure, Leona acts as counterpoint to the cynical Quentin, who has "lost the capacity for being surprised" (p. 260) and simply says "Oh, well" to whatever life offers. By contrast to Quentin's *mal d'esprit*, Leona exclaims, "I never just said, 'Oh, well,' I've always said 'Life!' to life, like a song to God, too, because I've lived in my lifetime and not been afraid of . . . changes" (p. 269). In her religious enthusiasm for life, Leona resembles Edgar Lee Masters' Lucinda Matlock ("It takes life to love Life"), even as the play itself, in structure and theme, recalls Masters' own collection of monologized lives, *Spoon River Anthology.*[32]

The play ends with the closing of the bar and the characters' dispersal from its sanctuary-port, as they set out on their separate voyages: Bobby on motorcycle to continue his quest to see the Pacific, and Leona in her "home on wheels" to continue her search for a surrogate brother to mother and love. In a final refutation of Quentin's deadened sensibilities, the play closes on a note of "surprise." As an act of kindness, Monk reluctantly permits the "filthy," derelict Violet to stay the night in his upstairs room, and she, in return, unexpectedly undergoes the cleansing ritual of a shower in preparation for their physical communion: a gesture of mutual consideration elevated to a small miracle, evoking, in the play's last moments, a religious sense of wonder or awe. *Small Craft Warnings*, then, like *Camino Real* and *The Night of the Iguana*, offers two comic attitudes which serve as viable alternatives to tragic despair or existential ennui: the capacity to "love life" enough to survive, endure, and "go on"; and faith in the human spirit's "surprising" ability for self-transcendence through acts of mutual kindness and consolation.

(5) A Lovely Sunday for Creve Coeur

In *A Lovely Sunday for Creve Coeur* (New York: New Directions, 1980), the romantic imagination which transfixed Laura Wingfield and destroyed Blanche DuBois is itself trivialized and debunked, their tragic fates averted by the comic strategy of accepting "second-best." The play's major conflict revolves around the social aspirations of Dorothea Gallaway--an "emotionally fragile" (p. 28), middle-aged high school teacher who spins romantic dreams around the school's "unprincipled" (p. 55) principal, Mr. T. Ralph Ellis--and the down-to-earth efforts of her *hausfrau* room-mate, "Bodey," to get her to settle for a life of "*Kirche, Küche, und Kinder*" (p. 15) with Bodey's twin brother: the ordinary, over-weight, but eminently reliable "Buddy." On this Sunday, as on every other Sunday, Buddy has invited Dorothea to picnic with him at the local St. Louis amusement park, Creve Coeur.

The ethereal Dorothea (who is just plain "Dottie" to the sensible Bodey) resembles another comic version or caricature of Blanche DuBois, while Bodey, like Stella, serves as her earthy antithesis. Accordingly, Blanche's romantic tragedy approaches parody as re-told by Dorothea. Frustrated by a youthful love with a sensitive "musical prodigy" afflicted with "premature ejacula-tion" (p. 51), Dorothea attempts to transform into a "magical" romance a one-night sexual encounter with Ralph in the reclining seat of his "Flying Cloud" parked on "Art Hill." Said to suffer from a "Southern Belle complex" (p. 68), Dorothea, like Blanche, insists that "Without romance in my life, I could no more live than I could without breath" (p. 15).

The ironic crux of the play turns on our knowledge that as

196

After Iguana

Dorothea waits expectantly for Ralph's phone call (as does Laura Wingfield for her gentleman caller or Blanche DuBois for the call from Shep Huntleigh), the announcement of his engagement to another woman has already appeared in the Sunday paper (a platitudinous parallel to the dramatized betrayals of Laura and Blanche by their idealized saviors); and that Bodey has torn out the article and disposed of it in the wastebasket. The play's climactic *anagnorisis* predictably depends on Dorothea's discovery of her loss. Unlike the protagonists of Williams' romantic tragedies, however, Dorothea is neither plunged into despair nor destroyed by the collapse of her romantic dreams. Instead, having found the announcement, she is merely "stunned for some moments" (p. 79); then, in a comic reversal of mood, she philosophically accepts her situation as "the way of the world" and determines to make the necessary adjustments to "go on . . . we must just go on, that's all that life seems to offer--and demand" (p. 81). In a flurry of activity, Dorothea "pulls herself together" and rushes to meet Buddy and Bodey for the Sunday outing, and a life that promises to be "just one long Creve Coeur picnic" (p. 15).

IV. Late Plays in the Comic Mode: A Critique

While the comic alternative to romantic disillusionment or tragic despair has always been an integral part of the dual vision of Williams' drama, in the plays after *Iguana*, the shift in emphasis from mythic loss to existential affirmation is at times so extreme as to approach self-parody: the parody of Williams' own formerly romantic themes, "larger-than-life-size" characterization, and the structural pattern of romantic tragedy itself. Whereas the internal conflicts between past and present, ideal and reality, mythicized memory and its mundane reenactment comprise the entire "action" of Williams' earlier plays, in his later work, both the protagonists' conflicts and their resolution or reversal are often condensed to momentary changes in mood. Thus, Blanche DuBois's fatal inability to reconcile her "belle reve" of the past with the harsh realities of the present is in *Small Craft*'s Leona Dawson reduced to a momentary conflict in which nostalgia is briefly evoked and quickly dispelled: "I cry! I cry! . . . No, I don't, I *don't* cry! . . . I'm proud that I've had something beautiful to remember as long as I live in my lifetime" (V, 247). The collapse of romantic dreams invested in a mythicized "gentleman caller" which results in devastating consequences for Laura Wingfield and Blanche DuBois only stuns "for some moments" the similarly be-

197

trayed Dorothea Gallaway in *Creve Coeur* before she "pulls herself together" and determines to "go on." Similarly, the tragic consequences previously experienced as inevitable by Williams' characters who found themselves "trapped by circumstances" are in *The Two-Character Play* abruptly reversed within seconds of the play's conclusion; thus, the play ends with its protagonists' embrace of reality rather than their violent destruction by it. In *Milk Train*, also, Flora GoForth resists until the very last moments of the play the summons of the "Angel of Death," Chris Flanders; then, in a transformation even more sudden than that effected by Hannah in Shannon, she reverses her position and demands with equal forcefulness his assistance in helping her accept her inevitable fate. Finally, in a reversal of *Streetcar*'s focus on Blanche DuBois's romantic tragedy, the demise of a romantic imagination grown effete, decadent, and grotesque goes unmourned altogether in *Kingdom of Earth*; and attention centers on Myrtle's "descent" to corruption, which is presented as a comic assent to the vulgar vitality of life.

The substitution in these plays of a comic peripeteia or abrupt reversal of a tragic situation for its inevitable fulfillment, or reenactment, lends a sense of contrivance to their comic outcomes. The comic reversal of romantic tragedy is realized with such rapidity and ease that it virtually denies any sense of the romantic disillusionment which had formerly been evoked not only in the tragic visions of *The Glass Menagerie*, *A Streetcar Named Desire*, and *Suddenly Last Summer*, but which had also been fully elicited in *Summer and Smoke*, *The Rose Tattoo*, *Camino Real*, and *The Night of the Iguana* before their final resolutions in the comic spirit of acceptance, accommodation, and endurance. Accordingly, the protagonists' easy acceptance of existential givens robs Williams' drama of that dual vision which had previously evoked a tragic sense of mythic loss even as it offered the viable alternative of comic compromise. According to Robert Heilman, such "acceptance" as the protagonists of these plays so readily embrace is meaningful "only if it implies difficulty and effort."[33] Such an implication would seem particularly important, when, as in these plays, a character's "acceptance of the world" is due to his resolution of an internal conflict rather than owing to an arbitrary, external complication of plot or to a supernatural *coup de grâce*. The facile achievement of the protagonists' acceptance trivializes the theme of "the negative heroism of plain survival,"[34] which is the existentialist philosophy projected in these plays. As a consequence, the "individuation" or psychic integration achieved by these protagonists without conflict, difficulty, or self-reflection lacks psychological authenticity.

It may be argued, however, that in at least three of these plays--*Small Craft Warnings*, *A Lovely Sunday for Creve Coeur*, and *Kingdom of Earth*--a comic context is established which justifies, in part, the short shrift given the resolution of a romantic or tragic personality's internal conflicts. According to Heilman, the context of comedy is not the "inner" world of a protagonist's mind and memory (which more properly belongs to tragedy) but the "solid, populated, representative" world-at-large, in which "the conflicts are not between impulses and imperatives that are elements of the psyche, but between individuals who are elements of society"; and where "the issue is not an individual's coming to spiritual terms with himself but his coming to working terms with other persons or groups of persons."[35] In these relationships, "the characters cannot be significantly troubled by inner splits," but act, finally, as if there were only one real course which they pursue with "wholeness." Thus, in the comic world, a character's conversion or change from past behavior derives from his pragmatic acknowledgment of his past foolishness as a "tactical error" or "practical misstep" rather than from his self-recognition of a moral fault or his reconciliation of a deep psychological division.

In both *Small Craft Warnings* and *Creve Coeur*, the context of a comic world is created through a shift in dramatic focus, from that on a solitary protagonist's inner world to one which includes the "populated" outer world. While the structural pattern which derives from a protagonist's internal conflict between a mythicized memory and mundane reality continues to inform these two plays, it does not organize their entire dramatic action nor does it constitute their single dramatic focus. Rather, the pattern is embedded in a larger context which serves to diffuse its singularity and lighten its intensity by comparison with the conflicts and relationships between others in the play. Thus, in *Small Craft Warnings*, although Leona Dawson's mythicized memory-story, its ironic reenactment, and the sudden resolution of her conflict between the ideal and the real forms a prominent part of the play's dramatic action, her story is only one of a number of others told by members of the play's microcosmic community; and the play's conclusion extends beyond a focus on the resolution of conflict *within* Leona's psyche to depict the reconciliation of differences *between* Monk and Violet. In the more farcical *Creve Coeur*, although the play's significant dramatic action derives from Dorothea

Gallaway's romantic desires and concludes with her sudden acceptance of a diminished reality, the play is as much a social comedy as an ironic romance, its broader theme of the importance of kindness and tolerance in relationships with others presented through the characterization of the down-to-earth Bodey, Dorothea's comic foil. The on-stage action of the play focuses on the encounters of Bodey with the play's other characters in her busy efforts to "make things right," while the "romantic agony" of Dorothea takes place largely behind the scenes. It is, finally, through Bodey's acts of kindness to the lonely Miss Gluck, her sensitivity to the ethereal Dorothea, and her instinctual aversion to the snobbish Helena that the play's comic mood is sustained. The context of the play is thus enlarged to encompass the interrelationship of four "spinsters" rather than focusing entirely on the conflicts within just one. In the larger context of the comic world, then, it may be argued that the parodic treatment of the romantic sensibility or the implausible metamorphosis to wholeness of a tragically divided self is justified in order to maintain the comic mood and realize its outcome of concord.

On the other hand, the comic parody of a tragically conceived character, or the miraculous transformation of a psychologically divided self to pragmatic wholeness, cannot be achieved without a concomitant mockery or diminution of the significance of the romantic personality's attitudes or sentiments. (Cf. Shakespeare's treatment of the "wisdom" of the melancholic Jaques in *As You Like It*; or, in a modern vein, Harold Pinter's absurdist treatment of the "intellectual equilibrium" maintained by *The Homecoming*'s "philosopher," Teddy, as he witnesses the literal violation of his wife and marriage.) In *Small Craft* and *Creve Coeur*, the quasi-philosophical utterances of Leona Dawson about the necessity of embracing "life," and those of Dorothea Gallaway about the need to accept and endure its limitations are given the weight of moral maxims and comprise moralistic themes. According to Northrop Frye, "It is . . . quite possible to have a moral comedy, but the result is often the kind of melodrama that we have described as comedy without humor, and which achieves its happy ending with a self-righteous tone that most comedy avoids."[36] Put more bluntly by G. Wilson Knight, "A moralistic comedy is a contradiction in terms."[37] In the last analysis, then, even in these two plays in which the conflicts within a single protagonist are subsumed in a larger comic world, there remains a fundamental contradiction between the effortless way the resolution of a potentially tragic internal conflict comes about, and the weighty moral significance given the subsequent acceptance of existential givens.

Only *Kingdom of Earth*, Williams' "funny melodrama," preserves the integrity of the comic world, by its sustained parodic treatment of the romantic sensibility, its conflicts, their resolution, *and* their significance. The play's comic outcome and theme of acceptance requires no instantaneous conversion of a divided personality, but derives organically from Myrtle's instinct for a self-preservation which she achieves with some effort, pursues with wholeness, and accepts without philosophical pretension. In structure, if not in stature, *Kingdom of Earth* fulfills Williams' comic vision.

V. The Evolution of the Pattern: From Mythic Past to Mundane Present

With these alterations in the mood, tone, and outcome of his fundamental structural pattern, Williams' dramatic development, in one sense, comes full circle: from the evocation of archetypal images of mythic wholeness, romantic transcendence, and spiritual redemption which are lamented as irrevocably lost in the plays of his predominantly tragic mode (1944-61) to a semblance of their restoration through themes of psychic integration, the acceptance of human limitations, and an existential will to survive in the plays of his predominantly comic mode (1962-79). As dramatically realized, however, Williams' comic vision after *Iguana* represents a movement from the mythic to the mundane: from romantic tragedy to the parody of "romantic agony," from a complex tragicomic vision to uncomplicated comic "acceptance," and from the psychic landscapes of an idyllic Belle Reve and a demonic Moon Lake to unrelieved confinement in a prosaic "kingdom of earth." In Williams' late works, then, the structural pattern that controls his earlier plays, tragic or comic, reveals signs of having reached exhaustion by its self-parody. According to Frye, parody is often "a sign that certain vogues in handling conventions are getting worn out."[38]

At the same time, signs of a new structural pattern are evident in Williams' plays of the sixties and seventies, a pattern based on a movement of "ascent" rather than "descent"; on the reversal of remembered experience rather than its reenactment; and on a comic outcome of concord rather than discord, integration rather than disintegration, and transformation rather than transfixion. Rather than suffering "the ultimately irresolvable tension of a longing for redemption,"[39] which characterizes the protagonists of Williams' earlier plays, the characters in his later plays readily resolve their conflicts by an embrace of "the comic choice," which, according to Robert Heilman, characteristically turns on "what is suitable, sensible, feasible; it does not often forget the convenient and the pragmatic."[40] In at least three of the five plays examined here, this comic vision gives rise to a context and focus that encompasses representatives of the entire community in its gaze rather than concentrating on a single "divided self"; one that is more concerned with the integration of a "society" than with the resolution of conflict within a single individual; and one which had been anticipated in *The Night of the Iguana* by the expressed philosophy of "looking out . . . not in" (IV, 355). In some of these later plays, then, it may be argued that Williams' dramatic vision reveals a shift from its former focus on the inner world of the tortured individual to a broader perspective of the "solid, populated, representative" world which is the scene of comedy.

This shift in focus, however, is neither entirely new nor entirely successful in realizing a coherent dramatic structure. In *Cat on a Hot Tin Roof*, Williams also attempts to capture "the interplay of live human beings" (III, 114) in a dark comic world of moral ambiguity rather than maintain focus on the personal "tragedy" (III, 168) of Brick Pollitt, the play's divided protagonist. In that play, however, as in much of Williams' later drama, a structural hiatus occurs because of a sudden shift in focus from the tragic conflicts of an individual protagonist to a wider perspective intended to encompass "the true quality of experience in a group of people" (III, 114). As indicated by the plays examined here, the components of this emergent structure in Williams' drama do not always cohere to provide the complexity of characterization, richness of meaning, sustained dramatic tension, and mythic resonance which characterize the best of his earlier plays.

Whereas Williams' most successful plays in the comic mode, such as *The Rose Tattoo* and *Camino Real*, present as gradual, difficult, and therefore meaningful the resolution of their protagonists' acceptance of a diminished reality, in such plays as *Milk Train, Small Craft Warnings*, and *A Lovely Sunday for Creve Coeur*, that resolution is presented as instantaneous, effortless, and consequently gratuitous. Even in *The Night of the Iguana*, which anticipates by the "miraculous" conversion of its protagonist

the comic resolution by sudden reversal which governs Williams'
drama thereafter, Shannon is depicted as undergoing a painful "dark
night of the soul" *before* his liberation from conflict. Of the
five plays exemplary of Williams' drama after *Iguana*, only *The Two-
Character Play* suggests a similar struggle to achieve a resolution
of conflict: Felice and Clare's resistance to concluding their
play, and their lives, not only gives depth to their conflict, but
also makes dramatically feasible (and, to a degree, psychologically
plausible) their final comic reversal of remembered experience
rather than their tragic reenactment of it. At the other extreme,
Kingdom of Earth resolves all problems of a discrepancy between the
conflicts of a romantic personality and the comic means to achieve
their resolution by reducing the entire pattern of a tragic "fall"
to parody.

The fundamental weakness, then, in Williams' drama after
Iguana seems to be that although the "old" structural pattern which
focuses on a protagonist's internal conflict between a mythicized
memory and mundane reality continues to inform his plays, it no
longer makes a significant contribution to or serves an indispens-
able function in the realization of their comic outcomes. Instead,
the comic outcomes of Williams' later plays most often come about
despite the intensity or significance of a character's romantic or
tragic conflicts, not as a result of his or her struggle to achieve
the comic resolution of those conflicts. Ultimately, the structural hiatus between the "old" pattern which continues to inform
these plays and the "new" components of Williams' comic vision
undermines the existentialist theme of "survival" which is the
consequence of their protagonists' "conversions"; those resolutions
of conflict achieved with neither difficulty nor effort serve only
to parody a tragic situation or reduce to platitude a comic one.

Thus, the development of Williams' drama--from *The Glass
Menagerie* to *A Lovely Sunday for Creve Coeur*--may be said to
recapitulate in its entirety the movement of the structural pattern
which informs each play individually: the movement of a "fall" from
the mythic to the mundane. The larger-than-life-size protagonists
of his earlier plays, who attempt to recapture the mythicized
memories of an idyllic past or to escape from the nightmares of a
demonic one, are replaced in Williams' later drama by lesser
figures--"small craft" or representatives of "the kingdom of earth"
--in whom lofty aspirations are reduced to schemes for survival.
Williams' dramatic vision shifts from a focus on the monumental
conflicts encountered by the mythic imagination in confrontation

with existential reality to an emphasis on the ready resolution of all conflict in the psychologically well-adjusted but dramatically platitudinous idea that "life goes on." Not only the tragic conflicts engendered by the romantic aspirations of a Blanche DuBois-- "I don't want realism. I want magic!" (I, 385)--but also the heroic efforts of such redemptive figures as "Maggie the Cat" and Hannah Jelkes to heal the division between the ideal and the real are in Williams' later drama rendered mundane and sententious by their expression in a Dorothea Gallaway's instantly-achieved resolve that "we must just go on, that's all that life seems to offer and--demand!" In these works after *Iguana*, the myths of death and rebirth, crucifixion and resurrection that underlie the structure of Williams' drama are trivialized, both by comparison with their archetypal forms of "divine" comedy and with Williams' own major plays in which his tragicomic vision restores to a thoroughly human comedy a measure of mythic significance.

NOTES

INTRODUCTION

[1] The terms "idyllic" and "demonic" derive from Northrop Frye as defined in his *The Secular Scripture: A Study of the Structure of Romance* (1976; rpt. Cambridge: Harvard Univ. Press, 1978), pp. 53ff; and in his *Anatomy of Criticism: Four Essays* (1957; rpt. Princeton: Princeton Univ. Press, 1971): "idyllic" imagery is illustrated in "Apocalyptic Imagery," pp. 141-46 and in "Analogical Imagery," pp. 151-58; "demonic" imagery is illustrated in "Archetypal Criticism: Theory of Myths," pp. 147-50.

[2] The phrase is Williams'; in his essay "The Timeless World of a Play," *Theatre*, II, 259, Williams states that "it is, perhaps more than anything else, the *arrest of time* which has taken place in a completed work of art that gives to certain plays their feeling of depth and significance."

[3] Esther Jackson, *The Broken World of Tennessee Williams* (Madison: Univ. of Wisconsin Press, 1965), p. 32, similarly observes that each of Williams' plays "takes the shape of a vision proceeding from the consciousness of the protagonist"; and, p. 69, she describes Williams' emotionally arrested characters as "transfixed": "As he [Williams] examines humanity through the patched glass of his synthetic myth, the playwright perceives a creature transfixed in a moment of stasis, halted at the point of transition in the process of becoming."

[4] As quoted by Robert Jennings, "*Playboy* Interview: Tennessee Williams," *Playboy*, April 1973, p. 80.

[5] Jackson, p. 55, similarly observes, "Throughout all his work, Williams follows a plan which theatricalizes--even ritualizes--ordinary experience"; see also Richard B. Vowles, "Tennessee Williams: The World of his Imagery," *Tulane Drama Review*, 3 (1958), 55, who perceptively concludes, "Perhaps Williams' major contribution to the theatre of today is his quiet transmutation of naturalism into ritual."

[6] *Anatomy*, p. 139.

[7] Jackson, p. 74, first used the term "shadow-images" to describe the "flawed image" of Williams' characters in relation to their archetypal prototypes: "Williams reveals his flawed image of man by showing his relationship to archetypal patterns. Throughout his work, Williams superimposes parallel visions--shadow images--of modern man." Jackson, p. 72, also first defined Williams' anti-heroic protagonists as "images of a humanity diminished by time and history."

[8] Jackson, p. 37, refers to Williams' composite characterization as "montage; that is, they are made up, after the manner of cinematic techniques, by the superimposition of figures one upon the other."

[9] T. S. Eliot, "Hamlet," in *Selected Essays: 1917-1932* (London, 1932; rpt. New York: Harcourt, 1950), pp. 124-25.

[10] Henry Popkin, "The Plays of Tennessee Williams," *Tulane Drama Review*, 4 (1960), 55-56, made a similar general observation about the climax of Williams' plays: "When truth enters the scene, it generally takes the form of a violent interruption of a hermetically sealed life of self-deception. Each play centers about an attack, a shock of some sort."

[11] The phrase is Frye's; see Chap. iv, "The Bottomless Dream: Themes of Descent," *Secular Scripture*, pp. [95]-126.

[12] *Anatomy*, p. 239.

[13] *Anatomy*, p. 223.

[14] Cf. Jackson, p. 54, who concludes,
> Williams has put together a kind of modern myth, a symbolic representation of the life of man in our time . . . [which] mirrors modern man's dilemma--his need for . . . a structure which can restore meaning to life and which can reconcile the conflict within reality itself.

[15] As quoted in *The Playwrights Speak*, ed. Walter W. Wager (New York: Delacorte, 1967), p. 232.

[16] Williams confirms his knowledge of Jung in "Letter 56; Nov. 3, 1943," in *Tennessee Williams' Letters to Donald Windham: 1940-*

1965, ed. D. Windham (New York: Holt, 1977), pp. 113-14:

> I am reading Jung now, the man with the
> cosmic-unconscious theory--you should try him--
> and I think he explains logically what Lawrence
> felt intuitively, that the dreadfully conscious and
> willful people with the over-developed minds are
> peculiarly dead and away from the only really warm
> and comforting things in human life. . . . The
> unconscious that wants other things is more and
> more lost and thwarted and so the hearts wither
> up.

[17] C[arl] G[ustave] Jung, "The Concept of the Collective Unconscious" (1936), in *The Archetypes and the Collective Unconscious*, Vol. IX, Pt. i, of *The Collected Works*, trans, R. F. C. Hull, ed. Sir Herbert Read, Michael Fordham, and Gerhard Adler, Bollingen Series, 20 (New York: Pantheon, 1959), p. 43, par. 90; and "Approaching the Unconscious" in *Man and His Symbols*, ed. C. G. Jung (Garden City, N.Y.: Windfall-Doubleday, 1964), p. 67.

[18] "Approaching the Unconscious," in *Man and His Symbols*, pp. 20-21.

[19] Jung, "Conscious, Unconscious and Individuation" (1939), in *The Archetypes*, IX, i, 275, par. 490, and 288, par. 523.

[20] Edward F. Edinger, *Ego and Archetype: Individuation and the Religious Function of the Psyche* (New York, 1972; rpt. Baltimore: Penguin, 1973), p. 7.

[21] *Ego and Archetype*, pp. 131ff. Jungian references to the images cited as archetypes of wholeness or psychic totality include the following: Jung, "The Phenomenology of the Spirit in Fairy Tales" (1948, rev. ed.), in *The Archetypes*, IX, i, 219, n. 14, states: "The mountain stands for the goal of the pilgrimage and ascent, hence it often has the psychological meaning of the self [the union of conscious and unconscious]"; Jung, "Concerning Mandala Symbolism" (1950), in *The Archetypes*, IX, i, 363, par. 652, comments on the significance of the rose as a psychological symbol:

> [The] rose, the Western equivalent of the lotus . . .
> corresponds to the 'Golden Flower' of Chinese al-
> chemy, the rose of the Rosicrucians, and the mystic
> flower in Dante's <u>Paradiso</u>. Rose and lotus are
> usually arranged in groups of four petals, indicating
> the squaring of the circle [the mandala archetype of
> wholeness] or the united opposites.

As regards the idealization of the Platonic relationship, Jung, "Concerning the Archetypes, [and] . . . the Anima Concept" (1954, rev. ed.), in *The Archetypes*, IX, i, 71, par. 146, observes that "homosexuality . . . a matter of incomplete detachment from the hermaphroditic archetype . . . preserves the archetype of the Original Man, which a one-sided sexual being has, up to a point, lost"; and, according to Joseph L. Henderson, "Ancient Myths and Modern Man," in *Man and His Symbols* pp. 149-51, the bird is a Jungian "symbol of transcendence," one of the symbols "which point to man's need for liberation from any state of being that is too immature, too fixed or final."

[22] See Edinger, pp. 37ff: "Encounters with reality frustrate inflated expectations and bring about an estrangement between ego and Self. This estrangement is symbolized by such images as a fall, an exile, an unhealing wound, a perpetual torture" (p. 37); however, "the experience of alienation is a necessary prelude to awareness of the Self" (p. 48), for "the ego must first be disidentified from the Self before the Self can be encountered as 'the other'" (p. 52).

[23] Jung, "The Relations between the Ego and the Unconscious" (1928), in *Two Essays on Analytical Psychology*, Vol. VII of *CW*, 2nd ed. (1953; rpt. New York: Pantheon, 1966), p. 174, par. 269.

[24] "Concerning Mandala Symbolism," in *The Archetypes*, IX, i, 382, par. 705.

[25] "A Study in the Process of Individuation" (1950, rev. ed.), in *The Archetypes*, IX, i, 351, par. 621.

[26] Tennessee Williams, "Desire and the Black Masseur," in his *One Arm and Other Stories* (New York: New Directions, 1954), p. 85.

[27] Cf. Benjamin Nelson, *Tennessee Williams: The Man and His Work* (New York: Ivan Obolensky, 1961), p. 111, who first pointed out that this passsage by Williams "represents a philosophy, or let us say an attitude toward man in his universe, which is to manifest itself in all his work."

[28] The phrase "broken world" derives from the poem "The Broken Tower" by Hart Crane; the fifth stanza containing the phrase serves as an epigraph to *A Streetcar Named Desire*:

> And so it was I entered the broken world
> To trace the visionary company of love, its voice
> An instant in the wind (I know not whither hurled)
> But not for long to hold each desperate choice.

Applied to Williams' plays, the phrase is a metaphor for the modern existential world which lacks a shared mythopoesis of transcendent meaning. The phrase was adopted by Esther Jackson for the title of her book *The Broken World of Tennessee Williams*, in which she advances the thesis that "Form in his [Williams'] drama is the imitation of the individual search for a way of redeeming a shattered universe" (pp. 26-27).

[30] As quoted by Jennings, p. 76.

[31] Williams, as quoted by Lincoln Barnett, "Tennessee Williams," *Life*, Feb. 16, 1948, p. 116.

CHAPTER ONE: *THE GLASS MENAGERIE*

[1] Cf. the interpretation of the thematic significance of Amanda's memory offered by Mary Ann Corrigan, "Memory, Dream, and Myth in the Plays of Tennnessee Williams," *Renascence*, 28 (1976), 156: "The events of *The Glass Menagerie* are enactments of Tom Wingfield's memories. . . . Within the memory sequences the further past has an effect on the present: Amanda Wingfield's reminiscences about the countless gentlemen who called on her in her youth determine her expectations for her daughter."

[2] Frye, *Secular Scripture*, p. 53.

[3] Frye, *Secular Scripture*, p. 53.

[4] The idea of the father in *The Glass Menagerie* as "Williams' God" is expressed by John J. Fritscher, "Some Attitudes and a Posture: Religious Metaphor and Ritual in Tennessee Williams' Query of the American God," *Modern Drama*, 13 (1970), 215.

[5] Erich Neumann, *The Great Mother: An Analysis of the Arche-*

type, trans. Ralph Manheim, Bollingen Series, 47 (New York: Pantheon, 1955), p. 75.

[6] See Frye, *Anatomy*, pp. 203-06.

[7] Edith Hamilton, *Mythology* (New York: Mentor-New American Library, 1942), p. 54.

[8] Neumann, p. 149.

[9] Frye, *Anatomy*, p. 152.

[10] Joseph Campbell, *The Hero with a Thousand Faces* (1949; rpt. New York: Meridian, 1956), pp. 60-62.

CHAPTER TWO: *A STREETCAR NAMED DESIRE*

[1] See Frye, Chap. iv, "The Bottomless Dream: Themes of Descent," in his *Secular Scripture*, pp. [95]-126; see also Chap. ii, "The Context of Romance," pp. [33]-61, and Chap. iii, "Our Lady of Pain: Heroes and Heroines of Romance," pp. [64]-93. Subsequent references to this work in my Chap. Two, Section I, are included in the text.

[2] Leonard Quirino, in his excellent study of the play's mythic symbolism and archetypal imagery, "The Cards Indicate a Voyage on *A Streetcar Named Desire*," in *Tennessee Williams: A Tribute*, ed. Jac Tharpe (Jackson: Univ. Press of Mississippi, 1977), p. 95, calls the play "a tragic parable of the pitiable and terrible fate of the human soul . . . incarnated in treacherous, decaying matter" and "seeking union with the stars." This volume is hereafter cited as *TW: A Tribute*.

[3] Williams refers to the "Tiger-Moth called Blanche" in "T. Williams's View of T. Bankhead," *New York Times*, Dec. 29, 1963; rpt. in *Where I Live: Selected Essays*, ed. Christine R. Day and Bob Woods (New York: New Directions, 1978), p. 153.

[4] Tennessee Williams, *Memoirs* (New York: Doubleday, 1975),

p. 252, concludes with this line in reference to his sister, Rose.

[5] See "Introduction," *Edgar Allan Poe*, ed. Philip Van Doren Stern (New York: Viking Portable Library-Viking, 1945), pp. xvii and xxi.

[6] Edgar Allan Poe, "The Poetic Principle" (1850), in *Edgar Allan Poe: Selected Prose and Poetry*, ed. W. H. Auden, rev. ed. (New York: Rinehart, 1950), p. 418.

[7] Maud Bodkin, *Archetypal Patterns in Poetry: Psychological Studies of Imagination* (London: Oxford Univ. Press, 1934), p. 56, so characterizes the crime of Cain.

[8] The phrase "broken world" derives from Hart Crane's poem "The Broken Tower," four lines of which serve as epigraph to the play; see above, Introduction, n. 28.

[9] See Edinger, pp. 7, 8, 10, 17-18; according to Edinger, p. 7, images of the Garden of Eden, paradise, or heaven all represent archetypes of that "original state of unconscious wholeness and perfection which is responsible for the nostalgia we all have toward our origins, both personal and historical."

[10] All quotations are from the verse translation of *The Aeneid of Virgil*, trans. Rolfe Humphries (New York: Scribner's, 1951). Subsequent page references to this volume are included in the text.

[11] Quirino, "The Cards Indicate a Voyage," in *TW: A Tribute*, pp. 78-79, so designates the symbolic significance of the poker game and shows how "the card game is used by Williams throughout *Streetcar* as a symbol of fate."

[12] See Britton J. Harwood, "Tragedy as Habit: *A Streetcar Named Desire*," in *TW: A Tribute*, p. 108: "The soldiers sprawling 'like daisies' on the lawn are in their own way 'Flores para los muertos.'"

[13] Edinger, p. 76.

[14] Sir James G. Frazer, *The New Golden Bough*, abridged, ed. Theodor H. Gaster (New York: Criterion, 1959), p. 355.

[15] Michael Grant, *Myths of the Greeks and Romans* (New York:

World, 1962), p. 278.

[16] Grant, p. 284.

[17] Hamilton, *Mythology*, p. 61.

[18] Grant, pp. 284 and 282.

[19] All references are to *The Bacchae*, trans. William Arrowsmith, in *Euripides V*, ed. David Grene and Richard Lattimore (Chicago: Univ. of Chicago Press, 1959), pp. 141-220.

[20] Quirino, "The Cards Indicate a Voyage," in *TW: A Tribute*, pp. 78-79.

[21] Hamilton, *Mythology*, p. 297.

[22] Quirino, "The Cards Indicate a Voyage," in *TW: A Tribute*, p. 90.

[23] Jung, "On the Psychogenesis of Schizophrenia" (1939), in *The Psychogenesis of Mental Disease*, Vol. III of *CW* (New York: Pantheon, 1960), p. 235.

[24] Quirino, "The Cards Indicate a Voyage," in *TW: A Tribute*, p. 87.

[25] Hamilton, *Mythology*, p. 270.

[26] Quirino, "The Cards Indicate a Voyage," in *TW: A Tribute*, p. 87.

[27] Hamilton, *Mythology*, p. 271.

[28] Hamilton, *Mythology*, p. 271.

[29] Henderson, in *Man and His Symbols*, p. 146.

[30] *Psychological Reflections: A Jung Anthology*, ed. Jolande Jacobi (London: Routledge and Kegan Paul, 1953), p. 293.

[31] C. Kerényi, "Kore," in C. G. Jung and C. Kerényi, *Essays on a Science of Mythology*, Bollingen Series, 22 (1949; rpt. Princeton: Princeton Univ. Press, 1969), p. 148.

[32] In *Memoirs*, p. 117, Williams echoes Blanche's romantic plan of being "buried at sea sewn up in a clean white sack and dropped overboard" (I, 410): admitting that he is "as much of an hysteric . . . as Blanche," Williams claimed that "a codicil to my will provides for the disposition of my body in this way. 'Sewn up in a clean white sack and dropped over board, twelve hours north of Havana, so that my bones may rest not too far from those of Hart Crane.'" At Williams' death, however, no such codicil was found (*St. Louis Post-Dispatch*, Mar. 3, 1983, p.1); despite his wishes, Williams is buried in Calvary Cemetary, St. Louis.

[33] Frye, *Anatomy*, p. 178.

[34] Frye, *Anatomy*, p. 176.

[35] Frye, *Anatomy*, p. 165.

[36] Frye, *Anatomy*, pp. 177-78.

[37] As quoted by Robert W. Corrigan, "Introduction," *Comedy: Meaning and Form*, ed. R. W. Corrigan (San Francisco: Chandler, 1965), p. 10.

[38] *Memoirs*, p. 125. In its original context, the statement refers to the conduct of Williams' sister Rose after her mental breakdown and subsequent lobotomy. "For nowadays the world is lit by lightning!" is one of Tom's final lines in *The Glass Menagerie* (I, 237); "A plague has stricken the moths" is the first line of Williams' poem, "Lament for the Moths," in *In the Winter of Cities* (New York: New Directions, 1956), p. 31; and the final reference to "Blanche . . . 'put away'" is, of course, specifically to Blanche DuBois, but also refers to the loss in the modern existential world of the romantic values she embodies. The final stanza of "Lament for the Moths" is a prayer for the return of such fragile, transcendent beauty:

> Give them, O mother of moths and mother of men,
> strength to enter the heavy world again,
> for delicate were the moths and badly wanted
> here in a world by mammoth figures haunted!

CHAPTER THREE: *THE ROSE TATTOO*

[1] Frye, *Anatomy*, p. 144

[2] *The Reader's Encyclopedia*, ed. William Rose Benét (New York: Crowell, 1955), p. 947.

[3] Dante, *The Divine Comedy*, in *The Portable Dante*, trans. Laurence Binyon, ed. Paolo Milano (New York: Viking, 1947), p. 488.

[4] Jung makes reference to the significance of the circle as an archetype of psychic wholeness throughout his works; for specific references, see "A Study in the Process of Individuation" (1934; rev. 1950) and "Concerning Mandala Symbolism" (1950), in *The Archetypes*, IX, i, 290-354 and 355-90, respectively.

[5] Jung, *Symbols of Transformation* (1911-12), Vol. V of *CW*, 286-88, gives an account of "the hysterical German nun [Anna Catherina Emmerich] who received the stigmata," and comments on the psychological experience of such hysteria:

> It is a well-known fact that hysterics substitute a physical pain for a psychic pain which is not felt because repressed. . . . The wounding and painful shafts do not come from outside, . . . but from the ambush of our own unconscious. . . . It is a well-known fact that scenes of mystic union with the Saviour are strongly tinged with erotic libido. Stigmatization amounts to an incubation with the Saviour, a slight modification of the ancient conception of the <u>unio mystica</u> as cohabitation with the god.

[6] Hugh Dickinson, *Myth on the Modern Stage* (Chicago: Univ. of Illinois Press, 1969), p. 282, makes the observation that "*The Rose Tattoo* derives its plot from Petronius' tale of the Widow of Ephesus, but it does not depend closely on it for its development or outcome." The myth of the dying and reviving god Dionysus *is* important to the play's development and outcome.

[7] "The Rose Tattoo," *Vogue*, March 15, 1951, p. 96.

[8] Frazer, *The New Golden Bough*, p. 352.

9 Frazer, p. 352.

10 Frazer, p. 355.

11 Frazer, p. 356.

12 "The Rose Tattoo," *Vogue*, p. 96.

CHAPTER FOUR: *CAT ON A HOT TIN ROOF*

1 W. Hamilton, trans., "Introduction," Plato, *The Symposium* (Baltimore: Penguin, 1951), p. 13.

2 W. Hamilton, in Plato, p. 12.

3 Historically, Jack Straw was "one of the leaders in the Peasants' Revolt of 1381," and his name soon came to signify "a man of straw, a worthless sort of person," according to *The Reader's Encyclopedia*, p. 550. Chaucer makes allusion to Jack Straw and the Peasants' Revolt in "The Nun's Priest's Tale" of *The Canterbury Tales* (1387-1400), in *The Works of Geoffrey Chaucer*, ed. F. N. Robinson, 2nd ed. (1957; rpt. Boston: Houghton-Mifflin, 1961), p. 205:

> So hydous was the noyse, a, benedicitee!
> Certes, he Jakke Straw and his meynee
> Ne made nevere shoutes half so shrille
> Whan that they wolden any Flemyng kille,
> As thilke day was maad upon the fox. (11.3393-97)

Appropriately, in the play Jack Straw represents a "revolt" against the prevailing taboo against homosexual relationships; at the same time, his homosexuality makes him "a worthless sort of person" in the eyes of a society "*disgusted* . . . by things like that" (III, 119). All the references to Jack Straw in Williams' play invest him with truly democratic, humane, and humanitarian values in direct contrast to the moral corruption, greed, and mendacity of an American society represented in microcosm by the Pollitt family and their circle.

[4] Hamilton, *Mythology*, pp. 88-89; Frazer, pp. 320-21.

[5] Hamilton, *Mythology*, p. 89.

[6] See Edinger, pp. 7-16.

[7] Plato, p. 64.

[8] Plato, p. 63.

[9] Plato, p. 62.

[10] For an analysis of Brick as Hippolytus, Maggie as a figure who evolves from an Artemis to an Aphrodite and a Phaedra, and Big Daddy as a Theseus, see Robert Hethmon, "The Foul Rag-and-Bone Shop of the Heart," *Drama Critique*, 8 (1965), 94-102.

[11] See Hamilton, *Mythology*, pp. 87-88.

[12] Edinger, p. 161.

[13] "Dying and Reviving Gods," in his *Golden Bough*, pp. 284-85.

[14] Plato, p. 94.

[15] See Frazer, pp. 285-89, 309-16, 322-29.

[16] *The New Larousse Encyclopedia of Mythology*, ed. Robert Graves (New York: Hamlyn, 1976), pp. 16-20.

[17] *Larousse*, p. 18.

[18] *Larousse*, p. 19.

[19] Alban Butler, "St. Margaret, or Marina, Virgin and Martyr (No Date)," in *Butler's Lives of the Saints*, ed., rev., and suppl. by Herbert Thurston, S. J., and Donald Attwater (New York: P. J. Kenedy, 1956), III, 152-53.

[20] See *Larousse*, pp. 36-37, for all references to Maggie as analogue of the Egyptian goddess Bast.

[21] *Larousse*, p. 121; the Roman goddess Diana, originally "a goddess of light, mountains, and woods," was rapidly hellenised,

according to *Larousse*, p. 211. As the Greek Artemis, her identification as a "goddess of light" was elevated to the status of a "moon-goddess" (*Larousse*, p. 121). However, according to *Larousse*, p. 121, the "lunar quality" of Artemis became less marked, as a special moon goddess, Selene, assumed that function; thus, in her aspect of "light-goddess," Artemis bore the same functions as Apollo: "Like him armed with bow and quiver, she bore the epithet *Apollousa*, the destructress; or *Iocheaira*, who liked to let fly with arrows, strike down mortals with her fearful darts, and assail their flocks with deadly disease." At the same time, "in her capacity of moon-goddess Artemis presided over childbirth, jointly with Ilithyia."

The point of all this information is that it serves to substantiate the complex paradoxical nature of Williams' Maggie as an ironic version of Diana-Artemis, who reverses or undermines the roles of the original goddess. As lunar goddess, Artemis was associated both with chastity and childbirth; with destruction (usually of women); and with the source of life: so, too, is Williams' Maggie. Thus, although Brick's preoccupation with the moon clearly signifies his yearning for a condition and sphere wholly beyond his reach, there is no essential contradiction in the idea that as a debased Diana, Maggie represents in one sense what Brick craves. She does, although ironically. Brick craves a pure, true, ideal love, non-existent in the sublunary sphere he inhabits; Maggie offers Brick an impure, inferior, but realizable version of that ideal. In so doing, Maggie fulfills the role of a debased, ironic, or sublunary version of Diana-Artemis, lunargoddess.

[22] Frazer, p. 301; see also Neumann, p. 275, who identifies Artemis as representing that aspect of the Great Goddess known as "the Lady of the Beasts," traditionally holding, sitting on, or incarnated as a lion: "As the Great Artemis and Diana, she is queen of the animal world." Isis also shares this aspect of the Great Mother, according to Neumann, p. 275.

[23] *Larousse*, p. 121.

[24] *Larousse*, p. 209.

[25] Hamilton, *Mythology*, p. 32.

[26] *Larousse*, pp. 120-21.

[27] Hamilton, *Mythology*, p. 31.

[28] *Larousse*, p. 121.

[29] See Hamilton, *Mythology*, pp. 137-39, for the story of Otis and Ephialtes.

[30] See Hamilton, *Mythology*, pp. 30-31, for all subsequent references to Apollo.

[31] Robert Heilman, "Chapter Five: Tennessee Williams," in his *The Iceman, The Arsonist, and the Troubled Agent: Tragedy and Melodrama on the Modern Stage* (Seattle: Univ. of Washington Press, 1973), p. 125; Heilman places Williams' original version of *Cat* in the tragic mode, beyond the melodramatic "disaster of personality" (p. 124), on the grounds that "His central character is the man who himself committed the originating deed and who is on the edge of acknowledging his own guilt" (p. 126).

[32] See Frye, *Anatomy*, pp. 23-29.

[33] Hamilton, *Mythology*, p. 239, refers to the *seven* sons and seven daughters of Niobe; *Larousse*, p. 121, reports *six*.

[34] *Larousse*, p. 19.

[35] Ernest Hemingway, *The Sun Also Rises* (1926; rpt. New York: Scribner's, 1954), p. 247.

[36] William Peterson, "Williams, Kazan, and the Two Cats," *New Theatre Magazine*, 7 (1967), 14-19, analyzes many of the play's parallel situations and repeated lines, including Brick's iteration of Big Daddy's line; Peterson makes a case for the superiority of Williams' original conclusion over the Broadway ending on this basis.

[37] Heilman, *The Iceman*, p. 122.

[38] Cf. my analysis of the two endings of *Cat* with the study of the two stage versions plus the film version of the play by William Sacksteder, "The Three Cats: A Study in Dramatic Structure," *Drama Survey*, 5 (1967), 252-66, which discusses the weaknesses of the two stage plays and makes a case for the greater dramatic integrity of the play's 1958 filmscript over either stage version.

[39] In the summer of 1974, *Cat on a Hot Tin Roof* was revived by the American Shakespeare Theatre in Stratford, Conn., and returned to Broadway that fall, reopening at the ANTA Theatre. For that revival, Williams made several revisions, published in *Cat on a Hot Tin Roof* (New York: New Directions, 1975). The most important revisions are to the play's controversial third act, in which Williams combines those parts of the Broadway ending which dramatize Big Daddy's return with his original ending in which no change takes place in Brick. The revisions consist largely of rearranging the verbatim lines from each ending to achieve this hybrid conclusion, adding very little new dialogue or action. As such, this "revised version" of the play neither addresses nor affects the problems raised in this analysis, and Brick remains at the end of Act II as in the original script: on the verge of a self-confrontation that never takes place.

[40] Walter Kerr, *New York Herald Tribune*, March 25, 1955, as quoted in Felicia Hardison Londré, *Tennessee Williams* (New York: Frederick Ungar, 1979), p. 127; see also Williams' response, "Critic Says 'Evasion,' Writer Says 'Mystery,'" *New York Herald Tribune*, April 17, 1955; rpt. in *Where I Live*, pp. 70-74, in which Williams defends the ambiguity of Brick's characterization by citing his "Note" subsequently appended to published editions of the play; he further confuses the issue of Brick's sexuality by adding that "Brick's overt sexual adjustment was, and must always remain, a heterosexual one," although "his sexual nature was not innately 'normal.'"

CHAPTER FIVE: *ORPHEUS DESCENDING*

[1] Nelson, p. 230, comments:

> For more than two acts, Orpheus Descending offers us the spectacle of two almost distinct dramas vying for dominance; but in the middle of the final act, the morality play emerges the dominant and the character of Lady Torrance and the story of her reawakening to life is lost in the symbolic hysteria which engulfs the proceedings.

[2] Paul Diel, *Symbolism in Greek Mythology*, trans. Vincent Stuart et al. (Paris, 1966; rpt. Boulder: Shambhala, 1980), p. 116.

[3] In the play's original version, *Battle of Angels*, Carol Cutrere is named Cassandra Whiteside.

[4] See Nancy Traubitz, "Myth as a Basis of Dramatic Structure in *Orpheus Descending*," *Modern Drama*, 19 (March 1976), 59-60.

[5] Dickinson, "Tennessee Williams: Orpheus as Savior," in his *Myth on the Modern Stage*, p. 308.

[6] Valentine Xavier's name has its source in Williams' ancestral lineage. In *Memoirs*, p. 12, Williams traces his father's direct descent from "the brother Valentine of Tennessee's first Governor John Sevier," his last name a variant of *Xavier*. According to Williams, his father's descendents became divided along religious lines, between Roman Catholics and Huguenots: "The Catholics remained Xaviers; the Huguenots changed their name to Sevier when they fled to England at the time of St. Bartholomew's Massacre. St. Francis Xavier . . . is the family's nearest claim to world reknown [sic]."

[7] Leonard Quirino, "Tennessee Williams' Persistent *Battle of Angels*," *Modern Drama*, 11 (May 1968), 31, identifies Val Xavier with "the martyred St. Valentine as 'love savior.'"

[8] *The Reader's Encyclopedia*, p. 979.

[9] Traubitz, p. 59.

[10] Mircea Eliade, *Myths, Dreams and Mysteries: The Encounter between Contemporary Faiths and Archaic Realities*, trans. Philip Mairet (1957; rpt. New York: Harper, 1960), p. 78.

[11] Eliade, *Myths, Dreams, and Mysteries*, pp. 60-61.

[12] Henderson, in *Man and His Symbols*, p. 151; see also Eliade, "The Magic Flight," in *Myths, Dreams, and Mysteries*, pp. 99-110.

[13] Eliade, *Myths, Dreams, and Mysteries*, p. 60.

[14] Tennessee Williams, "Heavenly Grass: from Blue Mountain Ballads" (1946), in *In The Winter of Cities*, p. 97.

[15] Henderson, in *Man and His Symbols*, p. 141.

[16] Henderson, in *Man and His Symbols*, pp. 142 and 145.

[17] Henderson, in *Man and His Symbols*, p. 148.

[18] Williams, "Orpheus Descending," in *In the Winter of Cities*, pp. 27-28.

[19] Quirino, "Persistent *Battle of Angels*," p. 27.

[20] Hamilton, *Mythology*, p. 57.

[21] In *Battle of Angels*, Lady's name was Myra, an anagram of Mary, which emphasized her association with the Virgin Mary; cf. Henry Popkin, p. 60, who also notes that Myra is "a variant of Mary," and finds the allusion retained in *Orpheus* through the suggestion of "Lady" as "Our Lady."

[22] Nelson, p. 238.

[23] Quirino, "Persistent *Battle of Angels*," p. 34.

[24] Brooks Atkinson, "Theatre: Rural Orpheus," *New York Times*, Mar. 22, 1957; rpt. in *New York Theatre Critics' Reviews*, 18 (1957), 310; hereafter cited as *NYTCR*.

[25] See Nelson, p. 230: "Williams presents a conglomeration of pagan and Christian symbolism and myth which obliterates almost all else in its intensity and confusion."

[26] John Chapman, "*Orpheus Descending* Has Fiery Scenes and Acting, But It Misses," *Daily News*, Mar. 22, 1957; rpt. in *NYTCR*, 18 (1957), 310.

[27] Dickinson, p. 291.

[28] For quoted material, see Dickinson, p. 291.

[29] Dickinson, p. 291, mentions most of these parallels, as well as others.

[30] Norman J. Fedder, *The Influence of D. H. Lawrence on*

Tennessee Williams (The Hague, Netherlands: Mouton, 1966), pp. 63-73, analyzes the parallels between *Battle of Angels-Orpheus Descending* and Lawrence's "The Fox" and *Lady Chatterly's Lover*. Williams himself, "The Past, the Present and the Perhaps," in *Theatre* III, 220, refers to both versions of his play as "the tale of a wild-spirited boy who wanders into a conventional community of the South and creates the commotion of a fox in a chicken coop."

[31]Foster Hirsch, *A Portrait of the Artist: The Plays of Tennessee Williams* (Port Washington, N.Y.: Kennikat Press, 1979), p. 21 quotes Williams as saying he had tried "to represent . . . one of Lawrence's main ideas which is the almost religious purity and beauty of the sexual relationship," but that "Somehow or other an effect almost the opposite . . . seemed to be created in the minds of some of its beholders."

CHAPTER SIX: *SUDDENLY LAST SUMMER*

[1] All references, except where otherwise noted, are to *Suddenly Last Summer* as published in *The Theatre of Tennessee Williams*, III (New York: New Directions, 1971), 343-423, which appears to be a revised edition of its original 1958 publication, although no citation of it as such is made by New Directions nor, to my knowledge, has it been noted in previous Williams' scholarship. Drewey Wayne Gunn, *Tennessee Williams: A Bibliography* (Metuchen, N.J.: Scarecrow, 1980), pp. 10-20, continues to cite the play's first edition, *Suddenly Last Summer* (New York: New Directions, 1958), pp. 13-88, as having the same contents as all subsequent publications of the play, including its revised version in *Theatre*. However, because the play has been reprinted so often since its initial publication, it is difficult to determine exactly when the revisions were made without a thorough collation of all the texts. No attempt is here made to present a comparative analysis of all texts of *SLS*; rather, the 1971 *Theatre* revisions significant to my discussion are compared to the 1958 text of *SLS* as reprinted in *Tennessee Williams: Four Plays* (New York: Signet-NAL, 1976), pp. [3]-93.

Several substantive changes and deletions appear in the 1971

Theatre edition of *SLS* which significantly alter the play's content and structure. All of these changes and deletions are confined to Scene i and fall within pp. 356-57 of *Theatre*, corresponding to pp. 17-20 of *SLS* (1958) as reprinted by Signet in *Tennessee Williams: Four Plays* (1976). These revisions include the following:

1) In the 1976 Signet reprint of *SLS* (1958), pp. 18-19, Dr. Cukrowicz tells a story of the first lobotomy he performed on a young girl, with which reenactment Catharine is threatened. This story is deleted from the 1971 *Theatre* edition.

2) In Signet, p. 17, Dr. Cukrowicz speaks the lines concerning the difficulty of man's search for God, emphasizing its particular difficulty for "doctors," adding that "doctors look for God, too." In *Theatre*, p. 357, Mrs. Venable speaks the lines concerning the difficulty of man's search for God, particularly for "poets." The line "doctors look for God, too" is deleted.

3) In Signet, p. 19, Dr. Cukrowicz is made to express shocked incredulity in response to Mrs. Venable's account of Sebastian's belief that he had found "God" reflected in the predatory spectacle enacted on the Galapagos Islands:

Doctor:

I can see how he might be, I think he would be disturbed if he thought he'd seen God's image, an equation of God, in that spectacle you watched in the Encantadas: creatures of the air hovering over and swooping down to devour creatures of the sea that had had the bad luck to be hatched on land and weren't able to scramble back into the sea fast enough to escape that massacre you witnessed, yes, I can see how such a spectacle could be equated with a good deal of--experience, existence!--but not with God! Can you?

In the 1971 *Theatre* edition, p. 357, Dr. Cukrowicz simply responds with a neutral expression of comprehension: "I see."

4) From the 1971 *Theatre* edition has been deleted a significant exchange between Dr. Cukrowicz and Mrs. Venable in which she explains to him what Sebastian meant by his identification of "God" with the spectacle on the Encantadas. That exchange is here quoted in full as it appears in the Signet reprint of *SLS* (1958), p. 20:

223

Doctor:

Did he mean we must rise above God?

Mrs. Venable:

He meant that God shows a savage face to people
and shouts some fierce things at them, it's all we
see or hear of Him. Isn't it all we ever really
see and hear of Him, now?--Nobody seems to
know why. . . .

Specific commentary on these revisions and deletions are made in
subsequent notes (see notes 5 and 69) and throughout my discussion
of the play (see Section XII of the text). However, the generali-
zation may be made that the predominant effect of these changes and
deletions is to diminish the characterization of Dr. Cukrowicz, and
thus reduce the significance of his functions--dramatic, symbolic,
thematic, and structural--in the 1971 *Theatre* edition of the play.

[2] Frye, *Anatomy*, p. 147. See also Leonard Quirino, "Chapter
Four: *Suddenly Last Summer*: The Play and the Myth," in his "The
Darkest Celebrations of Tennessee Williams," Diss. Brown 1964, pp.
125-27; Quirino first used Frye's designation and definition of the
"demonic" mode in reference to the play's imagery and symbolism. I
am indebted to Quirino for many fine insights into the mythic and
Jungian significance of characterization in the play and for leading me to relevant source material; based on these similar sources,
portions of my Sections VIII and IX parallel closely at some points
Quirino's [Part] III, "The Myth and Ritual of Attis and Cybele,"
pp. 168-74, and [Part] IV, "The Psychology of the Relationship of
Violet and Sebastian," pp. 174-79.

[3] Frye, *Anatomy*, pp. 148 and 149.

[4] I have followed textual authority in the spelling
of Catharine's name with a medial *a* rather than *e*. The
Theatre edition spells her name "Catharine" throughout the
play's text; the 1976 Signet rpt. of *SLS* the 1958 edition
also employs "Catharine" in the text (although the variant
"Catherine" appears in the list designating the "Cast of
Characters," p. [7], of the play's 1958 production).

[5] In the 1976 Signet-NAL reprint of the play's original 1958
edition, p. 20, Mrs. Venable is given dialogue deleted from the

1971 *Theatre* text, in which she explains more fully to Dr. Cukrowicz what Sebastian meant by equating the devouring of the sea turtles by the flesh-eating birds with "a clear image" of God: "He meant that God shows a savage face to people and shouts some fierce things at them, it's all we see or hear of Him . . . (see above, note 1 for complete passage). The deletion of this passage not only removes from Sebastian's "vision" the sense of modern existential *angst* occasioned by the "disappearance of God," but also removes what had been, perhaps, the single most significant phrase of the entire play in its original version: the "savage face" of God.

Although the term "savage" is retained in the *Theatre* text in its various references to the animal world--the "beasts, serpents and birds, all of savage nature" (p. 349); "the horrible savage cries" of the carnivorous birds (pp. 355-56)--its deletion in reference to "God" makes the symbolic associations between the naturalistic world and Sebastian's metaphysic less emphatic. For a specific description of the "God" Sebastian believes he sees in the Encantadas, we are left only with Catharine's reference to Sebastian's image of a "*terrible* sort of a . . . God . . . a--*cruel* one . . ." (p. 397). The substitution of the terms "terrible" and "cruel" for "savage" makes no denotative difference in the play's characterization of the modern "God," but it makes a substantial connotative difference: in the play's 1958 text, the term "savage" is made to reverberate with both naturalistic and "divine" significance.

[6] See Gilbert Debusscher, "Tennessee Williams as Hagiographer: An Aspect of Obliquity in Drama," *Revue des Langues Vivantes*, 40 (1974), 449-56; rpt. as "Tennessee Williams' Lives of the Saints: A Playwright's Obliquity," in *Tennessee Williams: A Collection of Critical Essays* (hereafter cited as *TW: A Collection*), pp. 149-57; Debusscher points out many correspondences between Sebastian Venable and his "name saint" and concludes that Williams' character represents the "debunked" counterpart of the martyred St. Sebastian. (Debusscher also finds ironic correspondences between *Milk Train*'s Christopher Flanders and St. Christopher, and between *Iguana*'s T. Lawrence Shannon and St. Laurence.)

[7] Butler, "St. Sebastian, Martyr (A.D. 288?)," *Lives of the Saints*, I, 128.

[8] Tatsumi Funatsu, "A Study of *Suddenly Last Summer*," *Fukuoka*

University Review of Literature and Science, 7 (1963), 359.

[9] Jung, *Symbols of Transformation*, V of *CW*, 291-92.

[10] Butler, I, 130.

[11] Butler, I, 130.

[12] Williams, "Letter 154: June 20, 1960," in *Letters to Donald Windham: 1940-1965*, p. 309: ". . . Sebastian's being eaten up by those whom he had eaten was the poetic abstraction of a truth which is truer than any factual one."

[13] Williams, "San Sebastiano de Sodoma," in *In The Winter of Cities*, p. 108.

[14] John Ower, "Erotic Mythology in the Poetry of Tennessee Williams," in *TW: A Tribute*, p. 613.

[15] Ower, in *TW: A Tribute*, p. 613.

[16] See Williams, "Desire and the Black Masseur," in his *One Arm and Other Stories*, pp. 83-94.

[17] "Desire and the Black Masseur," in *One Arm*, p. 85.

[18] Charles Darwin, *The Voyage of the Beagle*, ed. Charles W. Eliot, 2nd ed., The Harvard Classics, 29 (1840; rpt. New York: P. F. Collier, 1909), p. 407.

[19] Charles Darwin, *The Origin of Species*, ed. Charles W. Eliot, the Harvard Classics, 11 (1859; rpt. New York: P. F. Collier, 1909), p. 297.

[20] Paul J. Hurley, "*Suddenly Last Summer* as 'Morality Play,'" *Modern Drama*, 8 (1966), 396. (It is interesting to note as relevant to the textual study of *SLS* that although Hurley cites as the edition of the play he uses New York (1958), those passsages he quotes from the play agree in content with the 1971 *Theatre* edition; since his article was published in 1966, it follows that the revisions of *SLS* 1958 were made in or prior to that year.) See also Thomas P. Adler, "The Search for God in the Plays of Tennessee Williams," *Renascence*, 26 (1973), 48-56; rpt. in *TW: A Collection*, pp. 138-48, who describes Sebastian Venable, as well as *Iguana's*

Shannon and *Kingdom of Earth*'s Chicken, p. 141, as "three male characters . . . who become so obsessed with the evil in themselves and in those around them that they transfer this evil to God, creating a God devoid of any goodness or love." Adler, p. 142, concludes that this is "Williams' clearest warning that the worst possible evil is to become so obsessed with evil that you lose belief in any good or love, and thus risk being destroyed by your own vision of evil."

[21] Hurley, pp. 396 and 393.

[22] Herman Melville, *Moby Dick* (1851), ed. Harrison Hayford and Hershel Parker, A Norton Critical Edition (New York: W. W. Norton, 1967), p. 175.

[23] Melville, *Moby Dick*, p. 362.

[24] Melville, *Moby Dick*, pp. 262 and 255.

[25] Herman Melville, "The Encantadas or Enchanted Isles" (1854), in *Great Short Works of Herman Melville*, ed. Warner Berthoff (New York: Harper, 1969), p. 104.

[26] Melville, "The Encantadas or Enchanted Isles," p. 106.

[27] Melville, *Moby Dick*, p. 169.

[28] James R. Hurt, "*Suddenly Last Summer*: Williams and Melville," *Modern Drama*, 3 (1961), 400.

[29] Melville, *Moby Dick*, p. 169.

[30] Melville, *Moby Dick*, p. 354.

[31] Melville, *Moby Dick*, pp. 354-55.

[32] According to Butler, "St. Catherine of Alexandria," *Lives of the Saints*, IV, 420-21, the virgin martyr was sentenced to be killed on a spiked wheel (hence the "catherine-wheel"): "When she was placed on it, her bonds were miraculously loosed and the wheel broke, its spikes flying off and killing many of the onlookers." According to Christina Hole, *Saints in Folklore* (New York: M. Barrows-William Morrow, 1965), p. 75, the catherine-wheel, emblem of the saint's martyrdom, is an ancient fire symbol, "an image of

the life-giving sun." In the play, the image is ironically inverted to symbolize fiery destruction. St. Catherine of Alexandria is not the same figure as St. Catherine of Bologna (Virgin, A.D. 1463) to whom Catharine Holly is compared later in the text (see Section XI).

[33] Melville, *Moby Dick*, p. 169.

[34] The precise date of the play's dramatic present is not established in the text. However, the previous summer's date is established as 1935 by the reference to Sebastian's final "Poem of Summer" and its date (p. 407). Thus, the dramatic action probably takes place "between late summer and early fall" (p. 349) of 1936.

[35] Quirino, "The Darkest Celebrations," pp. 130-31, points out the specific references which extend the play's historical scope and concludes that "Williams is dramatizing from the outset . . . a vision of the timelessness of an action."

[36] Quirino, "The Darkest Celebrations," p. 133, explains the symbolic appropriateness of Mrs. Venable's insignia, her "starfish of diamonds" (p. 350), as an emblem of her rapacity. According to Quirino, pp. 133-34, "the starfish . . . feeds on aquatic animals such as crabs and mollusks by clinging to their shells with its tubular feet, exerting suction until the shells open and extruding its stomach to envelop the soft bodies of its victims." It is thus "emblematic of the function of the Venables." He also points out that "diamonds" are the means by which Mrs. Venable "wields her power."

[37] Several critics have explored the symbolism of the Venable name. Quirino, "The Darkest Celebrations," p. 133, ingeniously notes that Mrs. Venable's name sounds like "a Southern pronunciation of 'venerable'" and is justified as such by her "goddess-like fostering [of] the jungle values memorialized in this primeval garden by her god-like son, Sebastian." William Taylor, "Tennessee Williams: Academia on Broadway," in *Essays in Modern American Literature*, ed. Richard E. Langford (DeLand, Fla.: Stetson Univ. Press, 1963), pp. 92-93, traces the etymology of "venable" and also notes that Sebastian's name is derived from the Greek "Sebastos," meaning "august" or "venerable."

[38] Anthony S. Mercatante, *The Magic Garden: The Myth and*

Folklore of Flowers, Plants, Trees, and Herbs (New York: Harper, 1976), p. 70.

[39] Sigmund Freud, *The Interpretation of Dreams*, trans. A. A. Brill, rev. ed. (London, 1913; rpt. New York: Macmillan, 1948) p. 353.

[40] Quirino, "The Darkest Celebrations," p. 136: "Victims are portrayed as potential or actual victimizers in the play, and victimizers as potential or actual victims."

[41] In *Memoirs*, Williams speaks freely of his own psychiatric experiences. As he tells us, the production of *Suddenly Last Summer*, in conjunction with the one-act *Something Unspoken*, performed together under the title *Garden District* (1958), "was the first that I went into after the disaster of *Orpheus Descending* and my subsequent term of Freudian analysis" (p. 175). It is likely that many of the psychological ideas behind the relationship between Sebastian and Violet Venable, as well as the psychiatric methods used by Dr. Cukrowicz with Catharine, were in Williams' mind at this time. In recounting his subsequent breakdown in the sixties, Williams echoes several ideas pertinent to the psychological characterization of Violet and Sebastian. During his hospitalization in 1969, Williams put to his mother a question relevant to the relationship between Violet and Sebastian: "Why do women bring children into the world and then destroy them?" adding parenthetically, "I still consider this a rather good question" (p. 219). He also recalls during the same period his repeated chanting of the single word "redemption," and reflects that he may have been referring to "a redemption from the 'crime' of my love-life with boys and young men" (p. 220).

[42] Edinger, p. 6.

[43] Jung, *Symbols of Transformation*, V of *CW*, 304.

[44] Sigmund Freud, "Group Psychology and the Analysis of the Ego" (1921); rpt. in *A General Selection from the Works of Sigmund Freud*, ed. John Rickman, M. D. (Garden City, N.Y.: Anchor-Doubleday, 1957), p. 186.

[45] Cf. Quirino, "[Part] IV: The Psychology of the Relationship of Violet and Sebastian," in *The Darkest Celebrations*, pp. 174-79, who first explored the relationship's Jungian psychological

implications.

[46] Freud, "The Origin and Development of Psychoanalysis" (1910), in *A General Selection*, p. 31.

[47] Jung, *Symbols of Transformation*, V of *CW*, 312; Quirino, p. 175, similarly concludes:

> In a Jungian interpretation of the relationship, Mrs. Venable would be considered Sebastian's anima . . . [which] can contribute to the destruction of a man if he either allows himself to be too dominated by the venerability of the image or if, at the other extreme, he breaks his bond with it, as Sebastian attempted to do the summer he was destroyed, completely.

[48] Jung, *Symbols of Transformation*, V, 328.

[49] Jung, *Symbols of Transformation*, V, 251.

[50] Two Williams scholars have previously noted the playwright's use of the Attis-Cybele myth in this play. Quirino, "The Darkest Celebrations," was the first to identify and interpret the psychological relationship of the myth to the play; see "[Part] III: The Myth and Ritual of Attis and Cybele," pp. 168-74, of his "Chap. V: *Suddenly Last Summer*: The Play and the Myth": Quirino, p. 127, notes that

> Sebastian's blossoming forth with a poem every summer after nine months of pregnant preparation metaphorically parodies the function of a vegetation deity, and his relationship with his mother psychologizes the Attis-Cybele myth.

Subsequently, Constance Mary Drake, "Six Plays by Tennessee Williams: Myth in the Modern World," Diss. Ohio State Univ. 1970, relates Williams' use of the Attis-Cybele myth and Jungian archetypes in *Suddenly Last Summer* to her thesis of his recurrent use of myths concerning "the fertility god and goddess and related concepts of sacrifice and rebirth."

[51] Jung, *Symbols of Transformation*, V of *CW*, 423.

[52] Frazer, p. 311.

[53] Jung, *Symbols of Transformation*, V of *CW*, 424.

[54] Frazer, p. 311.

[55] Frazer, p. 313.

[56] Jung, *Symbols of Transformation*, V of *CW*, 246, n. 72.

[57] Tristram P. Coffin, *The Book of Christmas Folklore* (New York: Seabury Press, 1973), p. 23

[58] Lesley Gordon, *Green Magic: Flowers, Plants and Herbs in Lore and Legend* (New York: Viking, 1977), p. 39.

[59] Coffin, p. 23

[60] See Butler, "St. Catherine of Bologna, Virgin (A.D. 1463)," *Lives of the Saints*, I, 536-39; all subsequent references to this entry appear in the text of this chapter. In contrast to Quirino and other Williams scholars who find in Catharine Holly's "saintly" characterization a sole identification of her with St. Catherine of Alexandria (see Quirino, p. 190, note 17), based largely on the play's evocation of the image of the catherine-wheel (see above, note 32), I find many more similarities between the characterization of Catharine Holly as ironic saint and St. Catherine of Bologna (her place-name itself a pun on Catharine Holly's sainthood as specious or "baloney"?). Such an evocation of both saints is indicative of Williams' allusive, rather than allegorical, method (as well as his proclivity for puns).

[61] Hurt, p. 399, also suggests that "the play may be seen as a struggle for the soul of Catherine [sic] between the dead Sebastian and Dr. Cukrowicz."

[62] Calvin S. Hall, *A Primer of Freudian Psychology* (New York: New American Library, 1958), p. 31.

[63] Bruno Bettelheim, *The Uses of Enchantment: The Meaning and Importance of Fairy Tales* (1976; rpt. New York: Vintage-Random House, 1977), p. 172.

[64] Jung, *Modern Man in Search of a Soul*, trans. W. S. Dell and Cary F. Baynes (New York: Harvest-Harcourt, 1933), p. 234.

[65] Jung, *Modern Man in Search of a Soul*, p. 235.

[66] Quirino, "The Darkest Celebrations," p. 136, also notes that "In the blond doctor we are presented with another potential sacrifice to the cannibalistic elements of money and power," but that, "in his capacity to perform lobotomies, [he is] also . . . a potential cannibal and castrator."

[67] Harry Levin, *The Power of Blackness: Hawthorne, Poe, Melville* (New York: Vintage-Random House, 1958), p. 143.

[68] Williams, *Memoirs*, p. 251. There is little question that Catharine's characterization, insofar as it concerns her proposed lobotomy, is based on Williams' sister, Rose Isabel Williams. As is well known, Williams' sister, Rose, was subjected to a lobotomy, "one of the first performed in the States" (p. 48) which took place "in the late thirties" (p. 126). According to Williams, "having been so tragically becalmed by the prefrontal lobotomy" (p. 126), Rose was thereafter institutionalized in a series of public and private asylums. Like Catharine in *SLS*, Rose was initially placed in a "Catholic sanitarium" (p. 121) but was transferred in 1937 to the Missouri State Asylum, a facility similar to the institution Catharine is threatened with, and described by Williams as "too awful to believe" (p. 125). In commenting on Rose's lobotomy, Williams states: "I regard that as a tragically mistaken procedure, as I believe that without it Rose could have made a recovery and returned to what is called 'normal life,' which, despite its many assaults upon the vulnerable nature, is still preferable to an institution existence" (p. 251).

[69] All page references to *SLS* (1958) are to its reprint in *Tennessee Williams: Four Plays*, pp. [3]-93, and will be cited in the text by page number and publisher's imprint (Signet); see above, note 1, for complete publishing information.

[70] Catharine's allusive comment--"The truth's the one thing I have never resisted! . . . They say it's at the bottom of a bottomless well, you know" (p. 401)--is a paraphrase of a passage by Byron in "Canto the Second," stanza 84, of his mock-epic *Don Juan* (1824). The line appears, significantly, in that section vividly describing the desperate measures of a ship-wrecked crew to survive, which culminate in their cannibalizing each other. The pertinent stanza concludes,

If you had been in Turkey or in Spain
Or with a famish'd boat's-crew had your berth,
Or in the desert heard the camel's bell,
You'd wish yourself where Truth is--in a well"
(ll. 669-72).

CHAPTER SEVEN: *SWEET BIRD OF YOUTH*

[1] Peter L. Hays, "Tennessee Williams' Use of Myth in *Sweet Bird of Youth*," *Educational Theatre Journal*, 18 (1966), 256, similarly identifies the symbolic significance of Heavenly's name.

[2] Hays, p. 255, points out that all the characters are in some form "castrated," but does not relate the symbolic significance of castration to the play's theme of a diminished and demythicized modern world whose inhabitants have been "cut off" from heroic goals or spiritual values.

[3] Popkin, pp. 45-64, first identified Chance as an Adonis figure, "the classical ideal of male beauty," and identifies Williams' "favorite archetypal pattern" as the relationship between "a healthy, handsome man ['Adonis'] and a nervous older woman who is losing her looks" ['the Gargoyle'], who in this play corresponds to the Princess (p. 45). Hays explores in more detail the relationship between Chance and Adonis, basing his comparison primarily on their similar fate (castration) and on the many correlatives between Chance's story and the myths and rites of Adonis. I am indebted to Hays for his scholarship; however, my interpretation of the significance of the Chance-Adonis parallel is ultimately antithetical to his.

[4] See Hays, p. 256; Frazer, p. 286; Jane Harrison, *Myths of Greece and Rome* (Garden City, N.Y.: Doubleday, 1928), p. 19; and Hamilton, *Mythology*, pp. 32-33.

[5] See Hays, p. 256.

[6] Frazer, p. 297; Hays, p. 256.

[7] Hays, p. 256.

[8] Frazer, pp. 309-11.

[9] Frazer, p. 310.

[10] Hays, p. 256.

[11] Bettelheim, *The Uses of Enchantment*, p. 187, identifies Jack's "beanstalk" as a phallic symbol and offers a psychological interpretation of the fairy tale as a story of "the stages of development a boy has to go through to become an independent human being" (p. 190); see pp. 189-93 on "Jack and the Beanstalk."

[12] Bettelheim, p. 187.

[13] Bettelheim, p. 187.

[14] Bettelheim, p. 192.

[15] See Hays, pp. 257-58.

[16] Bettelheim, p. 190.

[17] Edith Hamilton, *The Echo of Greece* (New York: W. W. Norton, 1957), p. 130.

[18] Cf. Hays, p. 256.

[19] Hays, p. 256.

[20] See Tennessee Williams, "Sweet Bird of Youth," *Esquire*, April 1959, pp. [114]-155.

[21] J. E. Zimmerman, *Dictionary of Classical Mythology* (New York: Harper, 1964) p. 33.

[22] Frazer, p. 329; see also *Larousse*, p. 76.

[23] Hamilton, *Mythology*, p. 32.

[24] Hamilton, *Mythology*, p. 33.

[25] Neumann, p. 149.

[26] Frazer, p. 311.

[27] Neumann, p. 172.

[28] Bettelheim, p. 214; see also Bettelheim's psychological interpretation of "Sleeping Beauty," pp. 226 and 233-35.

[29] *Larousse*, p. 211; for a strikingly similar treatment of the ideal feminine archetype, cf. Williams' depiction of Heavenly in the whole of this passage (p. 51) to F. Scott Fitzgerald's image of Judy Jones as seen through the eyes of Dexter Green in "Winter Dreams," in *Short Story Masterpieces*, ed. Robert Penn Warren and Albert Erskine (1926; rpt. New York: Dell, 1975), p. 190:

> A low, pale oblong detached itself suddenly from the darkness of the Island, spitting forth the reverberate sound of a racing motorboat. Two white streamers of cleft water rolled themselves out behind it and almost immediately the boat was beside him. . . . Dexter raising himself on his arms was aware of a figure standing at the wheel, of two dark eyes regarding him over the lengthening space of water--then the boat had gone by and was sweeping in an immense and purposeless circle of spray round and round in the middle of the lake.

Significantly, the theme of Fitzgerald's story is also similar to that of Williams' play, the collapse of youthful dreams: "Even the grief he could have borne was left behind in the country of illusion, of youth, of the richness of life, where his winter dreams had flourished" (p. 206).

[30] Frazer, p. 293; Hays, p. 256.

[31] Robert Penn Warren, *All The King's Men* (1946; rpt. New York: Bantam, 1971), p. 4. Other similarities between the characters and events in Williams' play and Warren's novel are equally notable: Willie Stark's son is also named Tom; his wife (like Boss Finley's mistress), Lucy. Jack Burden, like Chance Wayne, carries with him an ideal memory of "his girl," an image also associated with the waters of the Gulf coast: "I had with me always that image of the little girl on the waters of the bay, all innocence and trustfulness, under the stormy sky" (p. 311), and "All the bright days by the water with the gulls flashing high were Anne Stanton" (p. 273). Like Boss Finley, Willie Stark builds a hospital to ameliorate (or disguise) his corrupt acts. He hires Adam Stanton,

reputable doctor, as director, just as Boss Finley promotes Dr. George Scudder to his "chief of staff" after he agrees to falsify the records of Heavenly's hysterectomy.

[32] Warren, *King's Men*, p. 91; in his own conversion story, pp. 91-92, Willie Stark is characterized in a manner strikingly similar to Boss Finley's self-description:

> And it came to him with the powerful voice of God's own lightning on a tragic time back in his own home county two years ago. . . . He looked in his heart and thought he might try to change things. . . . He was just a human, country boy, who believed like we have always believed back here in the hills that even the plainest, poorest fellow can be Governor if his fellow citizens find he has got the stuff and the character for the job.

Like Boss Finley, Willie Stark adopts the omnipotent image of "God-Almighty" (*King's Men*, p. 72).

[33] Bernard F. DuKore, "American Abelard: A Footnote to *Sweet Bird of Youth*," *College English*, 26 (1965), 630-34, first identified this parallel. DuKore believes the similarities between the play and the love story are too numerous to be coincidental and suggests several sources Williams may have used.

[34] The story of Abelard and Heloise is recounted in Marjorie Worthington, *The Immortal Lovers: Heloise and Abelard* (Garden City, N.Y.: Doubleday, 1960); D. W. Robertson, Jr., *Abelard and Heloise* (New York: Dial, 1972); and Regine Pernoud, *Heloise and Abelard*, trans. Peter Wiles (New York: Stein and Day, 1973).

[35] Worthington, p. 12.

[36] DuKore, pp. 632-33; see DuKore for several additional parallels between the two stories, among them the similarity between the name Abelard and the Princess' reference to "Franz Albertzart"; the "religious" concerns of Boss Finley which ironically link him with Fulbert, the canon of Notre Dame; and "the faint insinuation of the medieval" in the play's Moorish setting.

[37] Pernoud, "Abelard's Letter IV, Chap. iv," p. 166.

[38] Williams, "Sweet Bird of Youth," in *Esquire*, p. 130.

[39] Pernoud, "Heloise's Letter I, Chap. v," p. 234.

[40] DuKore, p. 632; see "Abelard's Love for Heloise," in *The Story of Abelard's Adversities* [Peter Abelard's Historia Calamitatum], trans. J. T. Muckle (Toronto: The Pontifical Institute of Medieval Studies, 1954), p. 25.

[41] Pernoud, "Heloise's Letter I, Chap. v," pp. 234-35.

[42] Worthington, p. 70.

[43] Williams, "Sweet Bird of Youth," in *Esquire*, p. 125.

[44] Peter Abelard, "The First Letter [of Abelard]," in *The Letters of Abelard and Heloise*, trans. C. K. Scott Moncrieff (1926; rpt. New York: Alfred A. Knopf, 1933), p. 20.

[45] See Edinger, p. 7.

[46] "Desire and the Black Masseur," p. 85.

[47] Hays, p. 256.

[48] Hays, p. 258.

[49] One possible reason for the ambiguity surrounding Chance Wayne's acceptance of responsibility for infecting Heavenly with venereal disease and, consequently, for the vagueness of his symbolic atonement for that defilement, may be that in the original "working script" of *Sweet Bird of Youth*, published in *Esquire*, April 1959, pp. [114]-155, Chance is, indeed, characterized as innocent of directly causing Heavenly's sexual defilement, though he remains guilty by association. In that original version, Heavenly's sexual desecration is attributed to her "gang-rape" by a group of drug-high Hollywood wolves who pick her up at the airport when she responds to Chance's plea to "come on out" to California. In a telephone dialogue between Heavenly and Chance (Act II, Scene ii, pp. 129-30), which is deleted from the play's final version, Heavenly reveals the assault to Chance, who had been unable to meet her at the airport himself because he was in jail, having been "caught in a raid" (p. 129), presumably for indulging in illegal sexual activities. In this original version, then, Chance is guilty only of appointing such sleazy characters as "Mr. Stars-of-

Tomorrow" and "Mr. Wet Back" to take care of Heavenly until his release, and of leading such a profligate and promiscuous way of life as would permit the opportunity for her violation.

Although Williams makes Chance the clearly guilty sexual partner in the play's final version, he seems to want to retain the sense of Chance's own victimization and lack of *direct* responsibility set forth in the original script, therefore characterizing both Chance and Heavenly as victims of "Time" and circumstance. The result is that Chance's promiscuity assumes the larger symbolic significance of reflecting an inescapably diseased and corrupt world to which he, like Heavenly, falls victim. At the same time, it reduces the significance of Chance's voluntary submission to castration as an act of *personal* atonement for Heavenly's defilement, for he never explicitly assumes responsibility for that act.

CHAPTER EIGHT: *THE NIGHT OF THE IGUANA*

[1] The phrase derives from the title of Frye's *The Secular Scripture*; I have, in Frye's own terminolgy, "displaced" his literary use of the phrase to give it metaphysical significance.

[2] As Jackson, p. 72, suggests, "Shannon follows the moral progression described by St. John of the Cross as the 'dark night of the soul.' He proceeds in contrary motion, in flight from the presence of God; but, like St. John, he finds that the 'way down' leads up."

[3] Frye, *Secular Scripture*, pp. 113 and 129.

[4] Frye, *Secular Scripture*, p. 157.

[5] See T. Adler, "The Search for God in the Plays of Tennessee Williams," in *TW: A Collection*, p. 148, who formulates Williams' "answer" to the question "Where's God?" in similar terms: "We must be like God to the other, and the other must be like God to us."

[6] St. John of the Cross, "Chapt. xviii," *Dark Night of the*

Soul (1582-88), trans, E. Allison Peers, 3rd rev. ed. (Garden City, N. Y.: Image-Doubleday, 1959), pp. 164-67; St. John, p. 165, compares spiritual elevation to a "ladder of love" upon which "to go down is to go up, and to go up, to go down, for he that humbles himself is exalted and he that exalts himself is humbled."

[7] As quoted in Lewis Funke and John E. Booth, "Williams on Williams," *Theatre Arts*, 46 (Jan. 1962), p. 72.

[8] Gerald Weales makes this observation in *The Jumping-Off Place: American Drama in the 1960's* (New York: Macmillan, 1969), pp. 3-14; rpt. as "Tennessee Williams' Achievement in the Sixties," in *TW: A Collection*, p. 63.

[9] Nancy Tischler, "A Gallery of Witches," in *TW: A Tribute*, p. 507.

[10] Frye, *Secular Scripture*, p. 142.

[11] Frye, *Secular Scripture*, p. 143.

[12] Neumann, pp. 75 and 80-81.

[13] Hamilton, *Mythology*, p. 126.

[14] In *Memoirs*, p. 99, Williams uses an image similar to Shannon's to describe what he calls "my greatest affliction, which is perhaps the major theme of my writings, the affliction of loneliness that follows me like my shadow, a very ponderous shadow too heavy to drag after me all of my days and nights." In the play, Maxine equates Shannon's "spook" with the "little shadow/ That goes in and out with me . . ." (p. 17) of Robert Louis Stevenson's child's poem, "My Shadow."

[15] Northrop Frye, *Fearful Symmetry: A Study of William Blake* (1947; rpt. Boston: Beacon Press, 1965), p. 37.

[16] Frye, *Fearful Symmetry*, pp. 61-63.

[17] Sigmund Freud, "Beyond the Pleasure Principle" (1920); rpt. in *A General Selection*, p. 149.

[18] Freud, "The Origin and Development of Psychoanalysis" (1909); rpt. in *A General Selection*, p. 26.

[19] Freud, "Types of Neurotic Nosogenesis" (1912); rpt. in *A General Selection*, p. 66.

[20] Freud, "The Ego and the Id" (1923); rpt. in *A General Selection*, pp. 232-33.

[21] Freud, "On Narcissism: An Introduction" (1914); rpt. in *A General Selection*, p. 119.

[22] Glenn Embrey, "The Subterranean World of *The Night of the Iguana*," in *TW: A Tribute*, p. 329.

[23] Embrey, in *TW: A Tribute*, p. 330. Significantly, Williams' own motivation for joining the Roman Catholic Church on January 6, 1969, after his prolonged nervous collapse in the sixties, was expressed in similar terms: "I wanted my goodness back." As quoted in Richard F. Leavitt, *The World of Tennessee Williams* (New York: Putnam's, 1978), p. 148.

[24] Freud, "The Origin of Psychoanalysis" (1910); rpt. in *A General Selection*, p. 30.

[25] Neumann, p. 149.

[26] See Embrey, in *TW: A Tribute*, p. 337.

[27] Neumann, p. 27.

[28] Neumann, pp. 172 and 65.

[29] Neumann, p. 65; see my remark on Williams' similar characterization of other male figures toward a negative anima-image in my Chap. Seven, Section III.

[30] Ingrid Rogers, *Tennessee Williams: A Moralist's Answer to the Perils of Life* (Frankfurt, Germany: Herbert Lang/Bern, 1976), pp. 105-11, compiles numerous examples of parallels between Christ and Shannon; she concludes, however, that the features of Shannon's Jesus-image are "mere pretensions" (p. 109). Rogers, p. 108, n.3, also cites George Hendrick, "Jesus and the Osiris-Isis Myth: Lawrence's *The Man Who Died* and Williams's *The Night of the Iguana*," *Anglia*, 84 (1966), p. 402, who suggests that the "T" in T. Lawrence Shannon represents a cross or crucifix. Along the

same line, Norman J. Fedder, *The Influence of D. H. Lawrence on Tennessee Williams*, p. 112, suggests that the "T" in Shannon's name stands for "Tennessee's" Lawrence, Shannon thereby representing Williams' characterization of D. H. Lawrence as "the gynephobe hero with the Christ complex" whom he had earlier depicted in his one-act play about Lawrence, *I Rise in Flame, Cried the Phoenix* (1941); rpt. in *Dragon Country: A Book of Plays* (New York: New Directions, 1970), pp. 59-75. Fedder points out that just as Hannah accuses Shannon of indulging in a "voluptuous" crucifixion, so Frieda derides Lawrence's similarly depicted Christ-complex in *I Rise in Flame*, p. 62: "You are getting so sentimental about yourself and so unappreciated and so misunderstood. You can't stand Jesus Christ because he beat you to it. Oh, how you would have loved to suffer the *original* crucifixion!"

[31] See Rogers, pp. 105-06.

[32] See Rogers, p. 108.

[33] Debusscher, in *TW: A Collection*, pp. 153-54, is the first to have made this observation and to trace the parallels between Shannon and St. Laurence.

[34] Butler, "St. Laurence, Martyr (A.D. 258)," III, 297-99.

[35] Butler, III, 298.

[36] Butler, III, 298.

[37] Edinger, p. 150.

[38] Edinger, p. 152.

[39] Edinger, p. 150.

[40] Edinger, pp. 253-54.

[41] Jung, "Psychotherapists or the Clergy" (1932), in *Psychology and Religion: West and East*, Vol. XI of *CW* (1958), p. 340, par. 522; see also, *Symbols of Transformation*, V of *CW*, 303, par. 460, in which Jung describes the cross or crucifix as the quintessential archetype of this crucial stage in the process of individuation:

> The cross, or whatever other heavy burden the
> hero carries, is <u>himself</u>, or rather <u>the</u> self,
> his wholeness, which is both God and animal--not
> merely the empirical man, but the totality of his
> being, which is rooted in his animal nature and
> reaches out beyond the merely human towards the
> divine. His wholeness implies a tremendous
> tension of opposites paradoxically at one with
> themselves, as in the cross, their most perfect
> symbol.

[42] Rogers, p. 109, notes that Shannon "takes the 'bitter cup that will not pass him,'" but she makes no comment on Shannon's subsequent responses.

[43] Neumann, pp. 4 and 65.

[44] Neumann, pp. 325 and 331.

[45] Eliade, "Androgyny and Wholeness," in his *Myths, Dreams, and Mysteries*, pp. 174-75.

[46] Eric Partridge, *Name This Child* (New York: Oxford Univ. Press, 1936), p. 26; and Elizabeth G. Withycombe, *The Oxford Dictionary of English Christian Names*, 2nd ed. (1950; rpt. Oxford: Clarendon Press, 1971), p. 138.

[47] Withycombe, p. 171; and Partridge, p. 122.

[48] Drake, pp. 106-07.

[49] Jung, "The Phenomenology of the Spirit in Fairy Tales," in *The Archetypes*, IX, i, of *CW*, 215 and 217-18.

[50] Jung, "The Phenomenology of the Spirit," in *The Archetypes*, IX, i, of *CW*, pp. 225-26.

[51] Both Nonno's name and characterization have an autobiographical source in Williams' ancestry and familial relations. According to Leavitt, p. 14, Williams' "paternal grandmother's people were early settlers of *Nantucket* Island; the *poet* Tristram *Coffin* was her [Williams' grandmother's] uncle." Also, Williams' father was named Cornelius *Coffin* Williams [all emphases mine]. As an amalgamation of these sources, Williams' Nonno in *Iguana* is a "poet" from "Nantucket" named Jonathan "Coffin."

Notes - Chapter Eight

Williams modelled his characterization of Jonathan Coffin, or "Nonno," after his grandfather, the Reverend Walter Edwin Dakin, a High Episcopal priest, whom, along with his grandmother ("Grand"), Williams in *Memoirs*, p. 110, credits as "the source of the greatest support and kindnesses to me all my life." Like Nonno, Williams' grandfather was "increasingly hard of hearing and nearly blind" in his elder years (Leavitt, p. 72). When Williams traveled with his elderly grandfather, he, like Hannah with Nonno, "lavished attention and consideration on the old gentleman; called him 'that ancient charmer' and indulged him by selecting only those dining places which still served on table linen" (Leavitt, p. 72). Similarly, Hannah caters to the genteel habits of Nonno, always carrying with her "linen napkins . . . in case we run into paper napkins as sometimes happens" (pp. 314-15). In *Memoirs*, pp. 146-47, Williams associates his grandfather with the philosopher Santayana, whom Williams met when Santayana was in his eighties, a semi-invalid, and whom he described as "a saintly old gentleman," like Nonno: "He had . . . infinite understanding and delicate humor and he seemed to accept his condition without the least bit of self-pity or chagrin. . . . His gentleness of presence, his innate kindliness, reminded me very strongly of my grandfather." Also in *Memoirs*, p. 147, Williams paraphrases Hannah's line about Nonno in reference to these real-life models of Nonno's character: "'Sometimes I've seen God in old faces,' said Hannah Jelkes. I think of Grandfather's face and Santayana's--and Grand's."

[52] Drake, p. 108, also makes the observation that "'Shannon' combines 'Hannah' and 'Nonno,'" but offers no interpretive comment on the wordplay; T. Adler, "The Search for God," in *TW: A Collection*, p. 148, suggests that "Williams gives to Shannon a name containing the alphabet letters needed to spell out 'Nonno' and 'Hannah'" in order to reinforce the play's theme of overcoming despair by recognizing "the interdependence of all people."

[53] Elsdon C. Smith, *Dictionary of American Family Names* (New York: Harper, 1956), p. 194.

[54] Angus Fletcher, *Allegory: The Theory of a Symbolic Mode* (1964; rpt. Ithaca: Cornell Paperbacks-Cornell Univ. Press, 1970), p. 356, n. 61.

[55] The phrase derives from the title of Jung's essay, "The Spiritual Problem of Modern Man" (1933), in *Civilization in Transi-*

tion, Vol. X of *CW* (1964), pp. 74-94.

[56] Jung, "Psychotherapists or the Clergy," in *Psychology and Religion*, XI, 331.

[57] Alan W. Watts, *The Way of Zen*, (1957; rpt. New York: Mentor-NAL, 1959), pp. 184 and 191.

[58] See Christmas Humphreys, *Buddhism* (1951; rpt. Middlesex, Eng.: Penguin, 1974); especially, "Introduction," pp. 11-23; "Twelve Principles of Buddhism," pp. 74-76; and "Buddhist Catechism," p. 71.

[59] Neumann, p. 332.

[60] Humphreys, p. 19.

[61] Embrey, in *TW: A Tribute*, p. 332.

[62] Embrey, in *TW: A Tribute*, p. 333.

[63] Cf. Embrey, in *TW: A Tribute*, p. 332.

[64] Williams is quoted in Hirsch, p. 70, as justifying the presence of the Nazi German family in the play on the grounds that they "offer a vivid counterpoint--as world conquerors--to the world-conquered protagonists of the play." My own opinion is that their inclusion undermines the play's central message of love's redemptive power, making grossly inadequate Hannah's philosophy of acceptance, endurance, and "a little understanding" (p. 352) in the face of such monstrous evil as is invoked by the very presence of the Nazis on holiday, ecstatic over the fire-bombing of Britain.

[65] According to Williams, "A Summer of Discovery," *New York Herald Tribune*, Dec. 24, 1961; rpt, in *Where I Live*, p. 147, *The Night of the Iguana* was, at one point in its composition, given the working title of "Two Acts of Grace," which Williams tells us refers to its central conversion scene between Hannah and Shannon in which "a pair of desperate people . . . had the humble nobility of each putting the other's desperation, during the course of a night, above his concern for his own," and Williams adds, "Being an unregenerate romanticist, . . . I can still think of nothing that gives more meaning to living."

[66] T. Adler, "The Search for God," in *TW: A Collection*, p. 148.

[67] T. Adler, "The Search for God," in *TW: A Collection*, p. 147, finds analogous the albatross which falls from the neck of Coleridge's Ancient Mariner and Shannon's gold cross, "his own albatross," which symbolizes "a perverted system of religion by which he feels condemned rather than redeemed" and which Shannon rips off in rage and frustration.

[68] In "A Summer of Discovery," p. 146, Williams identifies the autobiographical source of *Iguana* as his experience during the summer of 1940, when he discovered "that all which is most valuable in life is escaping from the narrow cubicle of one's self to a sort of verandah . . . beside another beleaguered human being, someone else who is in exile from the place and time of his heart's fulfillment." More succinctly, Williams is quoted in *Time*, Mar. 9, 1962, p. 53, as saying, "Hell is yourself. . . . When you ignore other people completely, that is hell."

[69] Jacob H. Adler, "*Night of the Iguana*: A New Tennessee Williams?" *Ramparts*, 1 (Nov. 1962), 63 and "Notes," p. 68.

[70] *Dark Night of the Soul*, p. 165.

[71] Robert Bechtold Heilman, *The Ways of the World: Comedy and Society* (Seattle: Univ. of Washington Press, 1978), pp. 82, 85, 86.

[72] Heilman, *Ways of the World*, pp. 82 and 83.

[73] As quoted in Howard Taubman, "Theatre Review" [of *Iguana*], *New York Times*, Jan. 7, 1962, Sec. 2, p. 1, col. 1.

[74] J. Adler, "A New Tennessee Williams," p. 68.

[75] Taubman, "Review," Sec. 2, p. 1, col. 1.

[76] Embrey, in *TW: A Tribute*, p. 334.

[77] Embrey, in *TW: A Tribute*, p. 338.

[78] Embrey, in *TW: A Tribute*, p. 334.

[79] J. Adler, "Notes" to "A New Tennessee Williams," p. 68.

[80] The phrase belongs to J. Adler, "A New Tennessee Williams," p. 68, who comments, "only Hannah wins out over her own personality, and hence banishes the power of naturalism."

[81] John Simon, "Review of *The Night of the Iguana*," *Theatre Arts*, March 1962, p. 57.

[82] Frye, *Secular Scripture*, p. 132.

CHAPTER NINE: AFTER *IGUANA*

[1] Heilman, *Ways of the World*, pp. 62 and 63; it must be noted that Heilman himself, "Chap. V: Tennessee Williams," in his *The Iceman*, pp. 115-41, classifies most of Williams' plays, including *Summer and Smoke* and *Camino Real*, as "the melodrama of the victim" or "disasters of personality." Although Heilman, *The Iceman*, pp. 120 and 128, makes brief mention of *The Rose Tattoo* and *Iguana* as "comedies," he does not examine the comic strain in Williams' drama either in this work or his in *Ways of the World*; nevertheless, the traits of "wholeness" and the attitudes of "acceptance" inherent in or achieved by such Williams characters as Stella Kowalski, Alma Winemiller, Maggie the Cat, Alexandra del Lago, Hannah Jelkes, and *Small Craft Warnings*' Leona Dawson clearly conform to Heilman's own criteria for defining comic characterization and structure as set forth in his *Ways of the World*.

[2] *Ways of the World*, pp. 89 and 50.

[3] *Ways of the World*, p. 241.

[4] *Ways of the World*, p. 90

[5] *Ways of the World*, p. 104.

[6] According to Heilman, *Ways of the World*, pp. 91-92, "Acceptance of the world may mean acceptance of second best, that is, making do with something less than a total good that one is capable of imagining"; see also Heilman's definition of "black comedy" as

"overacceptance," pp. 81-86.

⁷ Albert Camus, "The Myth of Sisyphus" (1942); rpt. in *The Myth of Sisyphus and Other Essays*, trans. Justin O'Brien (New York: Alfred A. Knopf, 1955), p. 121.

⁸ Dickinson, p. 179, discusses the device of dramatic recall in reference to the plays of Eugene O'Neill.

⁹ In his "Author's Note" (II, [7]) to the play, Williams explains that "aside from the characters having the same names and the locale remaining the same," *Eccentricities* is "a substantially different play" from its original version *Summer and Smoke*; and, he adds, "I prefer it. It is less conventional and melodramatic."

¹⁰ See my review of the Kansas University Theatre production of the revised *Eccentricities* in "KU and the Arts," *Lawrence Journal-World*, Feb. 27, 1978, p. 4.

¹¹ See Tennessee Williams, *The Eccentricities of a Nightingale*, rev. ed. (New York: Dramatists Play Service, 1977), pp. 50-51. This addition, one of a number of significant changes, also raises the question of interpreting Alma's characterization in terms of the so-called Proustian "Albertine strategy," the device of substituting women for men as symbolic embodiments of homosexual love; so named by Stanley Edgar Hyman because Marcel Proust in his *Remembrance of Things Past* was thought to have disguised the homosexual nature of his relationship with an "Albert" by naming him "Albertine." For a discussion of this device in the fiction of Williams and other modern writers, see Hyman, "Some Notes on the Albertine Strategy," *Hudson Review*, 6 (1953), 417-22.

¹² A parallel to Williams' "snake story" is an incident in Proust's *Remembrance of Things Past*: when "Marcel" loses "Albertine," he "envisions a python about to swallow a lion in a cage," according to Milton L. Miller, "Proust's Homosexuality," in *Homosexuality and Creative Genius*, ed. Dr. Hendrik M. Ruitenbeek (New York: Astor-Honor, Obolensky, 1967), p. 276; see Miller, pp. 267-77, for a discussion of the Freudian implications of this incident.

¹³ Eliot referred to the "mythical method" in his discussion of James Joyce's *Ulysses*, "Ulysses, Order, and Myth," *The Dial* (Nov. 1923), as "the most important expression which the present

age has found":

> In using the myth, in manipulating a continuous
> parallel between contemporaneity and antiquity,
> Mr. Joyce is pursuing a method which others must
> pursue after him. . . . It is simply a way of
> controlling, of ordering, of giving a shape and
> significance to the intense panorama of futility
> and anarchy which is contemporary history. . . .
> Instead of narrative method we may now use the
> mythical method.

As quoted in Jay Martin, "T. S. Eliot's *The Waste Land*," in *A Collection of Critical Essays on The Waste Land*, ed. J. Martin, Twentieth Century Interpretations (Englewood Cliffs, N. J.: Prentice-Hall, 1968), p. 7. See also Williams, "Letter 132: May 7, 1950," in *Letters to Donald Windham*, p. 260, in which Williams quotes from Eliot's "The Cocktail Party" the passage which begins, "Ah, but we die to each other daily"; Windham comments: "T. S. Eliot, one of Tennessee's phobias before his success, became one of his favorites afterward."

[14] For an excellent analysis of the ritual patterns and mythic symbolism of *Camino Real*, see Diane Turner, "The Mythic Vision in Tennessee Williams' *Camino Real*," in *TW: A Tribute*, pp. 237-51.

[15] "Foreword," *Memoirs*, pp. xvii-xviii; among the "circumstances" of Williams' life during the sixties were the death of his beloved companion Frank Merlo; drug and alcohol dependencies; a nervous breakdown and subsequent institutionalization; and his baptism as a Roman Catholic.

[16] As quoted in T. H. Wenning, "Unbeastly Williams," *Newsweek*, June 27, 1960, p. 96.

[17] Frye, *Anatomy*, p. 170.

[18] Williams, *Memoirs*, p. 212, writes in response to Walter Kerr's comment about *Slapstick Tragedy* that "Black comedy is not for Mr. Williams" the following: "It was I who invented American black comedy and he was surely smart enough to know it."

[19] Tennessee Williams, "Author's Notes" to *Out Cry*, unpublished, March 1970, unpaged; as quoted by Thomas P. Adler, "The Dialogue of Incompletion: Language in Tennessee Williams'

Later Plays," in *TW: A Collection*, pp. 81-82; see Adler's essay, pp. 74-85, for an excellent analysis of Williams' adaptation of "absurdist" techniques.

[20] Thomas Bullfinch, "The Age of Fable or Beauties of Mythology" (1855; rpt. New York: Mentor-NAL, 1962), pp. 164-65.

[21] Debusscher, pp. 154-55, notes the identification of Christopher Flanders with St. Christopher.

[22] Butler, "St. Christopher, Martyr (Date Unknown)," in his *Lives of the Saints*, III, 184-87.

[23] Martin Esslin, *The Theatre of the Absurd*, rev. ed. (1961; rpt. Garden City, N. Y.: Anchor-Doubleday, 1969), pp. 5-6, cites these "basic problems of existence" as the concern of both Existentialist drama and Theatre of the Absurd; the difference between the two genres rests in the *form* of their expression of these mutual concerns.

[24] Marie Delcourt, *Hermaphrodite: Myths and Rites of the Bisexual Figure in Classical Antiquity*, trans. Jennifer Nicholson (London: Studio Books, 1956), p. 81.

[25] See M. H. Abrams, *Natural Supernaturalism: Tradition and Revolution in Romantic Literature* (New York: W. W. Norton, 1971) pp. 45-46, 166-67.

[26] Jung, "The Personification of the Opposites" in *Mysterium Coniunctionis*, Vol XIV of *CW* (New York: Pantheon Books, 1963), p. 150, par. 178; see also p. 160, par. 188.

[27] For a Jungian interpretation of the play, see Rexford Stamper, "*The Two-Character Play*: Psychic Individuation," in *TW: A Tribute*, pp. 354-61.

[28] Williams, *Memoirs*, p. 40, refers to *Kingdom of Earth* as "my funny melodrama."

[29] George Niesen, "The Artist Against Reality in the Plays of Tennessee Williams," in *TW: A Tribute*, p. 475, observes that "*Kingdom of Earth* is very nearly a rerun of *Streetcar*, with Lot analogous to Blanche, Chicken to Stanley, and Myrtle to Stella."

[30] See Jerrold A. Phillips, "*Kingdom of Earth*: Some Approaches," in *TW: A Tribute*, p. 350; see also pp. 349-53, for his analysis of the play's symbolic allusions.

[31] Williams, *Memoirs*, p. 2, describes his own early experiences in New Orleans as one of many struggling young writers in the same metaphorical terms dramatized by *Small Craft Warnings*:

> . . . all of us disregarding the small craft warnings in the face of which we were continually sailing our small crafts, each with his crew of one, himself that crew and its captain. We were sailing along in our separate small crafts but we were in sight of each other and sometimes in touch, . . . and this gave us a warm sense of community.

[32] Norman J. Fedder, "Tennessee Williams' Dramatic Technique," in *TW: A Tribute*, p. 809, comments that "the play recalls Masters' poetic graveyard: a *Small Craft Anthology* of posthumous lives."

[33] *Ways of the World*, p. 178.

[34] Beate Hein Bennett, "Williams and European Drama: Infernalists and Forgers of Modern Myths," in *TW: A Tribute*, p. 445, observes that in post-World War II existential literature, "The negative heroism of plain survival became an art, and human dignity rested in the resilience the individual could muster."

[35] *Ways of the World*, p. 57; subsequent references are to pp. 55-57.

[36] Frye, *Anatomy*, p. 167.

[37] G. Wilson Knight, *The Golden Labyrinth: A Study of British Drama* (New York: W. W. Norton, 1962), p. 14; as quoted in Heilman, *Ways of the World*, p. 81.

[38] Frye, *Anatomy*, p. 103.

[39] Bennett, in *TW: A Tribute*, p. 441, cites this "tension" as the source of the "infernal" vision in literary and mythopoeic tradition: "The damnation lies in the ultimately irresolvable tension of a longing for redemption and the realization of the futility of that hope."

[40] *Ways of the World*, pp. 55-56.

INDEX TO THE PLAYS

Inclusive page numbers refer to those chapters or sections of chapters that comprise the main discussion of a play. Additional references in the text to plays discussed in Chapters One through Eight are not cited, nor are incidental references to other Williams plays.

University of Kansas Humanistic Studies Series

Back Issues

8/08 P